Stuck In Maleness

A Book Written For and About African American Men

Second Edition

Russell A. Ligon, Jr.

The names and identifying characterizations of certain individuals referenced in this publication have been changed, others may be fictitious. This publication contains the opinions and ideas of its author. It is sold with the understanding that neither the author nor the publisher is engaged in rendering legal tax, investment, insurance, financial, accounting, or other professional advice or services. If the reader requires such advice or services, competent professional should be consulted. Relevant laws vary from state to state. The strategies outlined in this book may not be suitable for every individual, and are not guaranteed or warranted to produce any particular results. No warranty is made with respect to the accuracy or completeness of the information contained herein, and both the author and publisher specifically disclaim responsibility for any liability, loss, or risk, personal or otherwise, which is incurred as a consequence, directly or indirectly, of the use and application of any of the contents of this book.

Stuck In Maleness: A Book Written For And About African American Men by Russell A. Ligon, Copyright 2013.

Scriptures referenced in this book are taken from the New King James Version of the Bible by Thomas Nelson, Inc. Copyright © 1982. Used by permission. "All rights reserved."

Dedication

The inspiration and motivation to write **Stuck In Maleness** came to me as the result of many experiences and influences that have shaped who I am as a man. But there are four sources of influence that stand out the most. First and foremost, I dedicate this book to God for creating me, giving me the many second, third, and fourth chances at getting my life together, carrying me through some extremely tough times, believing in me when I did not believe in myself, giving me strength to overcome when I didn't believe I could, for blessing me with His grace and mercy and for intervening in my life and making a way out of no way, when deep within my heart I know that I didn't deserve it, but He did it anyway.

I dedicate this book to the memory of my father, Russell A. "Daddy Russ" Ligon,Sr.,who continues to live on within me. When my father passed away in 2001, I was devastated. A co-worker of mine suggested, "Russell focus on your father's life and not his death." At the time I did not understand the wisdom of my co-worker's words but eventually they began to take on meaning in my life. At the beginning of my life my father would have been considered to be *"stuck in maleness"*. But by the end of his life in 2001, my father had become a lifelong worker, a dedicated husband and father, a friend, and a surrogate father and mentor to teenage males and young men in his community. My father was not rich and he did not own gigantic houses nor did he drive expensive cars but he was a good man and he gave me a wealth of insight, life examples and love. He was and still is my hero.

I also dedicate this book to my mother, Dora L. Hall, a strong black woman, who is the epitome of strength, good character, motherly love and patience. More than anyone else, my mother has experienced my own *"stuck in maleness"* behavior but she never wavered and has been a source of strength and encouragement through the toughest times of my life, and there have been many. Thanks, Mom.

I also dedicate this book to my daughters Cheritta Davis, Symone, Taylor, Jazzmyn, and to my son, Rouselle. You've seen me fall, and get back up, many times but never have I taken my eyes off of you because you were the reason I kept getting up. I love you all.

Finally, **Stuck In Maleness** is dedicated to all of the women who have been a part of my life and have, in one way or another, experienced my *"stuck in maleness"* thinking and behavior. You are a part of this book because you have been a part of my life. I want you to know that I appreciate you, respect you, love you, but most important, I honor you. Thank you for being a part of my life.

Russ Ligon
2014

Acknowledgements

There are always people in life who help us to accomplish the things that we do. What seems like an individual effort on our part, more often than not, involves many dedicated and supportive people behind the scenes. These special people do a lot of work to help bring a project to completion and, for the sake of the greater good, usually put up with difficult people like me while we go about trying to put our thoughts and views about a subject into a form that readers can understand and hopefully will appreciate. I thank Regina Price for printing out earlier drafts of **Stuck In Maleness** and for providing valuable feedback on the tone of **Stuck In Maleness** and how to better reach my readers. I thank Karen L. Forbes for assisting with typing, providing initial research material used in the book, and for her superior copy editing skills. I thank Kimberly A. Ferguson for providing meaningful anecdotes that I have included in **Stuck In Maleness** and for introducing the viewpoint that women can also benefit by reading **Stuck In Maleness** as well. I thank my mother Dora L. Hall for typing initial drafts of **Stuck In Maleness** and putting up with my impatience and insistence on why she wasn't typing faster than she was. I thank Gladies M. Melvin for helping with review of content, providing extensive research materials, and for providing ideas and feedback that have been incorporated into various places throughout the pages of **Stuck In Maleness**. Finally, I thank Mr. Ed Mann for providing clinical insight and ideas on how I could improve this second edition of **Stuck In Maleness** by addressing the person inside of the man. The sacrifice, efforts and hard work of all of these wonderful women, big or small, were powerful because without them **Stuck In Maleness** would still be stuck in my head or stuck on yellow legal paper, on napkins or scraps of pieces of paper that I often used to write down my ideas. Thank you so much, I couldn't have done it without you.

Table of Contents

Foreword 6
Introduction 7
Chapter 1   African American Men under Siege 11
Chapter 2   Issues of Domestic Violence 26
Chapter 3   Why So Many Faces? 36
Chapter 4   Myths and Misconceptions about Manhood 51
Chapter 5   What It Means To Be *Stuck In Maleness* 83
Chapter 6   How We Become *Stuck In Maleness* 95
Chapter 7   What It Means To Be A Man 122
Chapter 8   Men, Take Out The Trash – It Stinks! 164
Chapter 9   Manage the Karma in Your Life 181
Chapter 10   Attitude Is Everything! 192
Chapter 11   Men, Come Forth and Lead 208
Chapter 12   What Women Want 221
Chapter 13   One Size Doesn't Fit All 251
Chapter 14   Marriage or Shacking? 259
Chapter 15   The Spiritual Side of Manhood 276
Chapter 16   Final Thoughts 290
Bibliography 324
Appendix 329

Foreword

What we face today is more destructive than what we faced as black men in the years of civil unrest. Today, a monster in the form of disorganized organizations across the country has been unleashed to devour young black men (and women) all over America. Our change from for the people to for myself, or the "me-me" syndrome, has taken all of the caring out of our communities and made us other than what we originally professed to be.

It's past time to stand up and to really lead the youth in a real direction that has a real future. Those of us who are in a position to make changes have to start *NOW!* The first group didn't mean for this to be the outcome of what they started. Never was oppression on their agenda, instead it was brotherly love over oppression, destruction, or death. Let's get back to our roots, let's stand as we were meant to stand and that's tall. Unity of direction for a common purpose along with community, love, and a better future for the youth is what we stand for.

Russ Ligon has delved into the very heart of these matters, and emerged on the other side with a blueprint for success that can help African American men get back on track. **Stuck In Maleness** provides the mind-transforming insight that African American men need today in order to move forward into the future, and to effectively deal with ourselves, our women, our children and our families. Let's embrace him and the cause he stands for, which is ours.

Omar Supreme
The Law!

Introduction

"A journey of a thousand miles begins with a single step." ~ Lao-Tzu

The title of this edition of **Stuck In Maleness** could have been **Stuck In Maleness: A Book Written For African American Woman About African American Men.** As African American men we are often misunderstood and misrepresented by others, including African American women. We are sometimes accused of being complicated by our women, and we are; but not by design, rather through the experiences of being a male compounded by also being an African American male in American society. Almost at every junction in the writing of **Stuck In Maleness**, I have attempted to keep African American women in mind since our lives are so intricately intertwined and influenced by African American women as our mothers, sisters, wives, girlfriends, "baby mommas" and our friends, but I also recognize there are women from other cultures and backgrounds who are connected to us in some of these same roles as well. I hope all of the women who read **Stuck In Maleness: A Book Written For And About African American Men**, will read it with an open mind, a quest for insight and understanding into African American men and how we think, but most importantly, compassion and a commitment to make "adjustments" within their own minds and attitudes concerning the reality of what we really go through as men and how they can help make things better for us both.

Most African American men in the United States know of another African American male whose life has been troubled, even if it's their own. As African American men we cannot continue to ignore this fact and the impact it is having on the African American family. I've discovered that as African American men the way we view manhood is contributing to an epidemic of self-sabotaging and unmanly behaviors throughout our communities. Unmanly behaviors are affecting every facet of our lives including our relationships with women, our children and our families. Change is greatly needed because the existence of the African American family as a healthy and viable social unit is at risk if those changes are not forthcoming soon.

I've also discovered that while a considerable number of African American men have an unhealthy perspective about what it means to be a man, we also have "help" from larger societal forces that emasculate us as men and continue to remove key playing cards from the decks of our lives that are being replaced with false, deceptive, and misleading information about our manhood. This has been the case since our initial arrival in the United States as slaves over 400 years ago. Many of the recent generations of African American men either are unaware of this fact or have simply given in to the negative stereotype that has become a regular part of the American social diet. As a result of the combination of these two forces, African American men have experienced a precipitous rise in unemployment, incarcerations, divorce, substance abuse, black on black crime, domestic violence and the creation of multiple generations of African American children who are literally growing up fatherless.

These secret stakeholders that operate within our lives but out of public view have a different perspective about our manhood and they have a different plan on how to capitalize on the negative portrayal of African American men in American society. Daily, examples of the presence of these forces appear on the evening news, in newspapers, in how African American men are treated within the courts and the criminal justice system, in how the media depicts the life of African American men and most significantly, in the casual, almost neglectful way African American children experience the public education system in this country.

But the irony of this tragedy is that African American men (and some of our women) have become complicit co-conspirators in our own self-destruction. How *WE* view and understand our manhood is evidenced in how *WE* treat ourselves, how *WE* neglect our role as fathers and co-parents of our children, the disrespectful and damaging way *WE* relate to African American women, and the damaging attitude of entitlement that many brothers harbor today. Is someone else *REALLY* supposed to take care of us and clean up the mess that *WE* make of our life? I think not.

As an African American man, my life was troubled and for a period of time, I too was stuck into negative and self-defeating behaviors. Having fallen prey to the larger societal influences and to my own self-sabotaging thinking, my life had become a dysfunctional mess which reverberated into every area of my existence including my relationships with women, my children, employment, my finances and my involvement with the criminal justice system. Low self-worth and poor decision making had caused my life to break up into a thousand tiny dysfunctional pieces. Clearly I had lost my way. But through the grace of God and the insights He has revealed to me through the pages of this book and the many supportive people He placed in my way, I have been able to pick up those pieces and put my life back together again.

Moving forward we must begin to live responsibly in a healthy and more productive way so our children can have a chance to do the same in their lives. **Stuck In Maleness** reveals the forces behind the negative unmanly behaviors of many African American men, along with insightful and life changing steps on how to reclaim your manhood and transform your life into the man of vision, purpose and character that God designed you to be. If you do not provoke change in your life, change will provoke you.

Chapter 1
African American Men under Siege

There is a crisis growing in communities across the United States that threatens to destroy the African American family as we've historically known it. The crisis is manifesting its most and destructive effects on a systemic "institutional level" and on an individual "mental level" amongst African American men in ways that can only be described as epidemic. African American men are under siege and are losing the battle to maintain their manhood on many crucial fronts. The crisis is spreading and is no longer an isolated by-product of densely populated urban centers but is showing chronic symptoms in suburban and rural communities as well.

The present state of relations seen amongst African American men has mostly emerged during the past Civil Rights Movement such as, Dr. Martin Luther King, Jr., Malcolm X, Medgar Evers, Reverend Jesse Jackson, Adam Clayton Powell, Jr., and others has waned, which has left a void in race and culture-unifying leadership amongst African American men and the celebration of strength and character in our communities. However, since the end of the Civil Rights era, African American men have become plagued by low self-worth, low self-esteem, diminished racial and cultural pride, and a deterioration of core family values which is producing corrupted and dysfunctional images of manhood in the minds of increasingly large numbers of African American men.

What is more, these corrupted and dysfunctional images of manhood embraced today by African American men are spreading like wildfire to younger generations of African American boys (and girls). As this occurs it perpetuates the process of the destruction of African American men in society by ensuring the future supply of African American males that will be used and manipulated by others for profit, and further weakens the survival of the African American family as a healthy, and viable, social unit.

This is not the first time in history in which there have been large scale systemic efforts to unman African American men or to destroy the African American family. In 1619 in Jamestown, Virginia when the first slaves arrived from Africa (1), slave owners immediately sought to emasculate the slaves. While slaves were tied to trees or posted on auction blocks waiting to be sold, slave owners publicly beat them with horsewhips in front of their wives and children and other slaves until they submitted or until they fell into unconscious submission.

The purpose then, as it is today, was to break the will and spirit of slaves by treating them like animals in front of their wives and children and instilling fear in other would be rebellious slaves, less they receive the same treatment. Once this type of humiliating and degrading treatment became commonplace, slaves could be looked upon to keep each other down. The discriminatory treatment and self-sabotaging behaviors of African American men today is a reflection and continuation of processes set in motion many years ago back in 1619. The criminal justice system serves that purpose in the present society. Unlike slaves of the past who could buy their freedom or were set free by sympathetic whites, African American men who obtain a criminal record are quite often labeled for life and incur a lifetime of economic, social, political and even psychological ramifications to themselves and to their families.

In the 1800's during the Civil War era, the value of black soldiers was demonstrated when they were forcibly conscripted into the Confederate Army and forced to fight on the front lines with poor equipment and supplies while living in substandard housing conditions separated from white soldiers(2). Black soldiers were also the first to go into battle and were given the most hazardous details and incurred the most casualties.

At the turn of the century during the late 1880's and the early 1900's, during the boom years of the Industrial Revolution, both black men and women (Negroes) were employed as house servants, gardeners, nannies, washer women or chauffeurs by wealthy white people. Although blacks were permitted closer contact with white people and entrusted with performing as servants and caregivers for white people's children, blacks were still viewed as socially and mentally subservient and were always reminded of their inferior position to the white people they served. Despite black people's suitability for employment, privately they were viciously parodied in film, on stage, and through music. The black-faced white-teethed

Mr. Bojangles (3) and Aunt Jemima (4) characterizations were parodies meant to poke fun at blacks and caused both blacks and whites to view black people less seriously. Anything to keep black people (mainly black men) in fear of white people and to cause black people to think lowly of themselves as a race of people were regularly used by white society.

At the same time, during the Jim Crow era (taken from a racist minstrel song meant to poke fun at black people), black men were beaten, lynched, or burned (black women raped) as they were subjected to harsh social and legal sanctions to enforce racial discrimination against black people (5).

But it was during the rebellious Civil Rights era of the 60's, when black people(African Americans) led by a cadre of defiant black leaders, struggled for equality and equal rights treatment, which began to give way to progress and real change, and at the same time caused a renewed attack against black men. The United States government (who had formerly taken over the practices of white slave owners who were behind most of the assaults against blacks), while continuing their familiar strategy of "divide and conquer", no longer saw it convenient or feasible to openly meddle in the affairs of black people that could be linked directly to an agent or agency of the government. Instead, the FBI, led by J Edgar Hoover, began the practice of engaging "agent provocateurs" (some of whom were black stool pigeons) as tools to infiltrate black organizations or to blatantly murder black leaders whom they thought were "acting up", just like those slaves did back down on the plantation.

The purpose of agent provocateurs during the 60's (as is the case today) was to provide information to the government, keep black leaders (and people) suspicious and divided against each other and silence outspoken black leaders by causing a rift between members of black organizations or to obtain information to be used for blackmail or against black leaders in criminal prosecutions. Even in present day society African Americans are suspicious of each other and still find it difficult to support each other or to form cooperative associations and businesses.

This same trend is prevalent within African American families today whose members scramble to get their own apartment or car in order to be "independent" often to their financial detriment, while other ethnic groups live cooperatively and remain at home or move in with each other until each person is capable of purchasing their own home, business, or car.

Regardless of the tactics used, agents of the United States government used their vast communication networks, unlimited supply of money, and their ability to prosecute to make it costly or deadly for black men who publicly rebelled against the status quo of white people, organized or stood up for their civil and human rights.

What we need to understand is that there have been countless African American men and women who have rebelled, fought, organized, advocated and died for the right to freedom and self-realization in America that so many of our present day African American men and women take for granted by the frivolous and self-centered pursuit of "things", or trying to be something or someone that they are not. Countless past and present African American men and women have demonstrated the epitome of character, virtue, purpose, self-less and fearless leadership, including President Barack H. Obama, our first African American president, now in his second term in office.

But all of our African and African American predecessors must be either turning over in their graves or looking upon present generations of African American men with compassionate shame as many of us squander away several hundred years of progress to individualistic "it's all about me" acts of selfishness, self-hate and dishonor to those who came before them.

Today violence, substance abuse, gang membership, chronic unemployment, massive incarcerations, black on black crimes, domestic violence and the expectation of an early death have become the unwanted but constant bedfellows in the daily life of African American men. For some African American males the completion of high school or future attendance at college has become almost impossible and has given way to other dominant issues.

At the same time some African American men who have a high school education or even advanced education still compete for jobs against whites and other non-whites with college degrees and years of employment experience for the same jobs. Given the current racial and economic times, who do you think employers will hire? Who do you think will be the first to be laid off when employers have to make tough decisions to downsize their businesses?

The picture is more dismal for African American men who drop out of high school or who return to their communities after months or years of incarceration and may be disconnected from family, friends, and other social contacts that lend themselves towards sources of employment and support. In both scenarios, i.e., African American men without a criminal record, and, African American men with the label of a criminal record, both find themselves ready, willing and able to work, but unable to secure employment, despite their educational level or their criminal record.

The writer, despite a college degree and over 25 years of successful employment experience, at times found it difficult to secure employment to meet the needs of my family. But the reality of everyday life is that a key part of manhood or becoming a man is connected to one's ability to access employment that allows one to pay for "things" so you can meet the responsibilities that manhood implies, like paying for your own food, clothing, shelter, transportation, child care, for yourself and for your family.

When a man can't get a job and is not capable of obtaining these basic necessities, men, including others in his life such as his wife, lady or his "baby(s) momma", may begin to question the man's ability and right to call himself a man. Some men may begin to question their own adequacy as men when weeks of searching for a job turn into months of struggling to make ends meet without income and he has not been able to secure and/or maintain viable employment.

The thought of having your woman take care of you during those tough times can be humiliating but has become more prevalent in many African American households than many African American men would care to admit. I personally know how it feels when your children ask you for money for school trips or supplies or just to buy ice cream but you have to say, "No, daddy doesn't have any money. Go and ask your mother."

Because of these kinds of challenges, an increasing number of African American men have become dependent upon women to take care of them. Thinking in this way is not healthy as opposed to responsible men who may have temporarily fallen on hard times and need the understanding and financial support from their wife or lady until they can get themselves together. Partners in a healthy relationship are supposed to support each other when help is needed. But many African American men seem to have accepted dependence upon women as normal no matter how unmanly it appears to be. Some African American men refuse to be dependent on women in this way and simply make the choice to sell drugs which is equally unacceptable.

I do not condone selling drugs because drugs kill people and destroy relationships but I can understand why many of my brothers have turned to the drug trade as a way to make money to support themselves and their families. But like most other forms of illegal or criminal behavior the cost of selling drugs far outweighs the benefits. The benefits certainly don't last as long as the jail or prison sentence that usually comes with it when caught.

As a supplement to this discussion I have provided a summary of each chapter at the end of the book as a review and quick reference guide. In addition, in the Appendix there are some revealing background statistics on the state of affairs of African American men, and the African American family, that I know you will find interesting and useful towards understanding on a larger scale the nature of the many challenges African American men face in this country. Contained within those statistics are many telling reasons why we can no longer turn our backs on the state of affairs amongst African American men that could eventually threaten all of us as American citizens by eroding away the freedoms and quality of life that our ancestors sacrificed their lives so we could enjoy.

What makes the already tenuous condition of African American men in America more unstable is the impact that prolonged life on the streets and repeated incarcerations is having by hindering opportunities for maturity which are essential to healthy development into manhood. Conducting yourself as a man not only assumes knowledge of correct manly values and principles, but also consistent opportunities and experience in mainstream society in the various roles that are demanded of men. Hanging out on every street corner in America banging, selling drugs or sitting in a jail cell in a prison waiting for a correctional officer to tell you what to do, including when you can eat, drink or take a dump is not the kind of maturity-producing experiences that African American men need. Those are not the kind of maturing experiences conducive to healthy development into manhood.

Stuck In Maleness — Russell A. Ligon, Jr.

As African American men when we lack the proper understanding of manhood and what that manhood really means in our everyday life we tend to act out in self-centered and self-destructive ways. Not only is it harmful for us as men but lack of a proper understanding of manhood produces a lot of confusion in the lives of the people connected to us. This has been one of our problems as African American men in America, too much acting and pretending to be men based upon incomplete and incorrect manly values in place of engaging in real manly living.

I still cringe at the thought of all the negativity and confusion my own *"stuck in maleness"* behavior caused me and the people in my life. I have also observed behind prison walls and within society glaring examples of other African American men who lack perspective about life and embrace distorted ideas about what it means to be a man.

During childhood and the early teenage years, males have the opportunity to observe the interaction between their parents and learn what is expected of them as males, members of a family unit and as men. When that relationship is healthy and positive there are usually positive outcomes that follow. But many of our brothers are observing and experiencing the wrong behaviors.

When a father or another positive male role model cannot fill the void, the opportunity for those initial learning experiences are often replaced by a female interpretation of manly behavior or secondary influences from sources outside of the home. In the absence of a healthy sense of purpose for life or who they are as men,

African American youth have gravitated towards street life where they are manipulated and used and abused by others socially, politically and economically. What is more, African American males who have been incarcerated at an earlier age are more at risk to become *"stuck in maleness"* because they are more likely to have grown up without the structure and discipline provided by their father or a positive fatherly male role model during the formative years of childhood when they are most impressionable.

I am the product of parents who divorced when I was very young, before I was five years old. I did not have my father in my life at an early age and neither did my father have his father in his life. I also ended up in a juvenile facility at an early age. In addition, what I knew of my father and how I experienced him was through the jaded lenses of my mother's anger and negative attitude towards him. At such a young age I was not sophisticated enough in my thinking to figure out if my father was really a dead beat dad and neglected me and my siblings, or if he didn't come around because my mother made it too hostile and troublesome for him to be there, so my knowledge and understanding of manhood was limited and biased at best. My father's absence during those beginning years of my life, along with my lack of discipline and maturity had other consequences later during puberty when I acted out and became involved in illegal activities and was sent away to a juvenile facility for nearly three years.

But hanging in the streets or prison life isn't the best and most efficient way to learn about how to become a man. It wasn't for me and neither will it be for other African American men in this country. Gaining maturity and learning about manhood shouldn't be a "make it up as you go" kind of experience where you risk life or limb for yourself or for others. Growing up and becoming a man doesn't and should not have to be that way. This is especially so for men who are certain to be called upon later in life to perform the many roles that manhood implies and to take on other responsibilities as well. Throughout **Stuck In Maleness,** I will emphasize that manhood and becoming a man is not really about the man. Becoming a man is about responding with your God-given and learned skills and abilities to the people and circumstances of your life.

I've learned that as men whenever we mess up, there are a whole series of things that are set in motion that not only affect our lives but also the people in our lives that are tied to our purpose as men.

I said that I was going to leave all of the statistics in the Appendix for you to review at a later time but I must share with you now some information that I want you keep in mind as you proceed through the pages that follow. Think of how these individual factors have played out in your life growing up as a child and the present affect your *"stuck in maleness"* thinking and behavior is having on the people in your life right now. According to Children-our investment.org(6),homes without fathers ultimately affect children in numerous tragic ways:

- 63% of youth suicides are from fatherless homes
- 90% of all homeless and runaway children are from fatherless homes
- 85% of all children who show behavior disorders come from fatherless homes
- 80% of rapists with anger problems come from fatherless homes
- 71% of all high school dropouts come from fatherless homes
- 75% of all adolescent patients in chemical abuse centers come from fatherless homes
- 85% of all youths in prison come from fatherless homes

We must also recognize that many of our African American women suffer from some of the same kinds of issues (stuck in femaleness) that we do as men. When unhealthy thinking African American women become involved in relationships with men *"stuck in maleness"*, it reinforces the negative thinking and behavior patterns of both the man and the woman. When this occurs, it intensifies the corrupted images of manhood in the minds of African American men and makes it more difficult for them to break the cycle of destructive and poorly guided thinking because men will often overcompensate or become more ingrained in their behavior when they feel they have something to prove to a woman.

Because so many of our brothers harbor corrupted and dysfunctional ideas about manhood (and there is so much conflict between us and our women), 72% of African American children are born to unwed mothers (7). A larger number of the African American couples that I know have a "baby momma" or a "baby daddy" involved in their life from a pre-existing relationship, including the couples who are married.

But there is hope and a way out and there is hope with direction if we choose to take it. The Bible in Romans 12:2 says, *"Be ye transformed by the renewing of your mind."* A renewing of their mind is exactly the prescription for healing African American men in America need in order to become healthy and reverse the decaying state of the health of the African American family. Regardless of the seemingly overpowering and crippling influences of government, private industry, politics, policies, discriminatory policing or its agencies, change for the African American man must first originate within his own mind.

Manhood is the condition of a healthy mind. When the thoughts that African American men meditate upon daily are rooted in violence, drugs, alcohol, playing video games, music videos, sex, cars, "getting money", and so on, things that deceptively give the appearance of success, then real success will forever be out of his reach.

The crisis in the African American family (regardless of the larger social forces that I mentioned earlier) is mainly rooted in a crisis within the African American man's mind and the decisions he makes regarding his perception of his self-worth and self-esteem as a man. When the decisions African American men make and the imagery they expose their minds to is changed, and begins to reflect a healthy self-concept with positive character traits such as discipline, vision and purpose as their bedfellows, then the state of the African American family will begin to heal and change as well.

Stuck In Maleness meets the call as a prescription for healing the African American man's mind by providing curative insight into how many of us have become *"stuck in maleness"* and don't even know it. I have provided a relevant and understandable blueprint to uplift African American men out of the limiting and destructive confines of self-centered thinking, and childish behavior of misguided males, into men of vision, purpose and character. The first step to change comes with awareness of the problems and challenges that we face as African American men and the willingness and commitment to do something about them.

Chapter 2
Issues of Domestic Violence

When writing the first edition of **Stuck In Maleness**, I struggled with the idea of whether or not to include a discussion on the topic of domestic violence. I dreaded the thought of having to sort through mounds of literature, research materials and the many case studies written about domestic violence. I also thought that I was being sensitive to the people close to me who themselves have been victims of domestic violence. However, here in the second edition of **Stuck In Maleness** there is no struggle and my position is firm. I have concluded that I would do African American men, women, children, and those close to me a great disservice if I did not address a subject that has become omnipresent, menacing, and sometimes deadly, within an alarming number of African American households.

Domestic violence and abuse traumatizes and kills more than the target of its venom; it can devastate entire families and communities. Laying "hands" on women seems to have become more of an option to a lot of brothers as an acceptable form of communicating feelings of anger, dissatisfaction and even disrespect when dealing with women. I disagree and my purpose for including this chapter on domestic violence is not to point an accusing finger at

African American men because men from other cultures have some of the same issues. Neither is it my intention to portray African American women as victims because sometimes African American women are the perpetrators of domestic violence against men, although that is usually not the case.

There is nothing manly about beating up on women, so my purpose is to briefly discuss some of the bad programming within ourselves as men, and messages from within African American culture and the larger society, that may be causing us to think that way. Laying hands on our women is unmanly. It hinders our development as men and it hinders the psychological and emotional development of the person that is being abused. It's deceptive and unhealthy to think that putting down a woman and/or controlling and abusing another human being can elevate you as a man because it can't. Preying on the weak or dehumanizing another person until they are weak only makes you a bully or an abuser no matter how many ways you chop it up. But as men we can make adjustments in our thinking so that laying hands on a woman, or a child will not be considered acceptable manly behavior; committing violence against another person is a choice. In the previous chapter, *African American Men Under Siege*, I discussed how American society regularly and systematically punishes and emasculates African American men economically, legally, socially and psychologically for just being who we are. I'm pointing this out because people who have suffered experienced abuse, domination, or persecution often repeat the same behaviors onto others, in the same way as in domestic violence. I doubt very much if any brother ever wakes up in the morning thinking, "I'm going to put my foot up my woman's a__ today or maybe I'll smack my child around a bit." But as African American men we must understand the dynamics of what is happening to us in society and its influence on how we relate to the people in our life, especially if we personally have a history of domestic violence and abuse. Here are some revealing facts about domestic violence among African Americans in this country and why we need to continue to work on ourselves as men:

- African Americans, particularly African American women, experience violence resulting in death at the hands of family members more often than any other racial group in the U.S.
- Although the rate of intimate partner homicides among African Americans declined 69.2% from 1976 to 2005, African Americans disproportionately accounted for nearly a third of the intimate partner homicides that occurred in 2005.
- The rate of domestic violence in the African American community can be at least partly attributed to economic factors. Intimate partner violence occurs more often among low-income couples, particularly those in which the male partner is unemployed/underemployed, as well as couples living in poor neighborhoods.

- Alcoholism is related to domestic violence among African American couples more so than among Caucasian or Hispanic couples.
- Domestic violence re-occurs. Over 1/3 of the women who reported domestic violence admitted to being the victim of severe domestic violence earlier in the year (8).
- The number one killer of African American women ages 15 to 34 is homicide at the hands of a current or former intimate partner (9).
- An estimated 95 percent of domestic violence victims are female (10).

What is Domestic Violence and Abuse?

Domestic violence is a "pattern of abusive behavior in any relationship that is used by one partner to gain or maintain power and control over another intimate partner". Domestic violence can be physical, sexual, emotional, economic, or psychological actions or threats of actions that influence another person. This includes any behaviors that intimidate, manipulate, humiliate, isolate, frighten, terrorize, coerce, threaten, blame, hurt, injure, or wound someone(11).Domestic violence can be in many forms and are not limited to the physical act of laying hands on another person. As a matter of fact, the physical side of domestic violence and abuse are often secondary consequences to prolonged patterns of verbal, mental, sexual or economic abuse long before a hand is ever raised.

Where does domestic violence and abuse come from?

Abuse is a learned behavior and usually emerges out of a history of being abused or seeing others abused, such as a parent or relative. For various reasons the abuser perceives a sense of powerlessness or a loss of personal efficacy within themselves so they go about their relationships attempting to manipulate and control the behavior of others. Abusive and violent behavior can be learned through various sources such as:

- Childhood observations of domestic violence.
- One's own experience of victimization.
- Exposure to community, school, or peer group violence.
- Living in a culture of violence (e.g., violent movies or videogames, community norms, and cultural beliefs (12).

What is more, domestic violence and abusive behavior are often reinforced by cultural values and beliefs that are repeatedly communicated through the media and other societal institutions that tolerate it. Rap music lyrics, suggestive rap videos that objectify and portray women in submissive and sexually degrading positions, violent movies, and our insatiable diet for violent sports, all play a part in reinforcing the mindset of men who believe that women are not to be respected beyond their sexual or economic usefulness. The perpetrator's violence is further supported when peers, family members, or others in the community (e.g., co-workers, social service providers, police, or even clergy) minimize the abuse and fail to provide consequences. As a result, the abuser learns that not only is his behavior justified, but it is also acceptable. Earlier in this chapter, I stated that abuse is a learned behavior and usually emerges out of a history of being abused or seeing others abused. Those are undeniable facts and can be a starting point for us to understand the problem at hand. But I know that some of you will balk at the implication here, "but Russ, I haven't experienced abuse; I don't have a history of domestic violence or abuse in my family." That too may be an undeniable fact. But I'd like to go beyond the conventional view of domestic violence and suggest that you consider things on a broader scale. As a culture, and as African American men, we go through many of the same experiences that people who are being abused go through. The abuse and violence that we experience may not be relationship based but white people have been putting their foot in our a__ for years and they continue to do so today. Let's keep it real; although we instinctively know this fact, many of us block it out of our minds. Like someone being abused, many of us continue to perceive ourselves as powerless and we continue to our abuser in the same way. We don't change our behavior (or get out of the relationship) that we know is no longer healthy for us.

Instead, many of us displace our insecurities, lack of motivation, failure to plan, addictions, weaknesses, money problems, and our perception of impotence onto the people closest to us, mainly a woman because many of us feel that we have to prove our manhood to women, even if in a dysfunctional way. But manhood is an inside job and so is our sense of power and personal efficacy. Because a lot of us don't feel good about ourselves as men, or we are trying to hustle or come out of a bad situation, subconsciously many of us may perceive the only things we have under our control and influence are the women and children in our lives. It certainly is understandable; the frustration, alienation, and anger that some of us may feel when we can't secure a job or because the job we have doesn't provide the kind of income that allows us to be who we feel we should be. The challenge for us as men is to become better men by strengthening ourselves on the inside. Mental toughness is what we need to propel us forward in our relationships. We should not rely on our physical instincts and attributes as men to solve our relationship or family problems. Let's face it; most men are bigger and stronger than most women and most men are also usually more aggressive than most women and are more inclined to become physical. Being physical is a big part of our human nature as men which is nurtured and encouraged in just about every area of our development, including gym class, sports competitions, or the sports that we watch on television. But tossing a basketball into a hoop, throwing a football or lifting heavy weights does not imply that we should do the same with a woman or a child.

    Our manhood should be about character, discipline, restraint, and most importantly, respect towards self and others. When you choose to lay hands on a woman just because you're frustrated, angry, had a bad day, because she's "mouthing off", because you're intoxicated, because you perceived that she disrespected you or because she may have even laid hands on you, you have crossed the lower side of being a man and have delved into another dimension of thought. Your sense of a loss of power and control must be addressed within, not violently or abusively expressed onto a woman.

Domestic violence and abuse are also an unfortunate outcome when we choose to align ourselves with the wrong woman, for the wrong reasons. For example, you often hear brothers say, "I want a woman with a nice car, a career woman, a woman with her own home, you know, a "strong black woman" who's out there making that money." But as soon as she shows up into a brother's life, all of a sudden we start feeling intimidated, insecure, offended, or that she disrespected us with her mannerisms and self-confidence. But the truth be told, any visionless, purposeless, goal-less, lazy, or weak male is going to feel like that anyway, especially if he is unemployed, underemployed or may have self-worth or self-esteem issues. By not having a job, a healthy sense of self-worth, self-esteem, or self-control, this kind of man is more inclined to try to control and abuse women because of how he feels on the inside, although most men won't admit to that being the problem. This is why I've stated that the tendency to control or abuse a woman is an issue with us, not the woman.

Brothers, we need to check ourselves and check the way we are handling our business with our women and children. Many women (and men) who are being abused do not see themselves as victims and many abusers do not see themselves as abusers. Domestic violence is about one person in a relationship using a pattern of behaviors to control the other person. It can happen to people who are married, single, heterosexual, gay, living together, separated, or just dating. Some of us have gotten so used to putting on an image of being tough that we don't see the terror in our toughness when it comes to our relationships with women. Women are not other men, and we should not treat them that way. The following are some warning signs that may be suggestive that you have a problem with domestic violence and abuse or that you may be in a violent and abusive relationship. If you or your partner repeatedly uses one or more of the following to control the other you may be in an abusive relationship:

SIGNS THAT YOU'RE IN AN ABUSIVE RELATIONSHIP (13)	
Your Inner Thoughts and Feelings	Your Partner's Belittling Behavior
Do you:	Does your partner:
Feel afraid of your partner much of the time?	Humiliate or yell at you?
Avoid certain topics out of fear of angering your partner?	Criticize you and put you down?
Feel that you can't do anything right for your partner?	Treat you so badly that you're embarrassed for your friends or family to see?
Believe that you deserve to be hurt or mistreated?	Ignore or put down your opinions or accomplishments?
Wonder if you're the one who is crazy?	Blame you for their own abusive behavior?
Feel emotionally numb or helpless?	See you as property or a sex object, rather than as a person?
Hurt you, or threaten to hurt or kill you?	Control where you go or what you do?
Does your partner:	Does your partner:
Threaten to take your children away or harm them?	Keep you from seeing your friends or family?

SIGNS THAT YOU'RE IN AN ABUSIVE RELATIONSHIP (13)	
Your Partner's Violent Behavior or Threats	Your Partner's Controlling Behavior
Does your partner:	Does your partner:
Have a bad and unpredictable temper?	Act excessively jealous and possessive?
Threaten to commit suicide if you leave?	Limit your access to money, the phone, or the car?
Force you to have sex?	Constantly check up on you?
Destroy your belongings?	

As you continue to read through the pages of **Stuck In Maleness**, you will begin to learn more about yourself and why you think the way you do as a man. You will learn that some of the things that are a part of your thought process are childish and immature. They may also be unhealthy and dysfunctional, such as the case with issues of domestic violence and abuse. But most importantly you will gain insights into how to change your thinking and to become a better man. Part of being a man is learning from your mistakes and maturing as you go from one life experience to another. If you do find that you have an issue with one or more of the behaviors in the list above, check yourself and seek help from a professional counselor or therapist. There is nothing unmanly about getting help. Life is a terrible thing to waste.

Chapter Three
Why So Many Faces?

"No one comes to know himself through introspection.... rather, it is in dialogue, in his meeting with other persons. It is only by expressing his convictions to others that he becomes really conscious of them. He who would see himself clearly must open up to a confidant freely chosen and worthy of such trust. It may be a friend just as easily as a doctor: it may also be one's marital partner."(14)
~Paul Tournier, Swiss psychiatrist

The quote by Swiss psychiatrist Paul Tournier speaks volumes to the dilemma we're faced with daily, not only to be a man or a woman but also to the challenges we face with being human. The challenges of being a man, an African American man under siege, whether or not we are faced with *"stuck in maleness"* issues is secondary and irrelevant if we cannot come to terms with who we are as a person. On top of that we must find ways to balance the challenges of being a person along with the roles that we play in our daily lives such as employee, father, son, brother, husband, "baby daddy", and so on.

As men, and as African American men under siege with so many negative images in the world about who we are as men, it has become a normal part of our socialization process to develop "faces" or images that conceal who we really are as men on the inside. Growing up as children our parents, siblings or close relatives are usually the ones that initiate us into the practice of putting on faces or images when they say "Stop crying like a little girl", "Stop acting like a sissy", "Stop acting like you scared", "Stop acting like a punk," or "Stop acting up before them white people think you crazy."Intentional or not, the messages sent to us (and the messages we communicate to others) is that we are not acting right or that we are not expressing ourselves in an acceptable manner, so begins the process and habit of putting on a "face" to project an image that we think others will find acceptable. As men we are even more prone to these kinds of behaviors because of how we are socialized as males. If word gets out that you are weak or a punk it could make things hard for you in school, on the street or with the ladies. So along the road of our development we pick up the idea that boys don't cry, only girls do that; as males we have to be rough and tough all of the time or that it's not ok for us to be afraid, and so on.

Some of us men take the image too seriously and too far when we get ourselves caught in a vicious cycle of deception that can become confusing, expensive, and lonely when we use sex, drugs, money, cars and association or membership with certain groups of people as the basis of maintaining our image. The fact of the matter is that you cannot truly begin to change controlling and abusive behaviors or get "unstuck" out of maleness if you do not or cannot face up to the person on the inside of you. Manhood is an inside job and so is finding out who you are as a person.

You Gotta Know Who You Are

Many of the attitudes and behaviors that men *"stuck in maleness"* struggle with as adults, such as being controlling or abusive, started in childhood when we began getting messages from others that it was not ok for us to be ourselves. I have three older sisters and as a child they would rough me up at times when I did not respond to situations in the way they thought I should. I played football as a youth and many of the moves I used on the football field were grinded out at home dodging the wrath of my older sisters.

There are also many men and women, who experience the need to put on a face to cover up who they really are because of the sins of their parents. They may have developed a protective shield to hide the little boy, or little girl, inside of themselves while growing up but the habit of hiding their true identity continued to remain into adulthood. Growing up without a parent, not knowing who your parents are or being traumatized by the behavior and lifestyle of a chronically irresponsible, abusive or even violent parent certainly can instill a sense of incompleteness and/or anger in anyone. Everyone has a story about who they are and how they got to be the way they are.I certainly have my story to tell, but *YOU* and only *YOU* must come to know *YOUR* story, accept its existence, good or bad, and come to terms with how your story has affected you and how it is affecting the man and the person you are today. With that thought in mind, who are you? I really want you to give this some thought. No, you are not a "grown ass man", a "real nigga", " a pimp", a "drug dealer", an "addict", a "real man", a "Blood", a "Crip", a "cop", a "lawyer", or any of those things. Those are merely the images and faces that you or others have come to associate with your outer veneer. Some of those images and faces were given to you, and you bought into them at an early age, while others you chose for yourself or came about because of things you've done in life, while others were the result of circumstances beyond your control such as abuse or the sins of your parents.

What I am referring to is who you are on the *INSIDE*, the part of you that you conceal and hide from others. Who are you behind all of the faces that you present to your lady, your boys, your co-workers at the office, the students in your class or the homies on the block? Are you hurting inside because of abuse or domestic violence you experienced as a child? Are you angry at your parents for not being there for you when you were a kid? Do you feel that society or a particular person owes you something for the harms you've incurred in life? Have you been hiding yourself behind clothes, cars, women, or drugs and alcohol? If you are truly to be freed from the need to put on deceptive faces you must begin to recognize the feelings and emotions that are the lifeline to the faces and images that you project to others. Let me give you an example using myself. In public when I am at work or speaking somewhere, I tend to be focused, serious, and I usually have on my professional face. But in the safety of home I can be very sensitive. In fact I am usually the first one to cry or get mushy during a movie or when I hear a tragic story on the news. Yeah, I said it! Also, sometimes my first reaction to unknown or uncertain situations is fear. Fear is sometimes my initial reaction because I don't know how things are going to turn out or how I am going to handle a particular situation. But I've developed ways to overcome my initial fears by gathering more information, asking God to give me the strength to overcome them, or I simply take the plunge and work through my fears. I've come to accept that part of myself and I'm certainly comfortable with it because it's who I am. But that's me. So who is the *REAL* insert your name? I want you to think about this question and be honest with the answers you discover because only then will you be in position to change. I have a tee shirt that I wear sometimes that says, "*You Mad Bro?*" Every time that I wear that tee shirt I get feedback or a comment from the people around me. On several occasions I spontaneously answered honestly, "Yeah, I'm mad as hell!" Much to my surprise, most of the answers I receive are sincere and useful. What I am saying is that because I am honest about how I am feeling other people are honest with me. They challenge me to do something about my presumed anger. I'm challenging you to be honest with yourself about how you feel on the inside. If you find yourself angry, annoyed, fearful, anxious, sad, or whatever the situation might be, but you never do anything to *CHANGE* the circumstances behind those feelings, you will do both yourself and others a great deal of harm. You will continue to be just another angry, sad, "pissed off" person/brother/black man trapped inside of a male's body. The lifeline to putting on false images and faces to the world will always be there beneath your protective veneer until you decide to get honest with yourself and change it.

What is more, when you cannot be yourself, you in turn hinder and prevent the people in your life from expressing who they really are as well. The sins of our parents or the problems that we've had in childhood do not just go away, they become the sins and problems that we inflict onto the women and children in our life every time we walk through the front door after work and see our children doing their homework or watching television and when we climb into the bed next to our wife or partner. It probably gets very lonely inside pretending to be someone that you are not so come out and let the world know who you really are.

Inside-Out versus Outside-In

In the process of getting to know who the real you is on the inside, you will also learn things about yourself. Not only are you a sensitive, caring, angry, fearful, compassionate, loving, emotional person, but you may also learn that you may have developed some potentially negative faces, or behaviors, like being stubborn, mean, resentful, vindictive, argumentative, abusive or even controlling at times.

I knew a guy named Big Tank who seemed to always have an unnecessarily abrasive and sometimes mean way of relating to the women he dated. Big Tank's relationships with women didn't last long so he dated a lot. As a matter of fact, it was rare if you'd see Big Tank with the same woman more than twice. At first I couldn't understand why Big Tank went through so many women. Initially I thought that it was because Big Tank was a player and that he was just "using and abusing" women and getting rid of them after he got what he wanted from them, but I was only partially right in my assumption. When I thought about it, I realized that Big Tank always seemed to use his size and a tough guy veneer, or face, as a way of relating to people, certainly women. Later I learned the reasons why Big Tank may have been "excessive" in his demeanor towards women and why his relationships didn't last very long. Big Tank had been sexually assaulted as an 11 year-old boy by his baby sitter, a woman. On top of that Big Tank had what is generally known as a learning disability. Because of the learning disability Big Tank wasn't a good speller and he didn't do well when it came to filling out applications and applying for things that required a lot of detail. So as a defense mechanism and a way to cover up the real Big Tank on the inside, he used his size, looks and a tough guy image to deal with the people in his life, particularly women. Out in public it wasn't uncommon to see Big Tank's lady in front of him getting the tickets or paying for things while Big Tank chilled in the background or off to the side. That's because Big Tank was insecure and didn't want people to find out about his issues on the inside

Eventually, Big Tank's style of dealing with life, and women, from the protective face of a tough guy image got the best of him and, more than once, he got locked up for domestic violence for putting his hands on a woman. One of the challenges that we face when we become accustomed to hiding the real person inside is that we interact with others from the outside-in instead of the inside-out, just like Big Tank. What I mean is, that we tend to show people, for example our lady, an image of the person that we'd like them to see or an image of the person we believe they want to see instead of revealing who we really are. A lot of women, for example, may have the image of men or African American men as being very tough, masculine, macho or even emotionless. When we show them anything less than a tough guy persona we risk being perceived as a punk, a coward, or a p…y. I think you get the message. So instead of being ourselves many of us go into our relationships with women try to be cool, mean-spirited, cruel, excessively accommodating, controlling, intolerant or anything that fits the image we believe they want to see. That's what I mean about the outside-inside way of dealing with people

Certainly not all men handle things in the way Big Tank did but we all, more or less, can probably relate to the challenges of not always being ourselves. This is particularly so when it comes to things about ourselves that we perceive as embarrassing or very personal. The protective faces and images we put on do not always originate in childhood and may come about from experiences as adults. Every now and then I get a flashback from one such experience. A few years back my ex in a fit of anger at me for something petty, lashed out at me and threw some personal business of mine up in my face with the intent of hurting me. Her comments did hurt and they struck me in the chest like a Mack truck and my ego was badly injured. The rage I felt inside of me because of her betrayal of my trust in her, if outwardly expressed, could have been fatal. But the shock and embarrassment I also felt immobilized me where I stood and I haven't been the same since. Every time I meet someone new, those past experiences with my ex come to mind. I think that it is important to be honest with people about who you are or things that have occurred in your life but I do hesitate before I reveal sensitive information about myself to another person, especially to a woman. I've gotten better at about opening up to people and I've learned that everyone is not the same. Sometimes you must take risks with people but if you really don't want something to be known about you then don't put it out there. It is understandable that those kinds of experiences make us want to protect our inner self and keep the delicate and sensitive aspects of our life hidden away where we believe no one can harm us. But the longer you pretend to be someone that your are not the harder it becomes to break those habits which at some point may become harmful to us and they often do. Also, in the short term we might be able to get away with living our life behind false images and putting on deceptive faces but a long term pattern of suppressing your true feelings or your true self can lead to chronic stress, controlling behaviors, sleeping or eating disorders, depression or other dysfunctions like drug and alcohol abuse. In order to get in touch with the real you and to change the way you think about yourself, there are three points I'd like you to keep in mind: 1) If you don't make changes you will continue to have the same problems, 2) Your family and friends are supposed to respect and support the person that you are, not who they think you should be, and 3) You are not your environment.

Making Change

Some time ago, I was down to my last twenty dollars. My hooptie (my car) wasn't working and I had several things I needed to accomplish that day. First, I had to get to work but work was too far for me to walk. My plan after I got off work was to go over to my "baby momma's" house and spend some time with her. But her house was too far to get to by foot as well. When I thought about it, the problem wasn't that my car was out of operation or that I was down to my last twenty dollars. The problem was that I needed to take the bus and I couldn't get on the bus with a twenty dollar bill, so I needed change. When the first bus came along I asked the driver and the passengers on the bus for change but neither could accommodate my need for change. When the second bus came thirty minutes later I ran into the same problem, no one could provide change for me. Finally, I remembered there was a gas station about 15 minutes away by foot but in the other direction so I broke down and walked the thirty minutes round trip to the gas station and returned, change in hand. Then and only then was I able to catch the bus and make it to work and later to my "baby momma's" house as planned. The reason I told you this story was not to tell you about the activities of a day in my life or how difficult it is to get on a city bus with a twenty dollar bill and certainly not that I once drove a hooptie. I told you this story because the activities of the days of your life will continue to be the same if you do not begin to think outside of your usual way of doing things and make the needed "change" so that you can go on about your life in a healthy and productive manner. Making change is going to require you to break down your life (make change), your thought process, and the real outcome of the things that you do into the smallest pieces and sort through the parts of your thinking that are positive and productive for you from the parts of your thinking that are negative and may be causing you harm. Sometimes we can do this form of introspection and reflection and change ourselves, and sometimes we may need help of a support group or a professional counselor or therapist. If you need change for a twenty dollar bill or even a fifty, I can help you but change in your life will have to come from you no matter how much money that you have in your pocket or what you may read in a book.

You are not your environment

If you are going to make change in your life and get in touch with the person on the inside of you (which I strongly encourage you to do), you can no longer buy into the belief that you are merely a product of your environment. Rats, roaches, stray dogs, and so on are products of their environment because they function through inbred predispositions and instinct. You, my brother, are not a rat or roach no matter what neighborhood you come from. Unlike a rat or roach, you have the ability to think, make choices and decisions, reflect back on things you've experienced and you have the ability to plan ahead.

I am not saying that your environment can't or doesn't influence you or play a part in who and what you are but your environment is not a life sentence to failure, low grades, selling or using drugs, prison, being mean or abusive to women or others, a life of mediocrity or making excuses about why you can't do better. I've experienced some of those things but I didn't stay there because I wanted a better outcome for myself and for my children. I didn't write this book to reaffirm racial, cultural or gender stereotypes so you'd have an excuse to continue doing things the same way you've been doing them. This book is about making change in your life and my message is a call for you to take action. I know of men and women from the hood who made it and I know of men and women from the suburbs and working class families who have lived some very destructive and negative lifestyles but it was through the collective decisions they made in life that got them where they are, not simply a reaction to their environment.

If your friends don't support the REAL you, get new ones!

The second worst thing than not being yourself is caving into the views that other people have of you just so they will like you. Subconsciously, we all do this when we are in public or when we are around certain people, like white people, because we are socialized to be concerned about what other people will think of us. I learned the hard way that you cannot please most of the people most of the time, no matter how hard you try. But real friends, niggas, homies, women, or whoever, will accept you for who and what you are, no matter what. If you find yourself having to justify your beliefs, make excuses about your take on a situation to others or you find yourself constantly up against the ropes with your lady or your friends then get rid of them and get new ones.

I am not saying that you should dump the people in your life who may be genuinely attempting to help you but you just don't want to give up a negative behavior or lifestyle. Life is stressful enough (and much too short) without having the added burden of worrying about what another man or woman thinks of you. But if those people themselves are a negative influences on your life then you may need to send them walking, including family members that may have you trapped in the past. That may seem a bit harsh and I am sure that many of my readers will balk at my comments but so what? I recommend that they take my advice and apply it to their lives as well. I could say more about this topic but I am not. It's simple and straight forward, you just have to be willing to step out of your comfort zone and put it into practice. Remember, the people in your life are not going to change for you; *YOU* have to change for *YOU*. When you focus on being yourself and being good to you, you will begin to attract the kind of people to you that affirm who *YOU* are. My pastor says that "sometimes people simply cannot be happy for us." Because of their own insecurities they cannot stand to be happy for us, to celebrate our successes, what God has done for us, what He is doing in our life without feeling that it takes away from them. As a result they either try to interject themselves into our life, in our successes or they'll try and find a way to criticize us and put us down.

Setting Boundaries

In order to sort through the people in your life (family, friends, co-workers, colleagues or teammates) who will support your transition to becoming the real you, and to get rid of the people who will not, you gotta set some boundaries. Boundaries are like property lines or the markings that we see on the ground during construction or when a road is being repaired. Those markings, or boundaries, serve as communication to others that something is about to change or to be built on that location. Boundaries are everywhere and they tell us many things about the people who use them. When we see boundaries, for example the different colored jerseys that our favorite basketball or football teams wears, we are able to identify our team from their opponent, which side of the stands to sit on at a game and who is winning when we look up at the scoreboard. Dr. Henry Cloud and Dr. John Townsend in their book *Boundaries: When To Say Yes How To Say No To Take Control Of Your Life*(15) identified three basic types of boundaries that can start as a beginning point for getting in touch with the real you and learning to express the real you to the people in your life. Doing so will not only empower you to begin taking control of your life but setting boundaries for yourself and others can be a beginning point to making your life less stressful by reducing the conflicting emotions you might feel when people try to impose their views, opinions, or problems onto you and by empowering you to set limits for yourself. Drs. Cloud and Henry say that *"boundaries are personal property lines that define who you are and who you are not, and influence all areas of your life.*' **Physical boundaries** help you determine who may touch you and under what circumstances. **Mental** boundaries give you the freedom to have your own thoughts and opinions. **Emotional** boundaries help you deal with your own emotions and disengage from the harmful, manipulative emotions of others. For a full explanation of the subject of boundaries you might want to read their book but you may already see from the brief description the need to set boundaries in one or more areas of your life. I'll end this chapter with a quote from *The Art of Talking So That People Will Listen* by Paul W. Swets:

> *"Self-confidence enables one to speak his mind and listen fully to the thoughts of the other person. Unjust demands, extreme positions, judgmental attitudes—these are as contrary to self-confidence as night is today. Not needing to project or protect a false image, the self-confident person is more open to viewpoints different from his own, more able to speak with sincerity and integrity…..Self-confidence, like self-esteem, is not built in a day. The building process begins with drawing a blueprint of who you are, who you want to be, and how you want to come across to people. Taken one step at a time, the construction of self-confidence is relatively easy. Anyone can acquire more of it when he acts upon his own clear plan for development."* (16)

No matter how many secrets, sore spots or problems that you have in your head or in your past, doing nothing about them and covering them up with deceptive faces will continue to get you nowhere but stuck within yourself and stuck within the problems and issues that you hide from others. Until you deal with your issues on the inside and your particular issues with manhood, you will continue to hold other people, mainly the women in your life, hostage just for trusting you enough to have a relationship with them.

Chapter 4
Myths and Misconceptions About Manhood

"Turn away my eyes from looking at worthless things, and revive me in your way" (Psalm 119:37)

"Who do you think you're talking to? I'm a grown ass man!" said Charles, Felicia's husband, as he pounded on his chest with an open hand. Charles was angry at his wife for yelling at him in front of their three children. Charles had almost lost his job for getting to work late three days in a row after several nights of drinking and hanging out with his friends. Felicia yelled at Charles because he didn't put his family first who were dependent upon him for financial support. When it came to Charles' family, they always seemed to come "Honey, I'm sorry" second to his hangout buddies down at the bar.

Nick doesn't work at all. As a matter of fact, Nick hasn't held a job in three years. After dropping out of school five years ago, Nick gave up on starting his career for street life, especially when the economy went bad in 2007. Nick lives with his mother in a small two bedroom apartment above a furniture store and spends most of his time sleeping late into the afternoon or playing video games. At 24, Nick hustles for a living. Every day he waits until it gets dark outside and puts time in on the block near his apartment selling crack to the local fiends, the prostitutes and their tricks, or whoever will buy it. Actually, Nick doesn't like selling drugs and looks down on people who use drugs but he does it anyway. Selling drugs supports his ultra-flamboyant lifestyle and provides the ready cash to buy things for his girlfriend Trude, who always seems to want something.

Whenever Nick complains to Trude that he's going to give up selling drugs and go back to school, Trude withholds sex until he gives in to her demands. "Why you always tripping?" says Trude whenever Nick tries to change direction in his life.

Nick has been to the county jail twice for drug possession, but got off with 3 years probation. During Nick's last incarceration at the county jail, his mother went into his room and counted seventeen pairs of nearly new sneakers, and several pairs of Timberland boots of various styles and colors! Not surprising, Nick didn't have enough money to make bail so his mother had to borrow money from her pension.

Clarence is a 47 year-old government employee married to Debra, a 53 year-old pediatrician. As a doctor, Debra earns a lot more money than Clarence and is involved in a variety of civic and social activities. As the top income earner in the household, Debra pays most of the bills and usually picks up the tab whenever she and Clarence go out to dinner with friends. To their friends Clarence and Debra are the perfect couple, but privately things are quite different, at least they are in Clarence's mind. Clarence despises the fact that his wife earns considerably more money than he does and enjoys financial freedoms he doesn't. Clarence feels insecure with his wife Debra earning more money than he does and increasingly questions his ability as a man.

When Clarence isn't working, he often stays home and drinks. The only time that Clarence seems to be able to exert any control over Debra is when she's home away from her colleagues at work. When intoxicated, Clarence tends to become verbally abusive towards his wife, especially whenever she expresses concern about his drinking and insists that he get help.

These scenarios are but a few examples of African American men *"stuck in maleness"*. They occur every day in the lives of African American men in communities across America. I discovered that a lot of these situations occur with African American men because a lot of African American men have low self-worth and unhealthy ideas about what it means to be men. Many African American men are stuck into negative behaviors as men because they have a negative belief system about themselves and what it means to be a man.

Some of the negative thoughts we have about ourselves as men have to do with slavery, racism and how we have been treated as men in American society and some have to do with traumatic and/or unhealthy programming as children. In Chapter 1, I spoke at length about racism and how many African American men are being targeted by the police, the criminal justice system, the educational system and other stakeholders who have invested in the negative outcome of our lives in order to make a profit. In the same way that many of us have and/or are hustling in the street to make money, there are people hustling us, and pimping our lives in order to make a profit. But the rules of the game are different for them than they are for most African American men. For example, when it comes to the street drug trade, we get three to five years for committing a crime but they go undetected or get probation for committing the same crime but on a larger scale. "How he gonna get probation for five ounces of powder cocaine and I got five years with a three year stipulation for five grams of crack? He's the one I bought it from!" Guys that hustle in the streets know what I'm talking about.

And those of you who have been arrested or did time in prison know and understand how we are pimped and played out within the criminal justice system. At the same time, we are just as complicit in our own self-destruction as the people we complain about that target us on the streets and in the legal system. When I did wrong I knew what I was doing wasn't right and that it was a chance that I'd get caught.

Most African American men understand the connection between bad thoughts and bad behavior but we do what we want to do anyway, and worry about the consequences later because of the distorted and dysfunctional image that we have of ourselves as men. Having low self-worth and low self-esteem are lethal bedfellows when it comes expressing our manhood. I'm just keeping it real. But as you know, the consequences for acting now and thinking later have become much more severe, expensive and life changing than they were in the past. Everything I said at the beginning of this book is true. I provided the source information at the end of the book for anyone who may want to check behind me to see if I know what I'm talking about. And for those brothers who still want to remain stuck in their maleness game and want to continue to play the victim or point the finger of blame at others for what *YOU* must ultimately be held accountable for, your life, you need to grow up and stop playing with fire. One of the main reasons that I wrote this book was because I got tired of playing the victim, blaming "white people", my parents and sometimes a woman, for what was not going well in my life.

A big part of the reason why I was always trying to "get myself together" was because I had subconsciously and unknowingly given away my manhood and my powers of choice and decision making as a man over to other people. Subconsciously, I was looking for someone to "hook me up", to give me a break or for good fortune to just drop into my lap and that I would not have to do anything or make any decisions in my life. I've already addressed the fact that the criminal justice system is a business and that there is a financial motive to decisions regarding the incarceration of African American men, even when the law enforcement official is African American. That's because the criminal justice system, and the policies and practices they promulgate, are larger and exert a constraining influence over the decisions of any one person. Maintaining their job security and income is more important than you losing your job or going to jail. At the time, my parole officer knew I worked two jobs, had a steady residence, and otherwise didn't have any problems. But the fact of the matter was that I still gave my manhood and my power of choice over to him (or her) where I had to rely on their mercy when I got parole violations. Basically I put them in the position of deciding between my life and their job. What do you think they decided to do? What do you think that others will decide for you should you be in that situation?

In order for me to better understand the context of some of the negative, unmanly behaviors I was engaged in more clearly, I had to take a closer and honest look at myself and the imagery behind my thoughts that were causing me to think in an immature, unmanly and unproductive way. What I discovered was that the same thought process, or belief system, that caused me to go to prison several times was also the same system of thought that was causing me to think and act unmanly in my personal relationships with women and how I parented my children. I was not simply *"stuck in maleness"* in one area of my life without also being *"stuck in maleness"* in other areas as well and neither will that be the case for you. It doesn't matter what your position or station in life or how much money you make, unmanly thinking and behavior is just that, unmanly.

In order for us to fully stand up as men and to free ourselves from the grips of immature, unmanly, childish thinking and behaviors we must become aware of what is it that's causing us to be stuck; i.e., what is causing us to think and behave the way we do in the first place, otherwise we will continue "hustling backwards" as men and as a people or to be hustled by others all the way to the bank or the grave and we will have nothing in life to show for it but heartache and misery for ourselves and for our families.

I remember a training I attended years ago as a part of one of the positions I held at the time. While sitting in the class waiting for the instructor to appear I looked up at the chalk board and saw the letters K.I.S.S. written in large letters on the chalk board. They meant "KEEP IT SIMPLE STUPID." When I began seeking to understand this manhood thing and how I was going to change my life, I had to begin with the basics by starting with a basic understanding of manhood. So I am going to do the same thing here for you although some topics will require more detail than others.

In order for you to get the most out of **Stuck In Maleness**, I'd like to begin by discussing the meaning of several simple but powerful words that a lot of brothers seem to have a misunderstanding of and often misinterpret their meaning and how they apply to their life. Manhood [1] is composed of two primary qualities or characteristics:1) The attainment of a legal age (18) that classifies one as an adult male, and 2) Qualities associated with being a man. The first characteristic is a given and is achieved by the natural aging process and the act of puberty as our bodies change.

This is where I believe the main misconceptions about being a man with African American men begins. Males, in a rush to grow up believe that once they've reached 18 they are automatically men. Every kid in America knows when they will turn 18 because there are various legal and social benefits that come along with its attainment

---

[1] The condition of being an adult male (which has to do with our age); qualities associated with men (physical, intellectual, behavioral, character, maturity), manliness (17)

such as being able to purchase cigarettes, vote, work a full-time job or obtain a driver's license. Our bodies get bigger, some of us grow facial hair and our voices become deeper and we begin to sound like a man. In a word, we experience a physical growth spurt, mostly on the outside of our bodies that signals to the world that we've changed. That period is usually when we start wearing men sized shoes and can no longer get away with shopping in the boys section of the store, and we have to start buying our clothes in the men's section. "Dora Lee, look at that boy, he done grown up, he's a man now and he look just like his father." Many of you can remember those embarrassing but ego-reinforcing comments from relatives who knew you were on your way to becoming a man and other people were beginning to recognize it as well. Some of you may have to think back a little farther than others to recollect those days but remember you will. Those are physical changes that we go through but almost no emphasis is placed on the "qualitative" aspects associated with manhood, such as responsibility, leadership, honesty, sacrifice and character. People (including many of us men) just assume that we will pick up the other "stuff" along the way, but I've seen that in reality that is not what really happens. Manhood is more than achieving a chronological number, it is a condition of a man's mind and how it he responds to the circumstances of his life with his God-given learned and developed skills and abilities.

The mental picture or image[2] of manhood, which we now understand, must include both quantitative (age requirements) and qualitative (maturity) aspects in order to be accurate, but must also include the invaluable role of experience in the development of manhood as well. Now we are getting somewhere in understanding manhood, at least conceptually. But concepts without direction and the proper training and understanding of how we are as men and what it means to be a man is a recipe for disaster.

Our minds and the imagery behind our thoughts, becomes a powerful force that influences our attitudes and our behaviors through repetition and reinforcing experiences (negative or positive). The image making part of our brain recognizes patterns and converts our thoughts into a system of thought or belief system[3]. We conduct ourselves as men the way we do because that is how our minds have been trained to do so. When someone approaches you, your group, or even your family with ideas, information, or conduct that you disagree with, or you may not be familiar with, you might say, "Naw man, I don't get down like that, I don't do that kind of thing." That's because the information was contrary to your belief system. In a sense, the information that you've obtained about manhood so far has become your own personalized form of religion or belief system, negative or positive.

---

[2] A mental picture or conception; to call up a mental picture of; the power to imagine (18)

[3] An individual or institutional set of attitudes, behaviors and practices (19)

Stuck In Maleness — Russell A. Ligon, Jr.

Our belief system, mostly on a subconscious level, acts like the central processing unit of a computer and processes the images, thoughts and behaviors that are programmed into our minds into behaviors, attitudes and a certain mindset towards ourselves and others. Think about it, where did you get the programming for your understanding of manhood from? Did it come from your father, an uncle, an older brother, a pimp or drug dealer that you looked up to on the street, a gang, the church, or participating in a fraternity? These are very important questions that you must answer if you are to change your way of thinking and the kind of life you live as a man.

Let's take a look at Charles, Nick and Clarence, the men I introduced at the beginning of the chapter. How each of them chose to express their manhood was different and a reflection of how they were individually socialized, or "trained" to see themselves as men. Clarence became angry over how his wife spoke to him in front of their children, not how his behavior affected his family. Nick continued to sell drugs so he could buy "things" to keep the attention and sexual intimacy of his girlfriend Trude despite the real risk of incarceration. Clarence felt inferior and less of a man because of *his* perception of his wife's position and how much money she made in relation to himself, so he coped with these feelings by drinking and being abusive towards her which made him feel bigger. But you'll notice that in each case how these men felt about themselves was controlled by the imagery of manhood in their mind and was displaced onto other people. When your concept and understanding of manhood is tied up into things or the opinions of people outside of you, you have less control over your emotions and decision making and it makes it more difficult for you to take responsibility for your choices and your behavior. It also makes it easier to blame others for your problems and for you to do nothing about changing the circumstances of your life.

When we look at manhood as something outside of us, it reminds me of a game the kids at my school and I would play. We placed a popsicle-stick on the shoulder a boy (or girl) we were trying to pick a fight with. The instigating kid would give the popsicle stick a name like "this is your mother", a name that would get an emotional reaction out of the other kid. Then we'd pluck the popsicle stick off the other kid's shoulder. As the popsicle stick fell to the ground we'd say "I just knocked your mother onto the ground, what are you going to do about it, punk?" Usually this would be enough to tick the kid off or at least embarrass them enough to want to save face. Within minutes somebody got pushed or a punch would be thrown and a fight was on. Quite often the fight ended with a busted lip or a lump on someone's head. The fact of the matter is that neither the popsicle stick nor the words spoken over it possessed any special powers. But as boys we were unsophisticated in our thinking and immature in our emotional development, so we were easily provoked. The perception we had of ourselves gave the popsicle stick and the words spoken over it power over us. This is just like when your lady says "you're acting just like a child" or "you ain't no real man" and then you blow up at her like a crazed animal because you "felt" that she disrespected you. When your concept and definition of manhood is limited to how much money you have in your pocket, what kind of car you drive, the label on your jeans, or the words someone speaks to you, then almost anyone including an eight year-old will be able to say something that disrespects you every time. The challenge is to broaden our concept and understanding of manhood to include more than material things, words, or shallow comments. We alone are not guilty in this way of thinking because many of the women in our life play off of the same limited conceptions and perceptions of manhood as well. Women have a great deal of power over us and many use that power as conveniently as they use their hand to turn a doorknob to open a door or a key to unlock the sanctuary of a safe place. Manhood has more to do with character; how we think, how we behave and under what circumstances and whether we are selfish or selfless in relation to the people in our life. Charles, Nick, and Clarence reacted similarly, and so does tens of thousands of African American males who think of themselves as men. Individually Charles, Nick and Clarence are good adult males; they are just plagued by bad programming and imagery about what it means to be a man. Many of our brothers suffer from the same limiting and self-destructive thinking. They mistakenly believe that things, imitating people or various practices will give them an image or the power they lack within themselves. But in reality, they are *"stuck in maleness"* and are unable to free themselves from boyhood practices or to make the full transition into manhood because of bad programming along with the dysfunctional influences about manhood that society targets towards us.

This is the point made in James Allen's phenomenal book, *As a Man Thinketh*. Our manhood is merely a reflection of the quality and type of imagery that we carry around in our mind. The white man, bad parents, your ex or an unscrupulous "baby momma" cannot be the reason for you maintaining the status quo within your life. Allen says:

> *"Mind is the Master-power that molds and makes*
> *Man is Mind, and evermore he takes*
> *The tool of Thought, and shaping what he wills*
> *Brings forth a thousand joys, a thousand ills*
> *He thinks in secret, and it comes to pass:*
> *Environment is but his looking-glass (20)*

Misconceptions

There are two areas I've found that have an extremely powerful impact on the imagery and interpretation of appropriate manly behavior that are particularly prevalent amongst African American men. They are 1) Misconceptions and, 2) Myths. Many negative misconceptions[4] about manhood have become a part of dominant culture within the African American community and show up in the belief system of large numbers of men, and women, who buy into the behaviors indirectly.

These misconceptions are taken as truth, acted upon as if true, and passed on to siblings, family members, children and friends through generations of unsuspecting and gullible African American males (and females) as if they are truths. The problem with

---

[4] A misconception or to misconceive is to "interpret information incorrectly (21).

misconceptions is that when passed on and told to others, they are filtered through the mindset of the person who is providing the information and telling the story. Men, especially men *"stuck in maleness"*, have a tendency to exaggerate, inflate, or underrate an experience they've had based upon whatever fears, insecurities, or ulterior motives that they have about themselves. So when the drug dealer tells you "ain't no jobs out there, take these couple of bags of crack and sell it for me; I'll give you a cut", he's telling you or should I say "selling you" that story based upon his perception and assessment of the situation, which is filtered through his experiences, education, motivation, and what he desires and sees for his future. He's trying to justify his state of mind and his circumstances by seeking to distort your perception of yours.

African American men (and women) are hoodwinked, bamboozled and deceived on a daily basis more by people they know and claim to have their best interests at hand than many would care to admit. Let's look at ten common misconceptions about manhood that are prevalent amongst African American men (and some women) that must be corrected.

You're a man just because you call yourself one.

"I'm a grown a.. man!" Calling yourself a "grown a.... man" as Charles did makes you no more of a man than does calling yourself a millionaire when you barely have a dime to your name. Manhood is not a name game; it's an attitude and way of life that involves thinking and behaving responsibly. If you have to call yourself a man, constantly defend yourself as a man or justify your behavior as a man to another person, you're probably not much of a man anyway.

You're a man because you are 18 or older.

Turning 18, 21, or any other set age does not magically make you a man; it just makes you an adult male in the legal sense of the word. After reaching 18 in most cases you are able to engage in certain legal contracts, get your driver's license or purchase cigarettes or alcohol (age 21 in some places). There are many qualitative and maturational aspects of manhood that can only be obtained through direct exposure and experience.

You're a man because your lady, mother, father or some other person makes good money.

I've seen a great number of our brothers who mistakenly believe this misconception and they use it as a reason not to be responsible or productive themselves. The successes, failures, income or behavior of another person does not make *YOU* more or less of a man. It makes you a spoiled brat, a freeloader or maybe even a bum. When I was growing up, a person that chased after or relied on the success of another person was said to have "vapors"; they were chasing after or relying on the fumes or success of another person. Manhood is an "inside" job and refers to the qualities or state of mind of the man himself, not another person.

You're a man because you control your lady or "call the shots".

You cannot elevate yourself as a man by controlling or putting down another person; that just makes you a bully or an abuser. I've seen this kind of behavior in many men in their relationships with women and it rarely produces positive outcomes. Just think back to Big Tank and how he dealt with women. If you feel weak or inferior as a man on the inside, you will not and cannot become more of a man on the outside by attempting to change or control another person. Didn't you learn anything from slavery? You have to change your own thought process and exert better control over your own behavior. For example, Clarence the government employee felt inferior because his wife, the doctor, had more social status and made more money than him. Clarence had a competitive mindset (thoughts) and based his manhood solely upon how he felt about money. His wife made more money so he felt less of a man. Clarence's faulty and incomplete conception of what it means to be a man, and how he felt about himself, caused him to draw negative conclusions about himself. So he tries to feel better as a man by controlling and abusive behavior towards his wife. He should feel proud and blessed to have such a wife, who chose him, but…..

You're more of a man because you make lots of money

Earning a high income or having lots of money does provide a man (or any person) with the option to purchase "things" or to live in a way that others, who earn less money, cannot. Unless you use the options money provides wisely and responsively, like taking care of your children, family, investing or obtaining training or education, then it really doesn't matter how much money you make. Many "want to be men" in the world have been males with lots of money but used it to hurt people, including themselves. Money can buy you appearance but it cannot buy substance and character.

You're a man because of your physical characteristics

This is a big misconception because society places a high value on physical fitness and our love of sports. But brains, intelligence, manly virtue (character) and responsibility do not necessarily correlate with a male's physical size or how nice a body he has. There is more to the responsibilities of life (manly) than picking up weights or running up and down a basketball court if you cannot think and function properly off the court. Physical size and strength must be balanced with character and mental thoughts.

You're a man because you're a "player" or have a lot of women.

Nothing can be farther from the truth. Having a lot of women means that you do not know what or who you want in life, so you try everything or everyone, looking for "it." It could also mean that you don't feel good about yourself (low self-worth and low self-esteem) so you go about life seeking gratification or love, through numerous relations with multiple women. Been there, done that! At the end of the day you will be tired, lonely, possibly broke, or end up with multiple children by different women, or maybe even a sexually transmitted disease, but still left with *YOU*.

You're a man because you can drink a lot or hold your liquor.

Drinking before you are of legal age is illegal, period. Above and beyond the legal age factor (usually 21), the consumption of alcohol is based upon one's genetic makeup, physical size (or weight), tolerance and preference. If you violate either of these factors, especially in excess, you will get drunk, sick, pass out (black out) or injure yourself or someone else. Alcohol, alcohol-related injuries and accidents are the number one cause of death in the United States. If you repeatedly violate these factors, you risk developing a drinking problem, an alcoholic. Alcoholism (and drug addiction) can actually decrease sexual performance and will also decrease your ability to function as a man. History is filled with men (very rich men) who tried to defeat their problems with drugs and alcohol but didn't realize that they couldn't defeat either before it was too late. You have a chance.

You're a man because you're a father or have children.

This is a gross misconception of fact, particularly with high numbers of teen pregnancies and "babies having babies." Legal age, mutual consent, maturity and responsibility of both parties is the basic requirement here. The irresponsible behavior of a male cannot be counted as manly behavior although some young people do step up to the plate and do what is required of them. If you are married and/or are in a committed relationship with your lady and you are taking financial and emotional responsibility for your children, great; you da man! If on the other hand, you continue to sleep around with different women, and produce children, or you are with the same woman and you are producing children, but are not taking financial and emotional care of them, you are a deadbeat dad and a poor excuse for a man, period. One of the key elements of manhood is responsibility. Males make babies; men are responsible parents to their children.

You're a man because you've been to jail or done time in prison.

I will be the first to tell you that this misconception is just that, a misconception and has no truth in it at all. Individual cases aside, most of the brothers that go to jail or to prison did not get there because they conducted themselves as men in a responsible way. Sadly enough, if their time while incarcerated is not properly used to reflect, correct thinking errors, obtain training, and have a plan on how they will live responsibly in the future, most will come out the same way they went in, maybe worse. Manhood is the condition of a man's mind, not a reflection of his rap sheet, although a man can change if he chooses to. History is full of men who made mistakes or went to prison, but rose up to prominence or greatness after they were released from prison or released from unhealthy thinking and behaviors. Moses, Apostle Paul (Saul), Malcolm X, Don King, Charles S. Dutton, and many others. But the key point is that they changed their way of thinking. You probably know many others from your own life experiences as well.

Myths

Another powerful influence on how African American men view and define their manhood is through the creation and/or emulation of myths[5]. There are three points I'd like to point out concerning myths that are simple but must be grasped in order to understand the power and influence that myths have over the minds of African American men and how they view manhood.

One, myths like misconceptions have an element of truth or partial truths inherent in them that makes them believable, so it's easy for us to get sucked into them. Two, there is usually enough exaggeration and/or mystery surrounding myths and misconceptions, that the uninitiated will go out of their way to want to learn more about them and even imitate them in front of others as a way to be accepted. Three, there usually is a person, group or sub-culture that acts as an agent of communication and authority figure of the myth or the associated behavior(s). Family members, relatives and people in your hood are the more obvious sources of influence, but I want to go beyond those immediate sources and take a look at influences that often escape our perception but continue to have a tremendous influence over how we see ourselves as men.

I've identified three primary sources that promulgate much of the negative imagery about manhood, continue to propagate misconceptions about men, and that promote violent, disrespectful,

---

[5] A myth is usually legendary narrative that presents part of the beliefs of a people or explains a practice or natural phenomena; an imaginary (mental) or unverifiable person or thing. (22)

selfish, anti-authority, narcissistic and even misogynistic ways of thinking that are often contrary to the positive, disciplined family-oriented character and manly virtues that African American males so desperately need: 1) Movies; 2) Rap music; and, 3) Gangs.

Movies

In African American communities, particularly in urban areas amongst African American males, movies that depict action, sex, violence and crime, sell. Movies that portray organized crime involving the Mafia, bank robberies, drug-lords, turf wars, sex, money, guns and violence sell even more. I believe part of the attraction comes from movies is a desire to be like the characters portrayed in them and to have what those characters have and to do what the characters do, as seen through their fictional life styles. Many of the characters are modern day urban versions of Robin Hood who stole from the rich and gave to the poor, so the story goes. Just like the fictional Robin Hood character and his men, these modern day thugs and gangsters, are heroes (or heroines) to many brothers in the streets because they oppose the law; rob banks, drug cartels, jewelry stores, crack houses or because they're just bad.

These mostly fictional movie screen characters live lavish life styles surrounding themselves with expensive cars, beautiful women, pricey hotels, expensive clothing and any kind of "bling" their risky life styles can buy even if means degrading themselves, pimping their women or abusing those closest to them in order to make that all mighty dollar. The price is often lengthy jail terms or death but that does not seem to deter young African American males from their quest to bring these movie and television characters to life in their homes and on the streets of their local community.

Some of our brothers on street corners are so fascinated by these movie characters, for example Scarface played by Al Pacino, that they go out of their way to get tattoos on their bodies displaying the name of their favorite gangster movie character right alongside the tattoo of their mother, child or their baby's momma. Others go a little farther and make the decision to no longer use their "government name" in the street, but begin referring to themselves as "Scarface", "G-Money", "Nitty" "Cash", "Noriega", while others may just settle for a poster of Al Pacino or Marlon Brando from the "The Godfather" fame on their bedroom wall. I do understand that a lot of brothers use fictitious names on the street to keep from having to use their real name to avoid being caught; that's understandable. I've never really used an alias but I've been on the street hustling and doing things that I didn't want others to know about.

In these situations, manhood is not seen as positive and healthy character trait that you build within you. Instead, the focus is on how closely you can imitate and copy the behavior or "swagger" (no matter how degrading) of someone you admire or view as having the things that you desire for yourself. In an effort to make a name for himself or to appear credible, many of our brothers go to the extreme in violence or other forms of aggression in ways that often lead to irreparable harm to themselves, their families and to others.

This type of thinking and behavior can only make worse the fact that many of our brothers on the street are unemployed, living in poverty, and do not see a way out. Brothers on the street often do not see any alternative but to sell drugs, rob, steal or engage in other forms of criminal activity. Life in their families or on the street corner is so painful that they'd rather just be somebody else because it gives them a sense of identity and purpose that they lack within their own lives as men. But there is a strong man inside of you; he just has to be drawn out.

Rap Music

In its simplest form rap music is a form of artistic expression and communization. Rap artists, like the legendary singers and songwriters of the past and present, aim to write lyrics (or raps) that touch people's emotions, and resonate their hopes, dreams, and deepest feelings about a subject, be it personal, political or social in nature. What we remember most about a melody or rap is the hook. A hook is a catchy phrase from the song or rap that grabs the listener's attention and lingers in their mind. From this perspective, music, in this case rap music, is also a tool and instrument of communication, information and even education to its listeners, whether the message be negative or positive.

Rap music is not inherently a bad form of communication. As with many artistic expressions within the African American community, rap music emerged out of real life experiences of people on the street as a way to cope with poverty, unemployment, undelivered government promises, oppressive policies, or just as a way to have fun. I must admit that I have always had mixed feelings about rap music and the impact rap culture is having on shaping the attitudes and values about manhood of tens of thousands of African American men and women. I am from the "old school" of the 60's when the social, political, economic and musical environment was……different. But I've also learned that different is not necessarily better when you compare one generation to another. African American men of the 60's during the civil rights era are not the same as African American men of 2014, and they don't have to be.

As hip hop (as it was called then) and rap music evolved over the years, some rap artists used their popularity and access to larger audiences of young black people as a platform to educate the masses about social and political issues, as was the case with Boogie Down Productions and Public Enemy during the 90's. KRS-ONE, the head rapper of Boogie Down Productions called the term "edutainment" to describe their dual focus of entertaining listeners while simultaneously educating them about social, political and economic issues of the day within the African American community. Russell Simmons, former CEO of Def Jam Records, along with rappers Common, Chuck D, author Sista Soujah and Sean "P. Diddy" Combs, CEO of Bad Boy Entertainment, used their influence within the rap music community as a political force to form "Rap the Vote", a voter organizing and registration effort to get rap enthusiasts and other young people to vote during President Barack Obama's campaign for office in 2008.

However, in recent years rap music has departed from "edutainment" with the advent of so-called "Gangsta Rap." Gangsta Rap has been the subject of much national attention and controversy for its anti-authority messages and the fact that it's the source of most of the negativism that surrounds rap music. Gangsta rap artists and the incendiary lyrics they write (or spit) is where the profoundly subversive and negative influence of rap music is having on the minds of tens of thousands of African American males (and others) who listen to their music and watch their videos. Rap artists and record companies, for their part, are only concerned about sales and making money. These three-to-five minute films provide a lot of excitement and exposure for rap artists, along with live concerts, videos and CDs generate significant income to both record companies and to rappers themselves.

The problem with rap is that the lyrics and videos are often shocking, brutal and rife with misogamy, violence and anti-authority propaganda. Many rappers' rap videos feature bejeweled rappers throwing up gang signs while near naked women gyrate in the foreground or seductively pose atop expensive sports cars. Young impressionable African American males imitate and idolize the rappers in these videos just like the rappers themselves idolized and imitated people they saw on the big movie screen or on the streets of their hood. I must make it clear that I am not indicting hip hop or rap music. Rather I am pointing out some of the latent effects that rap music has on African American males' understanding and concept of what is appropriate manly behavior. Rap music and hip hop is ultra-materialistic, ego-driven, self-centered and over consuming. Those are the opposite values that we need as men in order to progress as men and in order for us to be of value and benefit to our families. The individuals that make it to the top in rap music are exceptional. Most African American men and women that listen to rap music are everyday people with everyday problems and everyday income at best. We need to focus on being better everyday men instead of the images associated with exceptional rappers.

Like soul music of the 60's and 70's, which became a vehicle for political awareness and social changes, hip hop and rap music have become the voice of change and empowerment to disenfranchised youth of the 80's, 90's and continues now in 2014. However, in recent years the original impetus and focus of entertainment and later, "edutainment" has been replaced by negativism, disrespectful, anti-authority and violent lyrics.

Unless refocused and redirected, rap music as a whole will continue to be a source of self-destruction and character corruption to the minds of many African American men (and women), particularly youth. African American males already have a target on their backs so we must be mindful of harmful influences to our minds. For a more detailed discussion and analysis of hip hop and rap music, see Michael Eric Dyson's "Reflecting Black: African American Cultural Criticism" (23). Following are several of the more salient, negative influences that I believe rap music and rap videos have on the lives of African American males and other.

Negative Influence of Rap Music

- Promotes disrespectful, rebellious, narcissistic, misogynistic and anti-authority attitudes.
- Promotes a false male bravado that African American males (and others) feel that they have to live up to in order to be accepted.
- Reinforces negative and degrading stereotypes about both African Americans and women in general.
- It has become a negative form of domination culture for millions of young people, primarily African American males.

Through its lyrics and videos, Rap music has become a primary gateway to substance abuse, gang affiliation and violent behavior. The following is an excerpt taken from gangsta rapper Sheek Looch of D-Block.

"You want me dead in right here do it bitch, let me bleed to a mother fuckin fluid list, I ain'tnew at this and don't give a fuck about you Sheek a run up and smack the shit outta you I live this shit niggas don't stop open niggas head with an octopus top, catch him all taped out there on the block."

Gangs

Similar negative attitudes and behaviors exist in African American males who become involved in gangs. Within the United States gangs have become one of the major perpetrators of violence, drug trafficking, degraders of women and disseminators of negative, anti-authority propaganda. The National Gang Center reports that gang activity within the United States has increased following a decline during the 90's. They state that the percent change in gang problem jurisdictions from 2002 to 2007 is as follows: + 12 percent in larger cities; +33 percent in suburban counties; +27 percent; percent in smaller cities; and +24 percent in rural counties (24).

On average, African Americans encompass 37 percent of gang membership in the United States (25) African American males(26). Members are generally between the ages of 12 and 24 although the larger percentage of gang members are adults (27).

Part of the attraction to African American males who join gangs is a sense of belonging, camaraderie and security. African American males often lack a father figure or strong male role model at home who can provide needed discipline, leadership and a clear, definable understanding of what it means to be a man. When this strong male role model is not present, African American males are more likely to seek that presence outside of their home.

For some African American males that presence and sense of belonging is found in school, artistic endeavors or through participation in competitive sports activities that provides for discipline, rules to follow, the opportunity for achievement, shared values and a sense of belonging to something bigger than one's self. At other times, however, that sense of belonging, discipline and leadership is found in gangs where the most dysfunctional and distorted images and practices of manhood prevail.

Pressured by unemployment, underemployment, lack of positive male role models, and the perception of a lack of alternative positive outlets, gang membership becomes more of an attraction. Access to money, leadership, authority, acceptance, shared values, a sense of belonging in a "family-like" atmosphere provides gang members with the access to support what they lack at home.

At the same time, some African American males through fear, intimidation, deception or the threat of violence, join for protection just so they will not become an open target to competing gangs seeking to claim turf or new members. Ironically, once a member of a gang, the opportunity to participate in self-directed, purposeful thinking and behavior associated with manhood is often forfeited in the interest of loyalty to the gang, group members or to group leaders.

Many young men (and women) quickly realize once they've become gang members is that gang life is more than they initially believed it to be. Depending upon the area or city the gang is located, economic conditions, access to legitimate means of employment, education or local community services, members can find themselves either encouraged to pursue academic, sports or work-related careers, or they can find themselves involved in hardcore drug trafficking, promotion of prostitution, robberies, hits on rival gang members or other criminal activities.

Although I have listed movies, rap music and joining gangs as individual and separate influences that negatively impact the concept and imagery of manhood amongst African American males, taken together they are concomitant co-conspirators that act to simultaneously corrupt African American males' minds with negative imagery about manhood. Most rap artists rise up from the streets of their hood but continue to rap about street life or other issues as they see them, from the perspective (filter) of their daily lives. Some rappers are also gang members or become gang members as they rise to fame.

Rappers, be they local or of national acclaim, continue to represent and rap about their respective "hoods" or "sets" just as they did before their celebrity. Some rap songs become anthems for various sets of a gang or for the gang as a whole, which just increases the songs' appeal to other sets or in other cities. In rap videos, gang members throwing up gang signs of their respective gang, or set, becomes a sign of respect and honor. It also shows defiance and disrespect to competing gang members or sets.

When all of these individual factors are brought together through rap music, rap videos, concerts, street activity, movies and the celebrity that increasing numbers of rappers and gang members achieve and enjoy, it has a magnetic draw on the minds of impressionable and gullible-minded African American males. The effect has been sort of a continuous religious revival across cultural, gender, age, economic and social lines that has drawn in other ethnic groups with African American males at the forefront as mascots and poster-figures of the archetypical gang member.

Movies, rap music and gang membership are but a few examples of the more common avenues of how myths and misconceptions can influence images of what it means to be a man amongst African American males. I am sure you can come up with examples of your own versions of myths and misconceptions. Defining your self-concept or your manhood on a pattern of misconceptions or myths can set the stage for the development of thinking errors. A thinking error is an attempt to reason or draw logical conclusions about an area of life based upon faulty or incomplete information. When you become stuck into these negative kinds of thinking patterns, everyone, including you, loses.

For many years I thought the same way and made some of the same mistakes far into adulthood. Thinking errors dominated my thought process and became formidable strongholds in my mind. I found myself struggling up and down personal and professional mountains that could either have been avoided, or scaled more effectively. Simply opening my mind to new ways of thinking and taking personal responsibility for my own destiny gave me purpose, focus, and a renewed sense of manhood. Sometimes as men we develop bad habits or get caught up into doing things a certain way, but don't understand why we are doing them. We develop these bad habits because we've always done them that way or because our friends or others are doing them, or we want to be popular, even though we know what we are doing is wrong.

This is a mistake and doing things just because others do them makes you a copycat and an imitator, not a man. What's more, African American males whose concept of manhood is merely based upon imitating the behaviors of others as we've discussed in relation to movies, rap music and gangs, especially if they have failed at and/or have given up on education, are more likely to take on attitudes and behaviors that involve or lead to unhealthy lifestyles.

In an effort to be accepted, to perceived as "down" or to make a name for themselves, African American males who engage in these mostly imitative behaviors and lifestyles are more likely to drink before legal age, drink excessively, experiment with drugs (especially marijuana), engage in premarital sex, become abusive towards women, have children out of wedlock, sell drugs or become involved in violent anti-authority behavior. Imitate no one; be original and learn to think for yourself. Real men do what's right, not what's popular or whatever they feel. If you fail to follow the laws and rules of society, then you will be forced into following the rules of a jail or prison and I can tell you from personal experience you don't want to do that.

Chapter 5
What It Means To Be *"Stuck In Maleness"*

I stated in Chapter 2 that you must become a healthy person on the inside before you can become a healthy man on the outside. In Chapter 3, I stated that manhood or becoming a man is not simply about imitating attitudes and behaviors of others, or attempting to live up to the myths, misconceptions, or the exaggerated stories we hear from our friends or others in the street, or the false images and stereotypes that are part of popular African American culture. Instead, manhood is a state of mind that directs and influences the attitudes, behavior and thinking pattern of a man to engage in healthy actions that are proactive and productive towards himself and/or the people that he is responsible for.

The inner state of the man's mind is translated into what is recognized on the outside as manliness or the behavior of a man. Nice clothes, a fancy car, the way you speak or how big or cut you are does not make the man. It never has and it never will.

Some of the qualities and characteristics associated with a man are self-motivation, selflessness, focused, principled, disciplined, moral, trustworthy, honest, integrity, spiritual; purposeful but most important, responsible. However, adult males I define as being *"stuck in maleness"* are males that have not, cannot or will not, make the full maturational transition from boyhood or the actions and behaviors expected of a boy or teen, into the thinking, attitude and mindset required and expected of a man. A man *"stuck in maleness"* will often be unaware of his behavior, unaware of the real impact his behavior is having on himself and others and he will oftentimes simply be unwilling to take personal responsibility for creating his own predicament. Are you *"stuck in maleness?"* Men *"stuck in maleness"* can be readily recognized by the "environment" of their life and/or by the impact they have on the environment of the people connected to them. "Grow up!" "Stop acting like a child", "Can't you be serious for 5 minutes?", "You're too old for that", "Stop trying to control me!" "Get a job, Negro" "You just a wanna be player", "It's not all about you!" are but a few of the expressions exclaimed by friends, family members, co-workers, and certainly loved ones who've experienced your *"stuck in maleness"* behavior. You may be able to relate to these kinds of comments from the people in your life even if you have been living in a manner that is inconsistent for someone expected of your age, position or realm of responsibility, even if only temporarily. Temporary behaviors can and often do create long term problems in our life regardless of how small or insignificant we think the problem is.

I have a friend whom I've known for over 15 years. Let's just call him Frank. I didn't see Frank for a few years until I ran into him at a cultural festival near my home. Back when I first met Frank he had a good job, drove a nice car and seemed to be an ok guy. Frank was easy going and confident and didn't seem to have any problems in life. During our first conversation Frank expressed an interest in purchasing real estate. This was during the mid-90's when the real estate market was healthy. I had done my research and I was on the verge of purchasing my first home, so I told Frank what I knew about real estate, purchasing a home, credit, mortgages, financing and the importance of the location of the property.

 At 36, Frank was single, didn't have any children, owned his car, lived alone in a one bedroom apartment in a nice part of town, and was getting by with one job. I suggested to Frank that he take a course in real estate or maybe purchase some books on investing in real estate and purchasing residential property. At the time Frank had saved up nearly six thousand dollars and revealed he was interested. I said "great" and commented that I thought he was in a good position to move forward if he wanted to. Over the next several years I saw Frank in passing a few times but never got a chance to really talk in depth about how things were going with him, until at the cultural festival. As I was walking out of the parking lot, just before I entered the festival area, I noticed a sharp looking late model Mercedes Benz with shiny custom rims and a limo tint on the windows. Moments later I ran into Frank.

 After talking a bit about the events at the festival, we talked about new developments in our lives. I spoke about the property I'd purchased and then sold for over double the price 7 years later, marriage, divorce, my children and some challenges I had to overcome. While talking with Frank, I happened to look in the direction of the parking lot and motioned with my head for Frank to look towards the nice Benz. "That's a nice ride, huh?" Frank said. "You diggin' my ride? That's my fourth Benz." I said "yeah, it's nice!" Frank offered to show me the inside of his car so we walked over and I listened as he pointed out the many luxury and safety features that were standard on his Mercedes Benz.

As it turned out, Frank had never pursued buying a house. Instead, he put the money he'd saved up as a down payment on a used Mercedes Benz. In order to qualify for the Mercedes, Frank had to trade in his old car (which was paid for) plus put up the $6000. He still ended up with a hefty car note but the car gave Frank more immediate satisfaction than the prospect of home ownership. The Mercedes Benz made Frank feel more successful and "look" more like the man he wanted to be. Frank revealed that two years after purchasing the Mercedes Benz he had already fathered three children by two different women, but he had not seen either of his children in over a year. When I asked Frank what happened to his interest in buying a house, especially now that he had children, he responded, "You know, Russ, I still want to get a house one day. But a brother gotta look good too. You know what I'm saying? You know I like them cars. My lady had a nice apartment at the time anyway." When probed further Frank went on to say that he was currently staying with his mother "temporarily" until he got back on his feet. I asked Frank if he had lost his job or had fallen on hard times but he said, "No, I'm still there coming up on 17 years." There is nothing wrong with driving a nice car, especially a Mercedes Benz, but it is more comforting to know that your children have a roof over their heads, food on the table and clothes on their backs. Frank felt feeding his ego was of a higher priority than his children. Between the rent on the one bedroom apartment, and the note on the Mercedes Benz, Frank was actually shelling out enough money a month for a mortgage on a decent size starter home that would have been more than enough space for him and his three children, even if he chose not to remain with either of their mothers. Frank went on to say that he was engaged to the mother of the two youngest children but she broke off their relationship because, as Frank put it, "Man she wanted me to sell my car so we could put a down payment on some dinky house that was still going to need a lot of work. I wasn't feeling that and I wasn't giving up my ride." Frank just didn't have any goals or aspirations beyond obtaining a flashy car.

Two years later Frank's ex bought a home and eventually married. Around the same time Frank began to get behind in his rent but never missed a payment on his car note. Frank said that he was "forced" to move in with his mother because his landlord wanted too much money for rent anyway. Frank suffers from thinking errors[6] and has a lot of misconceptions about the meaning and responsibility of manhood. Frank also believes that the qualities he lacks within himself can be compensated for by the purchase of external "things" and symbols of strength and power. The note on Frank's Mercedes Benz was nearly $800 monthly. In Frank's mind he could not make

---

[6] A thinking error is the tendency to reason or attempt to draw logical conclusions based upon faulty and/or incomplete information.

the payments for his rent because the landlord wanted too much money, but it was ok for him to pay $800 monthly for a car and freeload off of his mother.

Frank also believed he had to maintain his car payments because the Mercedes Benz was a symbol of his manhood. Somehow in Frank's mind the opportunity to purchase his own home was less valued as a symbol of success and manhood than was the car. What is more, over the years Frank continued to think the same way and purchased other cars still with no clear purpose or goal in mind other than to "look good", even if looking good caused him to do bad and become dependent upon the blind good will of his mother. Frank consistently hindered and sabotaged his progress in life, creating his own dependent state of mind and needs by maintaining a serious thinking error, his illusion of manhood. Frank is *"stuck in maleness"* and can't see his way out of it.

Jamal is a 32 year-old former high school football star from a suburban community in Dallas, Texas, who likes to compete. Although Jamal's football days are far behind him, his competitive spirit lingers on in his daily life. Jamal always seems to find a way to turn everything into a form of competition. Married 9 years, with a 7 year-old son, when not working at his job as a police officer, Jamal spends an excessive amount of time playing Xbox 360 or PlayStation. Jamal plays after work, on the weekends and sometimes before attending church services on Sunday. Jamal spends time with his wife and son, but only in activities involving some form of competition. Jamal plays well at everything he does but dislikes losing, even to his wife or son. Every time Jamal's wife kids around with him and wrestles in bed, he never lets her win, not even for fun. Whenever Jamal and his son shoot hoops outside in the driveway, he almost never lets his son win a game, not even as a way to boost his son's self-confidence. Jamal's wife has even observed Jamal block their son's shot before. Jamal's son prefers shooting foul shots because it's the only opportunity he gets to spend time with his dad and it's not totally competitive, and he actually will get an opportunity to walk away from the activity without feeling deflated.

Jamal's wife has repeatedly complained to him about his behavior and how it is affecting her and his relationship with their son. But Jamal can never seem to do things with his family for the fun of it; he always has to make things competitive. No matter what the activity, Jamal becomes obsessed with winning and showing how dominant he is. Whenever Jamal has been confronted about his behavior, he gets angry, blames his wife, and then he isolates himself and pouts for hours. Their son has begun to show similar behaviors. It never occurred to Jamal to lay back and enjoy time with his family, have fun just being in each other's company without a need to compete. Jamal is *"stuck in maleness"* but doesn't know it.

G-Money, as he likes to be called by his friends, is a drug dealer who lives in the projects in a small one bedroom apartment funded by Section 8 in a crime ridden city in central New Jersey. G-Money also is on public assistance so he receives a monthly stipend of $140 dollars a month and another $180 in food stamps. In order to maintain his public assistance benefits, G-Money is required to show proof that he is looking for employment, is in school, or in a training program. G-Money is in a training program but maintains the minimal amount of attendance so he doesn't get kicked out. On the side, G-Money sells drugs, crack cocaine and E-pills, out of his Section 8 funded apartment. G-Money has no real intention of getting a job. Between selling drugs and the string of women that make their way in and out of his bed, G-Money doesn't have any time for regular employment. Between the money G-Money makes from selling drugs, and the influence he has over his customers, especially the women, G-Money believes that he is sitting on top of the world.

G-Money has a six year-old daughter, born to one of his earlier customers when he first began selling drugs. He only pays a few dollars a week in child support because, beyond the benefits from welfare, he doesn't have any documented income. G-Money sees nothing wrong with selling and using drugs, abusing women, avoiding work, or avoiding the emotional and financial responsibility of providing for his daughter. G-Money has done twice done time in prison and the third time is just around the corner with his recent arrest for drug possession. But that doesn't faze G-Money because "nigga's got to do what he gotta do. Ain'tno jobs out there paying what I make. I don't even need welfare; as long as I keep my Section 8, I'm good."

At the beginning of the chapter, I provided a definition for what it means to be *"stuck in maleness"*. But definitions are only guides, conceptual frameworks to provide a focal point and a baseline of understanding. I provided the synopsis of the lives of these six men as an example and a way to bring to life the definition and meaning of being *"stuck in maleness"*. With this peek into the lives of Charles, Nick, Clarence, Frank, Jamal and G-Money, you may already recognize some aspects of your own attitudes, thinking, behaviors, or decision making patterns, and the impact they are having on you and others within your life. Are you *"stuck in maleness"*?

Remember, thinking errors are an attempt to draw logical conclusions based upon faulty and/or incomplete thinking. The imagery of our thoughts influences our behavior and produces real outcomes, good or bad, on our lives and the people connected to us. Over extended periods of time, thinking errors and being *"stuck in maleness"* may produce patterns of behavior that can also cause you to have emotional, mental, financial, and legal problems if they don't already exist in your life. To be *"stuck in maleness"* is when you have not, cannot or will not think and behave in mature ways consistent with the attitude, actions and thinking required and/or expected of mature, responsible men. Being *"stuck in maleness"* involves extreme forms of selfishness and self-centeredness that, over time, may also lead to substance abuse, control issues, harm to self and others, or it may lead to incarceration, violence or even death. This is certainly not a positive and productive image of manhood that you'd want your children or family to have of you but this quite often the case when these issues are not addressed. Men do what is right but they do what is right based upon a healthy and balanced mental perspective with respect and consideration for themselves and the other people in their life. When you're stuck into your maleness game, you have a tendency to develop tunnel vision, sabotage personal opportunities and overlook the needs of others. Below are additional points to further your understanding of the thinking and behavioral attributes and characteristics associated with men who may be considered *"stuck in maleness"*:

- Mamma's boy mentality.
- Player/womanizer mentality.
- Blames others for his problems.
- Views children and family as possessions.
- Avoids taking personal responsibility.
- Puts birth family over marriage family and children.
- Places loyalty to friends over his family.
- Uses lies and deception to create more of a manly appearance.
- Preys on women as a source of income and support.
- Refuses to take care of his children or spend time with them because he is on bad terms with their mother.
- Still lives with his parents (or guardian) after age 25, except for health or extended education purposes.
- Spends more time with your friends or hanging out with the boys than you do with your wife/girlfriend or children.

- Spends more time playing games than with your wife/girlfriend or children.
- Chronic incarcerations.
- Chronic unemployment or you refuse to work because you don't do certain kinds of work.
- You constantly brag or speak about what you're going to do but never accomplish anything.
- You blame your parents or others for your problems or for missed opportunities.
- You argue over petty issues although you know you're wrong.
- You use violence, intimidation or the threat of violence to solve problems.
- You're intimidated by or won't date or marry a woman who makes more money than you do or who appears more successful than you.
- You think and act based upon thinking errors.
- An attitude of entitlement.
- May be involved in a gang.

The list above is by no means exhaustive of all the possible attributes and characteristics associated with being *"stuck in maleness"*. This is also a beginning point to examine your own thinking and behavior to understand why you constantly aim, but miss the mark, become preoccupied with competition over compromise, react instead of respond, act without thinking or think without acting. Any behavior or thought process that causes you to hinder or prevent your own progress as a man or causes you to remain in a dependent state of mind can cause you to become *"stuck in maleness"*.

Chapter 6
How We Become *"Stuck In Maleness"*

In previous chapters I introduced you to Charles, who placed more emphasis on his image and feelings as a man than how he actually demonstrated responsible, manly behavior towards his family; Nick whose image of himself as a man was being manipulated by his girlfriend and the material things he could buy for her, and Clarence, who felt inferior as a man because his wife, a doctor, earned a higher income and enjoys a higher social status than he does. You also met Frank, who was obsessed with expensive cars and the appearance of power and success he derived from them; Jamal whose competitive nature and zeal for winning interfered with his ability to form a healthy bond and relationship with his wife and son; and G-Money whose image of manhood meant avoiding responsibility by selling drugs, preying on drug addicted women and getting over on the "system." All of these men have something in common with each other; they are all stuck into behaviors that hinder and prevent them from fully maturing into manhood. Their way of thinking keeps them from seeing life more realistically, placing the needs and happiness of their respective family members above their own selfish desires, in order to maintain an illusion of manhood supported by thinking errors.

You may recall from the preceding chapters that thinking errors are an attempt to draw logical conclusions concerning situations and the experiences of life based upon faulty or illusory thinking. But what causes thinking errors? What is the connection between thinking errors and men who become *"stuck in maleness"* and behaviors that hinder or prevent them from maturing into full manhood? I have identified four factors, when considered together, helps to explain why many African American men become *"stuck in maleness"*, which keeps them from maturing into the man they can be and enjoying the personal and professional successes they really desire. Some of these same factors, whether taken individually or grouped as a whole, can also provide meaningful insight into how these negative and destructive behaviors can be corrected and reversed given the right attitude and mindset to do so.

Physiology

The first factor upon consideration as to why African American men seem to disproportionately become *"stuck in maleness"* does not specifically apply to African American males but to all males in general. The factor lies within the recesses of our mind and how males generally process information. A medical study reported in 1998 by Gary Smalley and John Trent suggests that males have a tendency towards certain types of thinking.

"Medical studies have reported that during the eighteenth and twenty sixth week of pregnancy brain damage occurs to little boy *fetuses that forever separates the sexes. Sex-related hormones flood* a boy baby's brain causing the right side to recede slightly, destroying some of the connecting fibers. As a result, in most cases, a boy starts life more left brain oriented (the left brain houses more of the logical, analytical, factual and aggressive centers of thought)". (28)

What this study is saying is that most males, independent of social, racial and environmental factors start life with a tendency to think more from the left side of their brains than from the right side and the right brain houses more complex thinking functions such as the ability to multitask. While the study by researchers Smalley and Trent does not completely explain why some men become *"stuck in maleness"* and others do not, it does suggest that there is an increased inclination for men to think and reason one dimensionally, which is associated with one of the behavioral characteristics of men *"stuck in maleness"*. I can recall as an 18 year-old my mother warning me, "you need to stop being so narrow minded." The reason is that I had become interested in purchasing a car from a neighbor. The car was a red Ford Mustang. I had the money for the car but not enough to pay for the insurance coverage suggested to me by my stepfather, but I bought the car anyway with only liability coverage. All I could see was that beautiful red Mustang, and I wanted it. Two weeks later, while leaving the roller skating rink at 1a.m. with my girlfriend and her sisters, the car stalled because it had a bad starter motor. I didn't know anything about cars and neither did my stepfather so I was forced to leave my car in the parking lot of the skating rink overnight.

Several hours later the police called and notified my stepfather that someone had stolen my tires, my radio, and set my car on fire! What?! I was devastated. I was out of a car including all of the money I had put into it. But once the car was gone, all I thought about was the money I had lost. That car was more than a means of transportation, it allowed me to access people and places I would not normally have access to, it was a symbol of success, manhood, and an outward expression that my identity was changing. Before I got the car all I could think about was myself and the car I wanted, and after my hard earned money went up in smoke all I could think about was myself and the money I had lost. With most men physiologically predisposed to think and reason differently from women, what factors separate the men from each other and gives way to some men becoming *"stuck in maleness"* (as I have defined it) and others that not being the case?

Social/Environment
Self-Worth

The second factor, social and environmental influences, is composed of several sub-factors that I believe is at the root of the problem. They are self-worth, tendencies, choices, and self-sabotaging behaviors. Self-worth is the overall sense of value, deservedness, and self-respect that we have for ourselves. Our self-worth usually changes over time based upon our actions and the choices we make. Self-worth is a self-imposed value rating that we place on ourselves that we subconsciously carry around everywhere we go. You cannot increase your self-worth by dressing yourself in expensive clothing or buying a Ford Mustang, even though you might look better to others. Neither can you take away from your self-worth if you were to stand naked in the center of a busy intersection, although you might feel a little embarrassed by the honking horns, angry stares and laughter you will get from the people who see you. Your self-esteem might be a little damaged as well. But do not confuse self-worth with self-esteem. Unlike self-worth, self-esteem (associated with self-confidence) refers to liking or feeling good about yourself, your appearance, or your abilities. But self-esteem, just like self-worth, can change over time and can be influenced by a variety of situations.

Tendencies

Your sense of self-worth also shapes your thinking by creating "tendencies." Tendencies are your subconscious mind's inclination toward certain types of behavior, usually without your conscious awareness. As a younger man (I'm still a young man) I tended to choose women of a certain complexion. Subconsciously I chose and was attracted to women that resembled and reminded me of my mother, who is fair skinned. Today, I no longer do this but I am attracted to women of all sorts. Once I became aware of the filter that I subconsciously used when looking at women, I was able to change it. This is just an example; other men may have a tendency towards other behaviors, such as avoiding conflict, dressing a certain way, getting into trouble, or choose certain types of friends.

In everyday life, as you grow and mature, you choose your responses and reactions to situations. Those choices are reflected as further help to shape your sense of self-worth and become a part of your belief system towards life. Your sense of self-worth is not *real and* it's not a tangible "thing", so to speak, although it can and does have real consequences on your life. Self-worth is a perception that you have about your value and deservedness as a person. Consider an 8-ounce glass of water, filled to the 4-ounce mark (Figure 6-1). Is the glass half empty or half full? How you view the contents of the water in the glass resembles how you view your self-worth.

The fact is, the glass of water can be either half empty or half full depending upon how *you* perceive it. You may know people who instinctively seem to perceive situations in life from a positive perspective, and attract those kinds of experiences into their life, while others seem to always look at things negatively and attract a similar response from people.

Choices

We've already discussed the racist and discriminatory attitude of many towards African American men. Life certainly possess some very difficult and challenging circumstances for us but how we perceive situations, and the choices we make to react or respond to what we perceive is just as important in producing desired outcomes.

The issue with our self-worth is that subconsciously we choose or attract into our life those people and experiences we believe we deserve based upon the inner sense of value and deservedness we have of ourselves. Another way of saying it is....water (your inner self-worth) seeks its own level. Regardless of what others think of us, when we feel good about ourselves we will attract those kinds of experiences.

Figure 6-1

When you feel worthy and deserving as a man you will tend to make worth-enhancing and worth-producing choices. If you feel unworthy and undeserving, you tend to make destructive and limiting choices. Subconsciously, by the choices you make, you both reinforce your own sense of worth, and, you "train" other people to treat you the same way through all of the messages you send through body language, your tone of voice, and other subtle cues and behavior.

    This is why I stated earlier that water seeks its own level. What is your "water level?" Do you choose to hang out with the homies, go to work every day or to attend school? What kind of career path have you chosen for yourself? Drug dealer, pimp, player, criminal, government employee, security officer, postal worker, sanitation worker, mechanic, what? President Barack H. Obama didn't wake up one day and say to himself, "I'm going to be President of the United States." But he did choose to make the various academic, career, social (friends), economic and politically-based decisions that placed him in the position for others to perceive him that way. President Obama could just as easily have made choices that would have had him wearing a doo rag and a cut off tee-shirt while peering out the bars of a jail cell. Even if that were the case there are countless others, including myself, who have been in adverse situations but did not let a period or moment in time define their entire life. Instead, at various points mind-changing and life-changing decisions were made that place them on a different pathway. Those same choices are available to you.

Self-Sabotage and Getting Stuck

Everyone makes mistakes in life but a refusal to learn from them and make needed changes in choices and decision making reflects an unhealthy sense of self-worth (29). It is easy to see how men, especially African American men, can become "stuck" into certain types of thinking and behavior patterns on a subconscious level.

The reason I introduced myths and misconceptions about manhood in Chapter 3, is to point out many subtle cues contained within African American culture, and society in general, that speak negatively to the minds of impressionable African American males, men and females of all ages. My choice to discuss rap music and it's far reaching and mesmerizing influence over African American men, especially the younger generations of African American male children, was because of the negative and influential imagery contained in many of its lyrics.

Self-sabotage takes many forms, such as quitting school, joining a gang, refusing to work, choosing a spouse who physically, verbally or emotionally abuses you, spending more money than you have or earn, committing slow suicide with tobacco, alcohol, or other drugs, getting involved into crime, chronic incarcerations, hanging with the wrong crowd, or even just refusing to take advantage of and learning from previous mistakes. Both the inspiration and the motivation to finally commit to writing, **Stuck In Maleness** came after having ignored the wisdom contained in many of my own prior mistakes.

As males get older and begin to be stimulated by and interact within their environment, the quality of emotional, educational, social and environmental stimulation and reinforcement they experience becomes an increased factor in their daily thinking capabilities and how they perceive their sense of self. Additional insight can be found in the kind of imagery contained in your imagination. You learned in Chapter 4 that your imagination is composed of mental images or concepts. The information that is fed into your imagination becomes the oil that lubricates your self-concept and the power of your mind when you think. Dr. James P. Gills says of our imagination:

> *"These mental images or pictures powerfully influence our thoughts, our ideas, and our attitudes. Imaginations form a pattern of thinking and develop a whole mindset toward life which determines our creativity, our emotions, our outlook, our self-discipline, our ability to solve problems, and our ability to handle the choices we make every day" (30)*

What Dr. Gills is saying is clear -- our imaginations have an extremely powerful influence upon who we are, who we think we are and how we live our lives. So when our imaginations are messed up, especially when our self-worth is low, our thinking will be messed up as well. When our minds are filled with unhealthy concepts and imagery, our thinking will reflect that same ill state of health and so will the choices we make.

As we've seen many African American men are excessively exposed to misconceptions, myths, cultural and racial stereotypes and negative information from a variety of sources regarding what it means to be an African American man in American society. Movies, advertisements, rap music, rap videos, gang membership, news broadcasts of showing mug shots of African American male suspects being arrested, poor experiences in the educational system and more significantly, the widespread absence of fathers and/or positive male role models in the home during critical stages of development are common and ever present aspects of the African American male experience.

Not only are African American males exposed to an inordinate amount of negative and emasculating information about the African American male experience in advertisements, television, billboards, magazines, movies, music and but far worse, judging by the public conduct of African American males in recent years, many seem to believe the negative hype and have begun to demean themselves and self-sabotage their own access to successful experiences.

What is more, as we begin to understand the power of our imagination and the influence it plays in directing our behavior, it becomes more understandable the powerful role an unhealthy imagination and low self-worth has played in the lives of Charles, Nick, Clarence, Frank, Jamal and G-Money towards them becoming *"stuck in maleness"*. But mere exposure to certain kinds of stimulus doesn't seem to be enough to explain such a strong inclination towards the various kinds of self-centered and demeaning attitudes towards manhood that becoming *"stuck in maleness"* implies. So we must look deeper and take our examinations below the surface to where the real damage of these social and environmental influences takes place.

Strongholds

Our imagination is but one part of a larger "system of thought" that makes up who we are as a person and how we see ourselves as men. The part of our mind that provides support to the image making part of our brain is called our belief system. Our belief system can be defined as an individual "set" of values, principles, attitudes and practices (behaviors) that make up our thought process. I am not referring to one's religious belief system such as Christianity, Islam or Judaism, for example, although the belief system within our mind does take a religious-like hold of our thinking, attitudes and behavior.

Our belief system is considered to be a system because all of the individual parts that make up its various components, i.e., imagination, principles, values, attitudes and our actions work together in a systematic way to form what others recognize as our personality, attitude, and behavior patterns. We can have more than one belief system operating in our lives at one time. Contained within our belief system are "maps" (tendencies) composed of childhood experiences such as the influence of our parents, memorable events, traumatic experiences and the relationships within our family unit, for example, which is how and where the foundation of our self-worth is initially shaped and formed. Our mind subconsciously refers to those maps for direction just as we would look to the map of a city or state to find direction or the GPS in our car or on our cell phones.

When the maps of our belief system are healthy and balanced, so will the direction they provide to us. But when the maps of our belief system are filled with violence, fear, abuse, neglect, anger, poor role models, parents absent from home, or other events that may be traumatizing to our minds, especially during the developmental years of childhood, those experiences can become more pronounced tendencies or strongholds in our mind. As a whole, our belief system(s) forms a paradigm or model by which we "see" ourselves and the world around us. Stephen Covey in *The Habits of Highly Effective People* states that:

"Each of us has many, many maps in our head, which can be divided into two main categories: maps of the way things are, or realities, and maps of the way things should be, or values. We interpret everything we experience through these mental maps. We seldom question their accuracy; we're usually even unaware that we have them. We assume that the way we see things is the way they are, and the way they should be"(31).

Strongholds are like fortresses or defense mechanisms that our minds construct to protect itself from what it perceives as harmful situations (32). The direction our "maps" provide to our belief system will reflect the experiences that have affected our minds the most. Some men will go about their lives injured, broken, angry, lost or fearful; searching but never find what they lack inside. The institution of slavery, and it's offspring racial discrimination, and its impact on African Americans has produced what I believe are cultural strongholds that have and continue to influence how we think and view ourselves as African Americans, and certainly as African American men. This is the power exerted by low self-worth, low self-esteem, feelings of inadequacy or even inferiority complexes that can take root in a man's mind.

If Clarence was repeatedly told as a child that he was lazy or weak, or he'll never amount to anything, just like his father or that "White folk" ain't gone let him work downtown, true or not, he may begin to believe it. With this standard or expectation of conduct set for him by his mother and reinforced on a regular basis, subconsciously by low self-worth and self-sabotaging choices, he goes about life fulfilling the expectation that he believes has been set for him.

Strongholds are not isolated to one event or occurrence, meaning, there could be several strongholds of varying types operating within a man's mind simultaneously, and there usually are. Strongholds are like prisons within our minds. Most of us construct these prisons for ourselves. After we have become accustomed to and comfortable in these psychological cells we've constructed by our imagination, we accept the premise we've formed. And then our minds develop a belief system of attitudes, behaviors, principles and practices, negative or positive in order to keep our mind from crossing back over the threshold, or stronghold that has been constructed. We remain in the mess that we have created for ourselves and then we go about life, through our subconscious tendencies, trying to get others into the cell with us. Both African Americans and white people are equally guilty of this type of thinking. Family, friends or anyone who will buy into our belief system becomes a target or an attraction.

If nothing changes within our minds or within our environment that causes us to think differently about ourselves, the stronghold becomes even more engrained into our minds and our thinking, especially as we get older, set in our ways and preoccupied with maintaining a certain type of public image for ourselves. In the case of men *"stuck in maleness"*, anything that does not support our image or our version of manhood, i.e., athlete, pimp, hustler, player, husband, father, ladies' man, drug dealer, and so on, is promptly rejected and filtered out.

The longer we are exposed to these types of influences in our life, the more ingrained becomes the stronghold in our mind and our refusal to step back across the threshold of the prison we've constructed for ourselves. We become stuck, so to speak, in our maleness prison just like Charles, Nick, Clarence, Jamal and G-Money. We become our own jailors, always holding the key to our freedom but refusing to free ourselves because we've accepted, psychologically speaking, the sentence society or ourselves, has provided us. We become stuck into the various kinds of limiting maleness behaviors because we believe that's all that is available to us as African American men, even if only on a subconscious level.

The peculiar thought process and dysfunctional nature of the men *"stuck in maleness"* is usually obvious to everyone but him. To the man *"stuck in maleness"*, his way of thinking and the way he does things are normal, acceptable and make sense; it is other people that need to get with the program. Because "birds of a feather flock together", men *"stuck in maleness"* usually associate with other like-minded males or remain in settings in which they can be themselves or at least have the upper hand. This is one of the reasons gang membership is so popular and influential. It is also the same tendency (or stronghold) to want to fit in with others.

African American men *"stuck in maleness"* can and quite often are successful in a variety of professions, avocations and lifestyles, but only to the extent the goals and requirements of maintaining that success does not interfere with the imagery and demands of the strongholds needed to maintain its dominant position within their mind. The man *"stuck in maleness"* can work, attend school, church, be in a relationship or even run a successful business, it doesn't really matter. As long as he is able to "be himself" his perception or vision of manhood goes unchallenged. But when things get too uncomfortable or his thinking is challenged, the tendency to self-sabotage will rise up to reclaim a comfortable and dominant position in his life.

Some of the negative and/or traumatic experiences that may become the progenitors of low self-worth and stronghold and may become a catalyst for becoming *"stuck in maleness"* later in life are:

- Intense and/or prolonged verbal abuse.
- Physical abuse.
- Sexual assault and/or abuse.
- Prolonged emotional abuse by parent/authority figure.

- Substance abuse, especially at an early age.
- Repeated involvement and/or exposure to domestic violence.
- Repeated involvement and/or exposure to social violence.
- The absence of parent(s), especially father during childhood.
- Mental and/or physical disabilities.
- Over protecting, sheltering or spoiling.
- Early involvement into crime.
- Involvement in a gang or street lifestyle.

Racism and Cultural Influences

I have given considerable thought whether or not to discuss the influence of racism and African American culture as contributing factors to African American men who become *"stuck in maleness"*. In approaching the subject of racism as a contributing factor, there is the risk of using the somewhat worn out excuse of blaming slavery, the "white man" or others for what are essentially personal choices and decisions to engage in productive or counterproductive behaviors.

On the other hand, the suggestion to "blame the victim" for causing his own problems or setting himself up to be victimized, would be just as trite and incur similar uproar. I aim not to use either as a primary factor simply because categorizing slavery as the cause or perpetrator, and, African American males as victims does not provide African American men with the understanding into their own minds in order to avoid the psychological trap and lack of empowerment inherent in either perspective.

African American males need insight and a framework that, when applied, can provide them with the tools necessary to extricate them from the dysfunctional images of manhood that exist within African American culture and white society, and the perception of the need to imitate the behaviors of others. Acquiring more things or presenting more "bling" to the world does not mean that you are more of a man. Material or physical things cannot change your self-worth.

Manhood is about accepting personal responsibility and standing up to accept the consequences of choices you make, good or bad, and learning to move beyond them. I will preface my comments with a disclaimer and say that I do not believe nor am I suggesting that being an African American male, or a male from any other racial or ethnic group, is a decisive factor or cause to becoming *"stuck in maleness"* as I have defined it.

The long term experience of the institution of slavery amongst African Americans and the concomitant racial, social, educational and economic discrimination that followed has produced within African American men, more so than other males, a "cultural stronghold" and an increased propensity towards a syndrome of maladaptive behaviors that has the effect of exacerbating the *"stuck in maleness"* experience.

Remember, manhood has to do with the condition (healthy images, concepts) of a man's mind and his sense of value and deservedness as a human being. When a man's state of mind is not healthy, neither will be the man. No other ethnic or racial group within the United States have been abused, raped, beaten, murdered, burned, lynched, had their families torn apart and have had to deal with racial, social, economic and political discrimination for just for being the wrong color. And although physical brutality of previous years is no longer prevalent as it was in previous times, the social lynching and emasculation of African American men continues to run rampant at every level of American society.

African American males experience arrests, beatings, incarcerations, racial profiling, and discrimination within the media and the criminal justice system in ways that surpasses the atrocities of the past. The influences are omnipresent within American society and they have created, especially within large urban areas where there is a higher concentration of African American males, a mindset that greatly resembles a form of post-traumatic stress disorder. African American males experience and understand the realities of racism at an early age. They grow up knowing and understanding that they are "different" and that there is a target on their backs. Manhood is a condition of a man's mind and when you control a man's thinking you no longer have to worry about his behavior.

He will, as Carter G. Woodson stated in his monumental book, "*The Mis-Education of the Negro*":

"The Negro is so used to going through the back door of life that even when he comes upon a dwelling (house or building) in which there is no back door, his very nature will cause him to go and construct one for that very purpose (33).

What Dr. Woodson is saying is that the African American man's experiences from the institution of slavery and the later mis-educating influences of social, political, educational, economic and environmental racism has psychologically polluted his mind.. I have discerned sub-factors, or side effects that contributed to the mindset or nature that Dr. Woodson observed over 65 years ago, two of which (3 & 4) are still present within American society and exert a strong contributing influence upon African American males who become *"stuck in maleness"*.

The message to blacks from the institution of slavery was that black people were not worth much as human beings, certainly not in comparison to whites which justified black people's enslaved position and servitude during the period of time slavery was openly practiced and enforced in the United States.

Due to the presumed inferiority of African American people, a series of do's and don'ts and expectations of conduct we proscribed at every level of society. When blacks or Negroes, as we were called then, violated those proscriptions they promptly raped, beaten, burned, lynched, sometimes even without provocation. I believe this was done to instill fear and to cause us to think and feel inferior about ourselves in relation to whites.

To support the presumed inferior position of black people and their proscribed status, various social, educational, economic and political policies and practices were instituted at the national level that became widespread throughout American society. In March of 1857, the United States Supreme Court, led by Chief Justice Roger B. Taney, declared that all blacks — slaves as well as free — were not and could never become citizens of the United States.

In what is popularly known as the Dred Scott decision Chief Justice Roger B. Taney, declared that blacks "had no rights which the white man was bound to respect; and that the Negro might justly and lawfully be reduced to slavery for his benefit. He was bought and sold and treated as an ordinary article of merchandise and traffic, whenever profit could be made by it (34)."

The message that black people, especially the black males, were powerless to change their proscribed position in life was so widespread and reinforced through social, educational, economic and political racial discrimination that many blacks began to believe the demeaning message told to them by others.

Although the physical yoke of slavery has been far removed and racism has become less blatant and obvious, especially since the Civil Rights era of the late 50's, 60's and the early 70's, racism's harmful, crippling and emasculating grip on African Americans, particularly African American males, is still death-like and suffocating, despite the resurgence in recent years of African Americans on the political, educational, economic and social stages in America and the campaign and successful election of President Barak Obama to the White House for a second term in office.

These are monumental advances and point to the inherent power of mind over matter and the power of group consciousness. However, psychologically speaking, a significant number of African American men are plagued by a syndrome of conditions that interfere with their thinking that can be directly linked to influences of slavery, racism and the cultural adaptations by African Americans to both of these institutions.

A disproportionate number of African American males within the United States continue to suffer from low self-worth, low self-esteem, inferiority complexes, and attitude of entitlement, displaced anger and reverse racism (self-hate). These particular African American men continue to believe that they are powerless to effectuate meaningful and relevant change within their lives. This attitude of personal and social impotence is fueled in part by conditioning, and in part by the harsh realities of racism, discrimination, unemployment and underemployment in a society that continues to marginalize the existence of African American men. This impotence is also being influenced by the emergence of the new African American woman that no longer needs brothers to rescue them from their parent's house as was the case of times past.

Openly, African American males demean themselves and sabotage their access to successful experiences. African American men do this not because they are unlike other men who desire achievement and success in life, rather because they do not believe in themselves as men. Also, many African American women seem to feel that African American men no longer measure up to their standards or cannot operate at their level. The power of choice appears absent within them because strongholds within their individual experiences, magnified by their perception of societal and institutional barriers (strongholds), has made them believe they are powerless.

Far too many African American males do not believe that the powers God has given to every man also originated within them so they exert an extraordinary amount of time and effort imitating the attitudes and behaviors of other men, quite often other African American males who are also *"stuck in maleness".* Along with a change in self-worth and self-esteem, African American men need for African American women to support and encourage them and not beat them over their head about what they don't have or how they don't measure up. In the words of Nelson Mandela, *"If you talk to a man in a language he understands, that goes to his head. If you talk to him in his language, that goes to his heart."*

Along with the influences of African American women, this is the present day or 2013 version of the Negroes "nature" or unhealthy mindset as referred to by Dr. Woodson. If the African American male's mind is unhealthy so will be his interpretation and application of correct and appropriate manly behavior. The traumatic issues that have occurred in a man's life can keep him in a constant state of anger, resentment, sadness, grief or denial. As difficult as things may seem, you must move past these obstacles and seek positive change. If you do not provoke change in your life, experience has taught me that change will provoke you, usually in ways that you may not like or be prepared to deal with. What is more, the attitude that you take towards the occurrences in your life is more important, and can be much more powerful, than the facts of any individual circumstance.

Your attitude is everything! Forgive yourself and others, do not blame your parents, racism or any other "ism" for the individual choices that only you can be held accountable for. You must stop thinking and acting like little boys trapped in a man's body and take control and responsibility from where you are today. The Bible says: *"When I was a child I spoke as a child, I understood as a child, I thought as a child, but when I became a man I put away childish things."* (1 Corinthians 13:11)

My purpose for introducing this section as a contributing factor towards African American men who become *"stuck in maleness"* was not to blame slavery, white society or to point an accusing finger at racism. American history needs no help from me, the institution of slavery and its offspring racism, are well documented. African Americans, particularly African American men, need viable and sustaining solutions to solve the ongoing crisis within themselves, within the black family and within the communities we live in. *"Stuck in maleness"* is not about inciting one segment of American society against another. Political or social donnybrooks of an ethnic or racial character will not do today. American society and its many racial and ethnic groups, especially blacks and whites, are much too intertwined and interdependent.

However, I am speaking to African American men about how the residual effect of these institutions continues to affect his mind, his hopes, his goals, his aspirations in life and whether or not he (you) perceives himself worthy of them and possessing the internal power and perspective to pursue them. I am speaking to African American men, about real manhood and not the convenient practice of imitating what is popular on television, displayed in the media, rapped about on CDs, displayed in rap videos, practiced in gangs or idolized on street corners in America.

Real men do not resign themselves to the mere imitation of people or things, they originate with purpose and develop a vision to serve and to live spiritually (unselfishly).

The focus within this chapter has been to gain insight (vision) into understanding how you become *"stuck in maleness"* by the condition of your mind and the experiences of your life that prevent or hinder you from becoming the best man you can be, the man God designed and created you to be. For some of you, the issues surrounding becoming *"stuck in maleness"* centers around the absence of your father during the formative years of your childhood, while for others it may have been the occurrences of abuse, neglect, domestic violence, social violence, substance abuse or some other traumatic occurrence.

Some men can and do experience life-changing traumatic events during adult life. What is more, all African American males directly or indirectly have experienced and/or continue to experience the emasculating influences of the former institution of slavery and its present day progeny, the institution of racial, economic, political, educational, social and employment discrimination. You must use this discussion to better understand racism's controlling and stifling influence over the development of your mind into full manhood and not as an excuse towards apathy or taking the position of a victim.

Until healing occurs on the inside of you, you will continue to make the mistake of defining your sense of manhood through external means and the acquisition of things, or "bling" such as cars, video games, expensive (or fake) name brand clothing, nicknames, physical attributes, trophy-like items such as women or other possessions that give you the illusion of having what you lack as a man on the inside of you. This is particularly so when we as African American men spend billions of dollars of our money from employment, or from hustling on the street, buying products and services from some of the same people who seek to emasculate us or keep us mentally and physically *"stuck in maleness"* as men.

We obtained a glimpse into the lives of several African American males who are stuck in maleness. Charles, Nick, Clarence, Jamal, Frank and G-Money, sought the refuge through anger controlling behavior, alcohol, drugs, sexual promiscuity and the possession of material things. All are stuck into maleness-like thinking and behaviors.

The good news is there is a way out of these selfish, self-centered and self-defeating behaviors. The human mind is a terrible thing to waste by filling it with so much garbage but it is extremely resilient and adaptable. You can change your attitude, thinking, and learn a new way to live. Negative thinking patterns can be reversed and changed with awareness, practice, sacrifice and a commitment to become a better man, the man God designed and created you to be. But remember, it all begins in your mind. With the right awareness, the right tools, a blueprint for living and a clear and definable purpose for your life, you can and will overcome the shackles of being *"stuck in maleness"*.

Chapter 7
What It Means To Be A Man

"Be ye transformed by the renewing of your mind" (Romans 12:2)

In the first section of this book, Chapters 1-6, I discussed the fact that African American men are under attack in this country, that we all need to be mindful concerning issues of domestic violence, the need for us to address the person inside of the man, some of the myths and misconceptions we have about manhood, what it means to be *"stuck in maleness"* and how we can become stuck into the grips of negative maleness-like behavior.

This section of the book, covering Chapters 7-11, is about acquiring an understanding of the powers, tools, and blueprint you'll need in order to move out of being *"stuck in maleness"* and the steps you must take in order to transform your mind into thinking and functioning like the man God designed and created you to be. God did not design you or me as…..junk, or a chronically angry man, a criminal, an abuser, an alcoholic, a drug addict, a player or control freak, just to name a few of the many attributes of men *"stuck in maleness"*. There are many other attributes of being *"stuck in maleness"*, so do not think your particular form of being *"stuck in maleness"* does not qualify, because it does.

God designed and created all men for and with a purpose in life. The problem is that you and I got off track, or were not exposed to the correct information about manhood when we needed it most. Some of us were even brainwashed and deceived into believing we were unworthy as men and not entitled to certain qualities of life as was the case during times of slavery.

You were not made aware of your purpose as a man, and you became stuck into thinking and behavior patterns that were self-defeating, unproductive and unhealthy for you. Your present way of thinking may have also caused you to become counterproductive and even destructive to the people in your life who need and depend upon you the most, like your family.

Many of us as African American men have become accustomed to doing things in our life in selfish and self-serving ways, focusing only upon what *We* want, when *We* want it, and how *We* want it, which is one of the main symptoms of being *"stuck in maleness"*; it's all about *You!* But now it has become clear to *You*, because of the mess you've created for yourself, that you were or are….wrong in your assessment and belief about the circumstances of your life as a man. Manhood is not about you.

This is going to be a big step, a very important step towards transforming the way you think about manhood and it is going to require you to change the way you approach your life. But if you use and apply the information and tools in this book properly, it will help to transform the quality of your relationships with others and enable you to think and behave at a more focused and intentional level of thought and spirituality as a man, because you will no longer be satisfied with the way you presently think and view the circumstances of your life.

If you are not already a spiritual-minded man, you will become one. Just to be clear, what I mean by a "spiritual-minded man" is to possess or develop the insight (mental vision) to understand the purpose God has for your life as a man in relation to the people He has placed in it. Don't panic and skip to another chapter, or worse, close this book because I have suddenly mentioned God several times. Do not have any trepidation, no one is going to ask or force you to church this Sunday; that would be your choice. But you must keep an open mind; look where your best thinking has gotten you thus far!

No, this book is not about religion or any particular religious belief system. You can be Christian, Jewish, Jehovah's Witness, Muslim, Gentile, or you may practice another religious belief system, it doesn't really matter. What matters is that you change your present way of thinking about yourself as a man. I may use words or quotes from the Bible at times or other sources to illustrate certain points as I've done already but **Stuck In Maleness** is clearly about helping you to become a man when thinking and behaving like a self-serving male keeps getting you stuck in life and sabotaging your relationships with others.

Becoming a man (or a better man) is about becoming spiritual. The farther along you grow into manhood; the farther along you will grow spiritually because you will begin to know and understand that being a man is really not about you at all. I'm sorry to have to be the one to break the news to you, but somebody had to do it! Being a man is about understanding your purpose as a man, and using the powers, gifts, abilities, talents and skills God (call Him what you like) has provided you in order to serve Him by carrying out your purpose as a man towards the people and situations He has placed in your care.

These insights can get you un-stuck and on your way to a better quality of life. Whatever you've done in your previous life is no longer the primary issue. You cannot change your past anyway. Forget about it! Take it from me, I've already made the mistakes for you, it's not worth the effort or the consequences. That's part of the reason I've written this book. The other reason is that I've begun to learn from those mistakes and became a better man and so can you.

This is where you discover a new but simple blueprint, along with the tools and powers you already possess; when used properly, that can take you from the selfish, self-centered, inconsiderate and overly materialistic label that may be associated with your name into becoming a man, a real man. A man has a higher calling and level of responsibility than a male or a boy. There is no hocus pocus involved; there will not be any flashing lights but this journey is about enlightenment and acquiring insight (inner vision) that I hope will become life changing for you but you must be willing to change the way you currently think.

Your Toolkit – Powers

In the previous chapter on how we become *"stuck in maleness"*, I spoke about your belief system and the tremendous power it has in shaping your thinking, behavior, and the imagery (or picture) you have of yourself as a man. You also learned that your belief system, in particular your imagination of yourself as a man, has been shaped and greatly influenced by experiences from your childhood that may have left traumatic, unhealthy, and/or illusory impressions on your understanding of manhood.

In a sense, you are the sum of accumulated choices and decisions in your life's experiences, but most of the meaningful and powerful aspects of your personality, your development, your life as you know it, negative or positive, were likely set in motion during the developing years of your childhood. Unfortunately, you cannot go back into your mother's womb nor can you relive your childhood. We are not permitted "do-overs" as adults like when we were kids in the schoolyard playground playing kickball.

But you can change your belief system and the way you think of yourself through the choices that you make today.

The first set of tools that you will need in order to change the powerful influence of your present belief system and how it has hindered and prevented you from becoming the man that God designed and created you to be, you already have available to you. When God designed and created you He also gave you powers unknown to any other creature in the universe:

> He gave you the power to think.
>
> He gave you the power to love
>
> He gave you the power to will.
>
> He gave you the power to laugh.
>
> He gave you the power to imagine.
>
> He gave you the power to create.
>
> He gave you the power to plan.
>
> He gave you the power to pray. (35)

My African American brothers, through the gift of the power of choice you possess special powers with the inner ability to transform your immediate environment and your life into whatever you want it to become. There are many forces within society that send the message that we can or cannot do certain things or that we can or cannot experience certain kinds of successful living, but we can. There is no difference between the rich man and the poor man, the doctor and his patient, white men or black men, the criminal and his jailer, or you and men who fully experience their manhood and their purpose, but the power of the choices you make. How you use or abuse the power of choice that God has gifted you is your choice. The choice is exclusively yours. But what have you done with these tremendous powers?

From this day forward, you can no longer blame others for what has happened, or will happen, in your life. Bad parents, slavery, racism, growing up in poverty or living on the wrong side of the tracks, are now irrelevant factors because, these issues can be disempowered and overcome in your life by the intelligent, passionate and consistent application of your powers of choice.

You must learn to use your power of choice wisely; it is the most important tool in your toolkit. That does not mean that you will not encounter challenges or have to make tough decisions; everyone does. Start small and begin making better choices with simple things but do them more decisively and you will begin to see change. But making tough decisions and using, not abusing, your power of choice responsibly will yield powerful results.

Some things in your life may have come generously and with regularity but manhood is not about ease or convenience; it is about purpose. Your parents who raised you or others may have deceived you, they may have bamboozled you into believing that new clothes, shoes, cars, cell phones, money, living for free, and so on, without work, sacrifice, savings, and responsible decision making, are needs and entitlements owed to you by them or others. You are not entitled to anything. Your nakedness and your mind are gifts from above, that is all you should and can expect. You must lose your attitude of entitlement and expect nothing more than you are willing to pursue, sacrifice, save, or persevere for in a responsible manner.

You cannot just call yourself a "grown ass man" and expect results. Manhood is not to be demanded; rather it is to be earned and demonstrated by the development of your character through the consistent application of your purpose as a man without the expectation of return. You procreated the children, you take of them. They need food, clothing, Legos, dolls, bikes and braces.

You get a job and pay for them. They need love, guidance, and discipline; you provide it. They grow up health, happy, and responsible; there's your payment and reward and now you can feel proud because "You da man!"

If you honestly and soberly reflect back into your past life, you will see how the events in your life are mostly due to how you have used or abused your power of choice. But today is a new day; it's your birthday! You must no longer fret about yesterday or the opportunities that have escaped you. The milk that has been spilled is sour. From this day forward you must…..

> Choose to love….rather than hate.
> Choose to laugh….rather than cry.
> Choose to create….rather than destroy.
> Choose to persevere….rather than quit.
> Choose to praise….rather than gossip.
> Choose to heal….rather than wound.
> Choose to give….rather than steal.
> Choose to act….rather than procrastinate.
> Choose to grow….rather than rot.
> Choose to pray….rather than curse (36).
> Choose to live as a man rather than die *"stuck in maleness"*.

The pattern of each of these decisions that you make in your new life should not be abused and taken for granted as they were in your previous life. Each new choice that you make will become a new step towards maturity, regardless of your present age, or, a step back into the mediocrity and selfishness of being *"stuck in maleness"*. The choice is yours; the choice is exclusively yours.

Your Tool Kit – Belief System

The second set of tools that you have available to you is your belief system. You will recall that your belief system is composed of your self-worth, imagination, values, principles, actions (behaviors) attitude and your imagination. Your belief system is the guiding force of how you see yourself as a man and the choices you make in how you live your life. If your belief system is the guiding force of how you see yourself as a man, then your imagination is the power source that fuels your belief system.

Myths, misconceptions, and distorted ideas about manhood are previously what filled your imagination and caused the thinking errors that contributed to your becoming *"stuck in maleness"*. Reflect upon your present belief system and how you chose your friends, why you chose them, the things you do, the places you go and even the type of woman you find attractive and appealing. All of these choices that you've made over and over are a product of your belief system and how you view your self-worth. The type of friends, acquaintances and activities you've engaged in have lead you to believe that your choices have been good ones, because your friends, for the most part, are just like you. You chose them because you pursue and attract what you feel inside.

In everyday life we use tools to fix things that are broken and to make adjustments to items, such as appliances, that may not be working properly. You are not any different than an appliance in the sense that your imagination, your values, your principles, your behavior and your attitude and your sense of self-worth can be changed or adjusted to make you….work better. Your thoughts can be changed, to redirect the course of your life. Stated another way, your belief system must now become your "Navigation System" that you'll use to guide and direct your thinking and behavior towards becoming the man you were designed and created to be.

I do not believe that God designed you or any other African American man, to be a pimp, a player, a gangsta, a drug dealer or addict, a deadbeat dad, a criminal, an abuser of women, or whatever *"stuck in maleness"* attributes that have been associated with your name and way of life.

You are not alone; many African American men have found themselves making poor choices that placed them in bad situations. The main reason that keeps you and other men like you *"stuck in maleness"* are problems of lack. Lack means to be without what is needed, required or essential, especially to your development as a man.

There is no doubt that African American males are intelligent, competent, talented, and gifted in multiple areas of life, just as much as the next man. African American men often excel and dominate in sports. Every few years we hear of another African American male athlete who has begun to play in a sport previously dominated by others. But within a few years, he or others like him, become standouts and top performers, often exceeding their closest competition. Similar successes are also occurring in acting on the big screen of television and movies.

But we also we also see black males making headlines in negative areas of life as well, such as drug abuse, drug dealing, black on black crimes, or other forms of anti-social or criminal activity. But we need successes and standouts in everyday life, men who work every day, take care of their families and participate in their communities. But things can and will change. That is what **Stuck in Maleness** is about. Once you digest, incorporate into your mind and apply these simple but powerful principles to your mind, you will excel in other positive areas of life as well.

This book is written for and about you. Lack is where the greatest harm may have occurred to you during childhood, your teenage years or maybe during some part of your early adulthood. Lack has created and brought about the conditions that have caused you to become *"stuck in maleness"*, problems of lack. You lacked the awareness and the prospective of what your role as a man is supposed to be about. Problems of lack are the reason why it is important for us as African American men to have our father present when we are children and it is the same reason why we must be present in the lives of our children.

Children, especially African American male children, need a positive and consistent male role model in their lives that can teach them the correct values and what it means to be a man.

Try as she may, there are limitations to what a woman (or mother) can do to raise a boy into a man without the active involvement of a positive male role model. Along with modeling correct behavior, there are aggressive and masculine tendencies within males that only another male can recognize and be in the position to properly channel. With good intentions, many single mothers give their sons everything they want and pamper them beyond what is necessary or appropriate.

They attempt to make up for the absence (or lack) of their father or the presence of another positive male figure. This is a mistake; "things" cannot take the place of structure, discipline, the modeling of proper male behavior and the enforcement of age appropriate tasks and responsibilities at every juncture of growth and development.

When a man is not present in a boy's life to show him how to treat women, manage his emotions, manage his time, how to learn from his mistakes or model the provider and leader role, the boy will get the information from whatever sources that may be available to him. These sources of information are likely to be outside of his home life and are less likely to be accurate, healthy, or advantageous to the long-term well-being of the boy. This is one of the reasons that gang affiliation and membership has become so attractive to many African American male youth; the gang fills the sense of belonging, purpose, leadership, and even love that the boy or teen is not receiving from home.

The choices a boy makes to emulate another male, or gang member, and the information he obtains about manhood, how to conduct himself, treat women, etc., are not going to have the forethought and wisdom of a father to meet what the boy really needs. What is more, a father's presence is also needed to model appropriate and acceptable behavior for girls. A girl's first example of how women are to be treated by men and the behavior expected of men is by observing the interaction between her parents. Many fatherless girls grow up looking to replace the absence of their father's love, in relationships that become abusive. The loss of a father's presence in the home is felt by everyone.

So what are the areas of lack that are essential to correct and foster proper development into manhood? There are four of them. Together they form your blueprint for manhood and they must be used in conjunction with the tools of your belief system and your powers of choice. They are: Awareness, Purpose, Vision, and Responsibility.

Your Blueprint for Manhood
Awareness

Aristotle, a disciple of Plato said "know thyself". Self-awareness is the key to bring about change in your life. You cannot change anything about yourself, your circumstances or your environment if you lack the awareness of the problems in your life and the real impact they are having on you and others.

In addition, change will not be forthcoming if you do not accept the facts of whatever predicament you are in. If you do not accept the facts of the circumstances of your predicament, you will also be resistant to change and continue to falter in *"stuck in maleness"*. As men sometimes we can become so comfortable in our maleness behavior that we cannot see the immature and ridiculous nature of the mess we are creating for ourselves. Everyone around us can see the folly of our thinking and actions, but us.

Here's an example. Every morning for the past six months, Darryl's parents walked downstairs from their bedroom, crossed the living room on their way into the kitchen and passed their son sleeping on the sofa they bought years ago when he left for college. Now that Darryl was back he was only supposed to stay for a few weeks until he found an apartment. Darryl and his fiancé Tiana had broken off their engagement so Darryl moved out of their apartment. Although both Darryl and his former fiancé worked, Tiana handled paying the bills, scheduled all of their appointments and even took care of the food shopping and did all of the cooking. Darryl just forked over part of his check, ate, and complained whenever Tiana wanted to eat out, see a movie or take a short trip to a neighboring state. Now that Darryl and Tiana had broken up, Darryl did….nothing.

Darryl worked the first shift as a lab tech for a major pharmaceutical company. But about a month after taking over his parent's sofa, Darryl changed to the second shift so he wouldn't have to get up in the morning. Despite their romantic relationship and former plans of getting married, Tiana had been more of a surrogate mother to Darryl but she was no longer around to motivate him to do things he otherwise would not do. Darryl was a momma's boy and had gotten used to his mother doing everything for him since childhood. Darryl had broken off the engagement with Tiana because he thought she was too bossy. But Darryl also never initiated anything or took the lead in activities or projects without first making a fuss.

Darryl was 30 years-old and sleeping on his parent's sofa but he had no clue what he wanted to do in life or where he was going. Although she had arthritis and for the past ten years gotten used to no longer fussing over Darryl, Darryl's mother vacuumed the living room during the week just before she went to work. But this time Darryl's mother was not cleaning up after him; she was annoyed that he had taken up residence in her living room that she had meticulously been able to maintain over the years despite the weekly bible study group she held there with several members from her church.

For the past few weeks Darryl's mother seemed to spend a little longer vacuuming the living room, especially near the sofa where Darryl lay asleep. His old bedroom was gone. A few months after he graduated from college and started working, Darryl's father converted his old bedroom into a combination sewing room and TV room so his wife would not have to go up and down the stairs as much now that she had arthritis.

Darryl's father was not so subtle in his hints that it was time for Darryl to leave. Every time Darryl left dishes in the sink or made a mess in the kitchen, which was often, Darryl's father packed the dirty dishes into one of those plastic grocery bags from the supermarket, put all of the dirty dishes in it, then he placed the bag of dishes on top of the coffee table, in front of where Darryl was sleeping on the sofa.

Darryl's clothes were strewn on the floor or on the top of the coffee table. Sometimes the bag leaked onto Darryl's pants or stained his white lab coat, but Darryl's father didn't care. He wanted Darryl off of his wife's sofa and out of his house. Late one evening while lying in bed together, Darryl's father said to his wife in a sarcastic tone, "Somewhere along the way that boy got the impression that it was acceptable for a 30 year-old man, with a job, to come back home to sleep on his parent's sofa. I wonder where he got that bright idea from?"

Darryl's father had long ago admonished his wife for spoiling Darryl as a child. But Darryl's mother wanted him to have it "better" than she did; she didn't want her children to be without the things they needed. But instead, Darryl has become stuck in maleness and lacks the self-awareness or the motivation to see past his subconscious desire to remain dependent on others. You do not always need to have all of the answers to your problems; mistakes are inevitable. But you gotta know that you have a problem. Make the effort to remain aware of where you are in life. Men don't become stuck in maleness overnight. There are always signs or indications that you are beginning to slip a little. When you have awareness then you are in the position to make changes. A man should always be aware of where he is going because then he will be aware of when he begins to slip, make needed changes and adjustments in order to get back on track. This may mean changing the places you go, the things you do or the people who are a part of your circle. If you don't provoke change, change will provoke you.

What I am suggesting is that you must become educated about your life. Becoming educated about your life is learning to think and act in your own best interests. Now for all of you men *"stuck in maleness"*, take this comment as a contradiction to my earlier comments and misinterpret this as saying it's ok to be selfish and self-centered, hold up; I'm not saying that. Let me break it down for you in a way that you need to understand it. First of all, all three elements must be present and in operation.

We all know of people who think without acting. We see them sitting on the stoop or across from us at the table telling stories of what they *COULD DO* or what they been thinking about doing, but they never seem to do. With the second element, people who act without thinking usually end up having a whole lot of people pissed off at them, serving time in prison or dead. We don't need to spend a lot of time on that point.

Now, with the third element *I DO NOT MEAN* selfishness or self-centered behavior. What I mean is doing or engaging in thinking and behaviors that are in the best interest of your life. If you don't have a job, get one. It doesn't matter if you have a PhD and the only job available is working at McDonalds. Who cares? Certainly not the public utilities company who pumps gas and electricity to your apartment; certainly not the transit bus driver when you pay your fare; certainly not the cashier at the supermarket where you pay for groceries or disposable diapers for your little baby.

My grandparents Emma and Professor Morton had thirteen children together and neither one of them had higher than a third grade education. While several of my aunts and uncles are deceased, not one of them died as children or in their youth because my grandparents didn't provide food, clothing or shelter for their children. My grandparents also made sure that my mother and her siblings got their butts up every day to go to school walking, sometimes several miles, to the schoolhouse.

In retrospect many of all of our grandparents had doctorates and medical degrees... in the education of life. That's what we have to do, find a way to turn our street hustle, for those who do it, into a legitimate hustle to take care of ourselves and our families. But we gotta take our ego's out of it and do what is in our best interests as MEN, not dependent males, and so what if your lady makes more than you do. The totality of your character as a man is more than any individual element. Your value as a man is to be found in your self-worth, not merely the money contained in your wallet or the kind of car you drive.

Purpose

Every year the Sockeye salmon of Alaska make their way up rivers to the shallow waters. Dodging changing water temperatures, the baited hooks of eager fishermen and just before the waters calm, hungry bears trudging through the waters trying to catch and eat as many salmon as possible, the Sockeye salmon that make the journey to the calm, shallow waters lay their eggs for a new generation of baby salmon to begin the process all over again. The Sockeye salmon of Alaska have a purpose and the purpose is the procreation and preservation of its species.

In the same way as the salmon, God designed and **created every man for and with a purpose**. The main problem with African American men who are *"stuck in maleness"* is the absence of a clear and definable understanding of their purpose as a man. Without purpose in life, life becomes merely a series of random and disconnected events that lack meaning, intention or purpose.

The reason why your imagination, the head-lamp of your navigation system, has not worked properly for you is because it is filled with so many illusory and distorted myths and misconceptions and negative imagery about what it means to be a man. Low self-worth and your belief system has you thinking, believing, and engaging in unhealthy and dysfunctional things to yourself and to the people in your life.

Somewhere along the span of your life you were lead to believe that you were not a man if you didn't control or beat your woman, neglect your children, sell drugs, rob, steal, kill, destroy things, or a host of other false images about manhood that were a part of your former imagination, your former way of life. Those images were false; that is not what real manhood is about or what real men do. You were misled to believe that those are the things that African American men do but they are not; not real men, anyway.

Every day that God blesses you with the ability to breathe, place your feet on the floor and use your gifts, talents, senses, and intelligence, your powers should be filled with a sense of purpose and direction about your life. I do not believe that God designed you or I to get up every morning, place our feet on the floor beside our bed, sofa, cot or whatever, and merely think about how to get our next meal, drink, drug, woman, or the remote control to watch sports on television.

What a limitless and purposeless life. This is your wake-up call; this is your call to arms. The second part of transforming your mind and your life out of being *"stuck in maleness"* is to know and understand your purpose as a man. God designed and created you to be 1) A leader; 2) A provider; 3) A protector; 4) A teacher; and, 5) A companion and helpmate.

Leader

Of all the purposes of a man, the leadership role is the most significant role you must perform. Many of the problems faced by African American men, the African American family and the African American community are due to a lack of leadership. When a man fails to properly and effectively perform the leadership role in relation to himself, his family, and the people God has placed in his care, there is bound to be major problems.

Why? Let's take a look at the basic qualifications/job description of a leader.[7] Men are natural born leaders when it comes to our aggressive instincts, survival instincts, physical attributes and competition. Every day African American males survive in the hood,

---

[7] The ability to lead, guide or direct others towards a common goal or purpose (35)."

on the street corner, or on the basketball court. I've already mentioned how we excel in sports, the vast majority of African American millionaires originated in a sports-related field or are presently competitive, professional athletes.

But while the purpose of professional or even amateur athletes is competition, many falter off the playing field just like you may have because they still lack purpose as a man. The job description states "to lead others (family, children, co-workers, etc.) towards a common goal or purpose." Unfortunately, when you look at the news, listen to some rap music and watch some rap videos, walk down the street in many cities, or visit the many jails and prisons in this country, you will not see purpose-filled African American male leaders.

Many seem to think that their only purpose is self-destruction and the pursuit of illusory images of manhood. So I must ask, where have you led yourself, your children or your family recently? Have you led them to the poorhouse, to the crack house, to a place on someone's sofa, to the liquor cabinet, your stash in the garage, or did you just get up and leave and leave the leading to someone else? When was the last time (or have you ever) sat down at the kitchen table with your lady and the children to discuss your plans for them, what you're working on, and how it's going to get them to some future state of affairs?

Now, when was the last time you told your lady and/or your children you'd be back in a few minutes or an hour but didn't come back for several hours or more without explanation as to your whereabouts? If you have led them and/or yourself in a positive way, how did you become *"stuck in maleness"*? I am not trying to put you down or to make you feel bad about things that you've done or may have not done for your children or your family. But my beloved brothers, you cannot call yourself a man, a "grown ass man", if you are not performing your leadership role effectively or not at all, but in order to lead them you first must first learn how to lead yourself. Without knowing and understanding your purpose as a man, you cannot even lead yourself.

The absence of African American men who know and understand how to lead themselves, and of course their families, has been one of the main problems contributing to the crisis within the African American family: males who either fail to step up to the plate and lead within their respective families and/or males who lack the purpose and responsibility of manhood to lead, but do it anyway.

The ability to lead is a gift from God that is to be shared with other people. This is the principle reason why I've continued to emphasize throughout the pages of this book that being a man, a real man, is not about you. When a man leads, he sets the tone for his family, the household and how the overall atmosphere of the family will be. When you lead you keep a bird's eye view of things but zoom in on specific situations as needed. Leadership is not about barking out instructions or just telling people what to do, although giving instructions, and delegating certain responsibilities, or directing people to do things is a part of leadership. In most cases, you lead in conjunction with others such as your wife or partner.

When you don't step up the plate and take on your leadership role, you deny others the benefit of the direction and guidance that you otherwise can provide them. When you don't perform this very vital role within your family, somebody else will. It could be a man, or it could be another lost male *"stuck in maleness"*, such as an abuser, drug addict, con man, or it could be strangers from a series of government agencies providing services because your wife or lady has been forced to apply for welfare.

Welfare services usually come with "conditions" in order for the recipient to receive, or continue to receive, the requested benefits. In times past, such a practice started a negative trend in African American households where the woman was receiving benefits but the husband or father was unemployed or underemployed and was not able to support his family. If social workers came to the home and the unemployed husband/father was there, the woman may not receive her benefits. Eventually some African American men began to stay away longer, for various reasons of their own, while some women began to accept living on public assistance as a normal and acceptable way of life. Some men began to take advantage of this opportunity and make their way to several women at a time, resting in whatever household they could lay their head the longest. At the same time, not all men are to blame. Some women had multiple "friends" and used the arrangement to get extra money and live higher than their monthly welfare benefits would allow.

These practices by both African American women and men continue to go on today. That's where a lot of African American men end up with child support arrears or go through a series of petty incarcerations for child support warrants. Men, step up to the plate and lead before someone else does.

The area that men within the African American family need the most change is in their ability to lead responsibly. You created the child, got into the relationship or the apartment but can't take care of either. You acted before you thought, and now you and everyone else in your care must suffer as well. Been there, done that. Or you confuse your leadership role with the boss role and want to tell people what to do, how to do it, and when to do it, in a hostile, aggressive, or even abusive manner, and then feel that you are doing your job. One of the key attributes of leaders is that they model within their own character the behaviors, attributes and values that they expect of others. Most importantly, the values of trust, respect, honesty, integrity, patience and teamwork must be a regular part of your leadership vocabulary and behaviors. In order to lead, you must lead with character.

What is your leadership style? Is your style appropriate to the people you're leading and the direction you are trying to take them? Do you threaten or intimidate? Are you controlling? A disciplinarian? A micro-manager? Laid back? All of these are important questions and greatly influence your leadership as a man. The most important question is where are you leading your family or other group towards? Do you have a vision and goals? Have you discussed with your wife, lady, children or others your plans or the direction you'd like to take in life?

Leading also means that you must possess the insight and ability to coach members of your family or group in the best ways for them to participate in achieving the family's or group's goals. A good leader does not try to do everything himself but delegates or even co-leads if his wife, lady or team member possesses knowledge and expertise to accomplish a particular task.

You might be a good money maker but be a poor money manager. If you let your ego or pride get in the way and continue to lead where you can't, then you're leading irresponsibly. Put yourself in the position where you can lead best. Base your leadership on a system(s) that you already know works, like the Bible, Quran, or Torah, for example, or wisdom obtained from an academic or spiritual advisor/mentor. Remember, manhood is not about you. A leader is someone who leads, guides and directs others towards a common goal or purpose. African American men must learn how to lead themselves and their families.

Provider

Other than leader, a provider is the most significant role for a man and his family, yet, for African American males it has been also the most controversial. Providing for yourself and the needs of your family is probably the most visible expression of your manhood. There is no question as to what must be done to provide for your family but get a job, if you don't already have one. You get up every work day and go to work, period. When you can't or won't perform this very vital part of manly responsibility, you are bound to have problems in your household and in your relationship. If you cannot obtain employment in your regular line of work (a legal line of work), then opt to flip burgers, mop floors, perform construction work, dig ditches, or even wash cars; it doesn't matter. Manhood is not about ego; it's about providing.

You should never resign yourself into thinking or believing that it's okay for your lady or the children to get on welfare unless it is absolutely the last resort, for example, because your family or your child's wellbeing is at risk. Far too many African American men neglect taking care of their children and far too many African American women abuse public assistance and use it as regular income in the same way that others use the emergency room for nonemergency care.

As a man, you should learn to plan and to use a budget in order to maximize the resources by not shopping in corner bodegas or local convenience stores instead of shopping at BJ's, Costco, or Sam's Club, where the unit price per item most often a fraction of the price paid locally. A similar argument can be made for accessing health and life insurance. We must provide in a way that keeps our families out of the crisis mentality of daily survival into thinking and providing for an improved quality of life over the long term.

One of the main reasons for divorce in America is money problems. Compared to other ethnic groups, African American families tend to be more financially unstable due to income disparities and poor spending and saving habits. So when you don't work, or work but blow your money at the strip joint, the bar, the crap or poker game, or using and abusing drugs and alcohol, you make your family unstable. The money that could be used for needed payments, purchases, or emergency situations is now in someone else's pocket or has gone up in smoke.

Part of being a good provider is not just making money but knowing what to do with it, how to make it grow. What I am saying is to become more financially literate and versatile in how you earn money and how to make better use of the money that you earn. If you don't have the time or the interest to take a class in business, finance, or real estate, then buy a book on one of those subjects and study on your own. You can learn a lot from reading financial publications such as Black Enterprise, Money Magazine, Smart Money, for example, and taking the time to read the business section of your local newspaper to gain insight (mental vision) on what's going on in the world and your local community. If you don't already use a budget, make one, and stick to it. Black folks (I'm sorry, African Americans) have a tendency to spend an excessive amount of money on "things" that make them look or feel good, instead of just doing better by making better financial choices. This behavior is a part of the illusory imagery in our minds that needs to be transformed, chasing "things" or trying to be something or someone that you are not.

When you begin to see and understand that your real value and worth as a man is on the "inside", it will lessen your tendency to the habit of adorning yourself with worthless, expensive clothing and jewelry that is often tossed in a closet, lost, or misplaced, $50, $80, and sometimes hundreds of dollars laying wrinkled at the bottom of a dirty clothes basket.

    Another point on your role as provider -- men, you cannot allow your wife, lady, or others to stress you out to spend money or to purchase things that do not have anything to do with the vision and goals you have for your family. This is why it is so very important for you to align yourself with the right woman and not just someone who looks good, makes a lot of money or simply provides gratification in the bedroom. If you have a beer or Pink Champagne budget for the moment and your wife or lady has Crystal taste or if she is very materialistic, she is going to put pressure on you step up to *HER WAY* of doing things. It's not wise to be with someone that expects you to live above your means or to put unnecessary pressure and strain on the relationship/marriage or on your finances.

    It is so very important for you to know and understand your purpose and roles as a man. There is absolutely nothing wrong with purchasing nice items for your wife, lady, or children when the money is there to do so, but not at the expense of the stability of the household or at the expense of undue mental or emotional stress. The dysfunction within the African American family mostly comes when the African American man doesn't know, understand, and actively live his various roles as a man. This is also a part of your teacher role, to teach your family in the best ways to maximize financial resources.

    Bling doesn't have anything to do with paying the light bill, the rent or mortgage, putting food on the table, clothes on the children's backs and gas in the car. If you change your habits with money and focus on priorities and not "appearances", you can better provide for yourself and your family without stressing yourself out or worse, turning to crime. There are plenty of African American men in prison serving time for crimes they committed in the name of maintaining or pursuing an image to impress a woman with "things" instead of demonstrating good manly character.

In your provider role is where you have to be a leader and develop a spine (if you don't have one) and re-focus the troops, remind them of the vision you have for the family and for them as individuals. It's about setting and keeping focus on the goals for the family and for individual members of your family. African American people are not as broke and needy as they have to be; an overwhelming desire to keep up with the "Joneses" and financial illiteracy is probably closer to the truth.

For men in relationships in which your wife or lady earns more than you, so what? Keep your focus on your portion of providing for the family. Her earning more money does not and cannot make you less of a man unless you simply don't know and understand your role as a man. Manhood is a condition of a man's mind and his purpose.

If she earns more money than you, great — then that's the way it is. Income is but one factor in your position as a man. You should not feel inferior if she earns more money; feel inferior or inadequate if you're not doing anything. Stop hating on women.

Maybe she took the time to go to college or took extra training so she could make more money. She could also be in a high paying profession or has been at her job for a long time. Don't hate on your wife or lady because things are or have worked out for her in that area of her life. Do your part and provide to the best of your ability.

The reality is that in many households it takes two incomes to make ends meet. The bill collector or the cashier at the supermarket does not care whose check, or how much, or where the money comes from as long as the bill is paid. And should you and your wife or lady break up or if the relationship does not prosper as planned, you are still responsible for taking care of any children the two of you produced, regardless of whatever your feeling may be towards your wife; lady, ex or whatever the situation may be. The children did not ask to be born and still need your love, structure, discipline and financial support. If you have a job, pay up and cut back on your lifestyle. If you don't have a job, get one.

Teacher

Your role as a teacher is probably the most neglected, least talked about but the most important role for you as a father of your children, step-children, etc. Failure to perform the teacher role, along with leadership, is where the most damage occurs in the black family when the man is absent from his family or when he fails to teach his children due to neglect or ignorance. Not having a father or a father figure, who took the time to teach about manhood and life may have been part of the reason that you became *"stuck in maleness"*. However, moving forward, this vital part of your purpose as a man cannot be neglected. It is your job and responsibility to teach your children, in partnership with your wife or lady, the facts of life and the information they need to know in order to be the best they can be.

You begin by teaching your children the values that are important for character development, such as honesty, integrity, respect, and trust. You do this by the consistency between what you say to your children and the behavior that you and your lady models in their everyday life. You and your lady may have a system of rewards and punishments that the two of you use to teach your children. That system could be based in general or it could be based upon the values and principles of your particular religious belief system. Oftentimes this becomes a great benefit to you as a leader and as a teacher because your religious belief system will likely already have values and principles that contain wisdom that you practice and desire for your family to live by.

Church on Sunday and Bible study may be a part of your teacher routine or going to the mosque on Fridays. You don't necessarily need to do everything but you do need to know from what sources or resources to obtain the correct information and influences needed to empower your mind and to teach/lead your family. Teaching your children about God and how conduct themselves in a virtuous way is extremely important for building good character and setting the stage for a fulfilling life. Teach your children to be thankful, grateful and appreciative of the simple things of life. Most importantly, teach them about God. Quite often we cannot do *EVERYTHING* by ourselves and will need to draw on the strength and limitless power of God.

How you conduct yourself at home with your wife or lady also becomes the basis by which your children relate to each other, how they behave in public, how they resolve conflicts amongst themselves and others, and how open and responsive they are to correction. It is the job of both parents to correct and discipline their children, although the job usually falls upon the man. Everyday of your lives you and your wife or lady are modeling behaviors that your children absorb like sponges, good or bad.

The value of money, financial literacy, the ability to delay gratification and to be frugal with spending are directly related to how you live yourself, along with the values that you teach them. What is more, you are teaching your son(s) how to be men and you are teaching your daughter(s) what to expect from men and how men are supposed to treat their women. Every little gesture or response in the minds of children impresses them with information on how to behave and the behavior they should expect from others. Teach your children or someone else will.

Protector

It is your job as a man to protect your family. You must protect them from the harm that may come to them from the outside the family unit, and you sometimes must protect them from the harm they bring to themselves. In your provider role you must protect the physical safety of your family by providing a roof over their heads in a safe and comfortable environment that you can afford. It is your responsibility to make sure that the house or apartment you provide for them is free of hazards within the home and if possible, in a community free of social violence, racial disturbances and crime. It is your job to teach your children basic safety techniques and to provide them with the tools needed to protect them when they are outside of your presence.

What is even more significant than the physical hazards of their environment is that you protect them emotionally by creating a social environment within the home where they are free to learn and express themselves as individuals without fear of rejection or putdowns. You must also protect their innocence by not exposing them to drugs, alcohol, abuse, neglect or violence within the home and assure that they are not preyed upon by others. And when your children get ahead of themselves by fault of their own or by negative influences from others, step in to make things right as best as you can; it's your job to protect them.

Finally, you must establish and enforce rules within your household. Establishing rules and teaching your children to abide by them not only to protect them from themselves, but also to teach them that freedom and success within society at large comes with rules and laws that must be obeyed.

Companion/Helpmate

Men, you can perform all the other roles of your purpose as a man, but if you don't take the time to be a friend and helper to your wife or lady, you are still acting a manner suggestive of being *"stuck in maleness"*. Manhood and becoming a man IS NOT ABOUT THE MAN. Unfortunately, many brothers make this mistake by believing that because they pay the bills, fix the car, discipline the children and put a few nights a week in the sack they don't have to do anything else. Just as men are by nature more left brain oriented and tend to be more aggressive and logical in their thinking, women, conversely, are more right brain oriented and tend to be more complex in their thinking and are more emotional.

Most women can cook, clean, tend to the children, wash clothes, and make a shopping list while carrying on a conversation with two different people (I've observed this). But nothing can be more rewarding and soothing to their sense of womanhood than to have an intimate conversation with their mate, especially while relaxing on the sofa or lying in bed. Listen what they have to say and make a sincere effort to follow along, no matter how many times she may switch back and forth between different subjects. Sometimes it's not what she's saying to you but how much attention and interest you show to what she's saying. What is more, take the time to ask her about her day and take an interest in her job or other things that interest her. Compliment your wife or lady and remind her how much you love and appreciate her as your mate and as a person, and show it.

Without asking, do the laundry, wash the dishes, take the kids to the park, run her bath water, prepare dinner or order take-out and give her opportunities to relax and enjoy the much needed extra attention. Flowers or special treats are nice but actually do things for her that confirm that she is your special person, your companion and help mate. This topic will be discussed in further detail in Chapter 11, "*What Women Want*".

Vision

"I float like a butterfly, I sting like a bee, your hands can't hit what your eyes can't see. Now you see me, now you don't, you think you will, but I know you won't." ~ Muhammad Ali

The third area of lack that must become a part of your Blueprint for Manhood is vision. Muhammad Ali, the greatest heavyweight boxer of all time, uttered the above quote over 40 years ago. But the central point of Muhammad Ali's flagrant words were unquestionable; you cannot hit a target you cannot see. That is what having a vision for your life and a purpose is about. When you know what you're aiming at, you have an increased ability to hit the target. But what is vision and what does it have to do with your Blueprint for Manhood?

Vision is a mental image created by our imagination. An example is having a vision of purchasing a home for your family and seeing your children grow up and go off to college or maybe starting your own business and making enough money to retire and travel around the world. A vision is something you hold within your mind's eye. But unlike a dream, a vision is transferred into the "let me see how I can make this a reality" part of your mind. Having a vision propels you to take action and taking steps to bring the vision to fruition. Myles Munroe, author of *The Principles and Power of Vision: Keys to Achieving Personal and Corporate Destiny* states:

"God not only created each person on earth with a distinct design, but He also placed in everyone a unique vision. No person can give you this vision. It is only God-given. You can go to as many seminars as possible and receive all kinds of wonderful instruction, but no one except God can give you the idea you were born to fulfill.

The poor man, the rich man, the black man, the white man— every person has a dream in his heart. Your vision may already be clear to you, or it may still be buried somewhere deep in your heart, waiting to be discovered. Fulfilling this dream is what gives purpose and meaning to life. In other words, the very substance of life is to for you to find God's purpose and fulfill it. Until you do that, you are not really living"(36).

In order to make your vision your reality, you must set goals for you and your family that will create the focus and movement that will help you to begin achieving your vision. What is more, the goals that you set to aid in the achievement of your vision must meet certain criteria. They must be: 1) realistic; 2) achievable in your lifetime; and, 3) measurable.

Realistic

For your goals to be realistic, they must be something that you can actually do. If you are 40 years of age and stand at 5'5" tall and your goal is to become a NBA basketball player, that is not realistic. About 99% of NBA players retire or are injured and cannot play by their mid to late 30's. What's more, no one has ever started an NBA basketball career at age 40, no matter how good they were. For the same 40 year-old man to say that he wants to purchase his first single family home by the time he is 42, even in today's volatile economy and unstable housing market, is realistic because there are plenty of houses on the market available at many different price levels.

Achievable

The goal must also be something that you can actually achieve in your lifetime, like earning your bachelor's degree by age 50. Whereas, becoming a multi-billionaire by age 50, but you presently only have $100 in the bank, is theoretically possible but highly unlikely for even the most gifted investor.

Measurable

Your goal must be measurable. You must be able to determine if you are making any progress towards achieving your goal. If your goal is to purchase a $300,000 home by age 40 and you're presently 36 with $10,000 saved towards an expected $30,000 down payment, then your progress and the likelihood of your success can be determined.

When you have self-awareness, you know and understand your purpose as a man; to lead, to provide, to teach, to protect and to be a companion/helpmate to your wife or lady, coupled with a vision for yourself and your family. You are then in the unique position of having the tools – your powers (power of choice) and your belief system and your Blueprint for Manhood to think and act as the man God designed and created you to be.

Response-Ability

One of the key issues underlying the crisis within the African family and the African American community is the lack (there goes that word again) of responsibility on the part of African American men (males) in situations and under circumstances where they are needed. Because of our tendency to think one dimensionally, African American men almost instinctively place themselves in situations without the knowledge to perform the roles required of them. An example of this phenomenon is the disproportionate number of black female headed households and/or African American men who father children by multiple women. Lacking a sense of responsibility is how and why so many African American men find themselves *"stuck in maleness"* and struggling with otherwise avoidable and unnecessary interpersonal and legal issues.

In order for African American men to function properly and to adequately and effectively perform their role as men, and as head of their family, they must and should possess *ALL* of the key elements of lack thus far discussed: 1) Awareness; 2) Purpose; 3) Vision; and, 4) Responsibility.

Together, they are your navigation system, the tools and the blueprint to move you out of being *"stuck in maleness"*, into responsible manhood. You have already possessed within you, the powers and the tools; they are your God-given abilities. You have always had these abilities. The problem is that you have been brainwashed, deceived, and bamboozled by slavery, racism, the educational system, and in some cases your parents, to believe that you did not have the ability, but you now know this to be a lie. What you lacked is the response power of your mind to know and understand your purpose as a man.

Previously you have only been acting like a fool and taking on the role of a misguided jester seeking fun, games, and laughter. But with awareness of your purpose as a man through your Blueprint for Manhood, you can now respond with ability. Responding with ability means that you as a man and leader possess the awareness of your power of choice, the understanding of how your belief system works and a blueprint for manhood, to call forth and match up with your abilities as a man. You have vision, you can now "see" where you are going in life and you can now better navigate the choices and decision of full manhood.

Faltering in any of these elements will hinder you from handling your business as a man in a responsible manner. If you lose your knowledge of self, you're done; you forget or stop performing your purpose, you're done; you lose sight of where you're going in life and why, you're done.

Men, record these key areas of lack, and their subcomponents, deep within your mind and within your imagination. Begin to perform them immediately, not tomorrow, next week, but immediately. Utilize your power of choice and your belief system and your blueprint for manhood to begin transforming your own life. You must meditate upon these concepts and principles in the same way you used to meditate upon clothes, cars, women, drugs, alcohol, video games, and the myths and misconceptions about manhood that were formerly a part of your mental diet. *"As a man thinketh, so is he."*

My suggestion is to begin applying this mind and life-changing information without announcement, fanfare, or warning and without the expectation of recognition or reward. Do it because you want and need to become a better man. This is your purpose, your job, the position that was always required of you. Your reward is that God woke you up this morning and gave you a second chance at life. Yes, others will see the changes in you. They will begin to see the change in your attitude but you must resist the temptation to bask in accolades. Smile, be humble, and keep it moving because being a man is not about you.

Below are the final parts that you must practice in order to remain Response-Able, and to keep your navigation system (your purpose) and your position as a man in place. Becoming a man (it's a lifelong process) is not a day job, a part-time job, or something that you do when you "feel" like doing it; it's a 24 hour, 7 day a week, 365 day a year….drop it like it's hot….lifestyle and way of thinking, until you drop commitment towards excellence. Whew! That took a lot out of me.

Acceptance

In order for your new roles to work properly, you must accept the responsibility and embrace all of the elements as your own, no matter what. Not just when things are going well for you or when others are looking; you must proceed with honestly and integrity at every step of the way, even when it hurts or when you are less motivated. Some aspects of your new roles will seem thrust upon you in many ways, including legally. But it's best that you willingly accept the responsibility as your own because you are more

Sacrifice

Nothing, absolutely nothing that you do or work towards is going to come exactly in the way or at the time that you want it to. You will need to make choices and sacrifice some things over others. When you are clear about your purpose as a man and you become committed to achieving your vision, you learn to sacrifice some things over others because it's all leading towards the achievement of your goals and realizing your vision.

Discipline

In the same way that your belief system must become your Navigation System, along with your Blueprint for Manhood to guide you through the shark invested waters of life, it also must become a means of thought discipline to help you to remain focused and self-motivated. Stay the course no matter the distractions or problems that you might encounter. In the beginning, disciplining your mind to your new way of thinking and responding correctly to situations will be your biggest challenge until your self-awareness, your purpose, your vision and your sense of responding with ability becomes second nature. No matter what your age, occupation, or how smart you think you are, practice, brother practice, so you can get this thing right. Manhood is a condition of your mind and becoming the man God designed and created you to be is really not about you.

Chapter 8
Man, Take Out The Trash – It Stinks!

You are already clean because of the word which I have spoken to you (John 15:3)

Nothing can stink up a kitchen more than trash that has been in the trash can for too long. After a few hours of sitting in the trashcan, a bag of trash can bring you to your knees. Your mind is not much different than a bag of smelly trash. If you continue to fill it with trash or garbage and don't take it out, it will begin to stink up your life as well.

Trash

So, what is trash? Trash is something of little worth or value, garbage or food waste (that's where the smell comes from). Psychologically speaking, trash is unresolved negative emotions from the past that you continue to carry around in your mind. Unresolved emotions are emotional experiences such as anger, grief, resentment, guilt or traumatic experiences that you don't have closure on or may not have fully come to terms with the changes they have caused in your life. These issues may be from the past or distant past but they continue to remain fresh in your mind, often on a subconscious level, and stink up your present outlook and attitude towards life. No matter how much vision, purpose or how focused you become on achieving goals in life, you can continue to be stuck in some areas in some areas of your life if these issues continue to go unresolved.

So before you get started along your journey you must address the unresolved issues, problems, or people that take up unnecessary space in your mind. These issues can overburden your mind and hinder your ability to effectively and maturely function in a healthy manner.

When triggered, our emotions toward negative and stress-inducing feelings can come back to us at any time as if the event or experience occurred recently. When they do, the emotional trash can cloud judgment and interfere with decision making. Trash can also affect your ability to socialize or relate to people in your everyday life, such as your wife, lady, or children. It can also influence how you cope with stressful situations at home or on the job. These emotional experiences usually begin to occur when we are very young and gradually build up over a period of time. During our daily experiences our minds can become filled with all sorts of negative or agitating occurrences that we don't quite fully resolve. An argument with our lady, an overdue bill, a run in with a supervisor at work, the death of a loved one can all begin to pile up within the confines of our mind and begin to eat away at our sense of internal control and peace of mind. Other examples are traumatic experiences from childhood, grief over a failed relationship or PTSD (post-traumatic stress disorder) from having served in the military during war time. In these situations it may be necessary to seek professional help through therapy. Involvement in therapy or a support group can help you to work through some of these hidden emotions. Awareness of these unresolved thoughts itself, can become the beginning point to releasing their grip on your mind and the influence they have over your life. Some of the emotions that become trash are grief, resentment, anger, guilt and fear.

Grief

Grief is emotional pain and distress caused by bereavement or the lost of someone or something. We can experience grief over the death of a family member, relative, friend or even the loss of a relationship with a friend or losing a job that played a big part in how we see our self as a man. Grief is a natural emotional reaction to sudden or traumatic changes in our life due to loss but how you cope with these sudden and traumatic changes in life can become challenging.

Several years ago I went through some very trying personal times when I lost my eldest sister to liver disease. At the time of my sister's death I had already going through some tough times in my personal life. I was incarcerated and unable to visit her while she was in the hospital or to attend her funeral when she passed away. The circumstances I was dealing with while incarcerated were challenging enough so I tried to intellectualize my sister's her death and block it out of my mind but I never really had any closure. Later when circumstances changed I tried to revisit my sister's death logically but not emotionally.

Before I was able to catch my breath from my sister's death, less than a year later, a little over a month after 9/11, I lost my father due to complications from emphysema. My father had been a smoker for over 50 years. He stopped smoking about a year before his death in an attempt to improve his health but the damage to his lungs had already been done. I was close to both my sister and my father. In different ways they were like best friends. Losing two best friends was like receiving two blows to the head while suffocating from a loss of air.

Because I couldn't see clearly during that time and I didn't get any help for my grief, I lost my way. I felt lonely and empty without my two best friends, so I chose to keep my feelings bottled up to myself the best I could. That didn't last too long so I found a new friend, Scotch Whiskey. After a while Scotch didn't quite do the job so I turned to substance abuse. Drugs didn't do it either and I ended up with more problems than I started with. Neither drugs nor alcohol brought my deceased family members back. When the drinking and drugs wore off the loneliness and the emptiness was still there.

The denial of my grief and later, substance abuse, went on for several years until I was forced to address them. I have since come to terms with the death of my beloved relatives and I've found healthier and more productive ways to cope with their deaths and to remember them. Through tough love, counseling and support groups, I was able to come to terms with my grief and its impact on substance abuse. Today I honor my sister and father's life in a healthy way and I am no longer imprisoned by their deaths or the substance abuse I unsuccessfully tried to free me.

When the moment arises in our life when we must let go of someone or something, we automatically try to hold on. We emotionally clamp down and try to hold on, thinking that we can hold people or things frozen in time, possibly until we can let go on our own terms, but it doesn't work that way. Life continues to go on whether we accept the changes in our circumstances or not.

Attempting to hold on to or prevent change or loss from occurring, can actually cause us to become stuck. That is partly when the trash can begin to accumulate in us emotionally. Not only do we clog up and stink up our minds, but we also hinder the enjoyment of new experiences and new people from entering our life. Said another way, you cannot fully enjoy the people who continue to be in your life in a happy and joyous way when you're carrying around "corpses" from the past.

The same applies to romantic relationships. Today I understand why we are encouraged to wait before starting a new relationship after the old one has gone sour. There is a sense of loss, or grief, that we have to allow to heal. We have to close the one emotional door before we open another. It's not fair to you or to your potential new love. You could be cheating the both of you out of a potentially rewarding new relationship.

Guilt

Guilt or a feeling of responsibility for wrong doing permeates the lives of many people. Feelings of guilt could be for things you've done to someone or actions you should have taken, but didn't. In any event, the feeling can hang around to haunt you or become a tool of manipulation that ill-intended people use against you for their own purposes. Either way, when unresolved, guilt can clutter up your mind and smell up your life like rotting trash.

A friend of mine, let's call him Al, has been in and out of jail in recent years for a series of minor offenses that caused him to be incarcerated for several months at a time. This took place for about 5 years. To outsiders, Al had a lot going for himself and people could not understand why Al kept finding himself in jail for what seemed to be avoidable situations. "Al, you're too smart for that. How do you keep getting yourself into these stupid situations?" was the usual comment when it was learned that Al had recently called collect again from the county jail. As it turned out, Al had been carrying around a great deal of guilt, or trash, from a sundry of traumatic experiences, dating back from his childhood to as recent as a few years ago, but not many people knew about Al's past.

As a very private kind of guy, Al did not talk much about his past and his pride kept him from talking much about his feelings. The few times Al had let his guard down and opened up about his past, his trust was betrayed so he clammed back up again.

On one occasion when Al let his guard down and opened up about things that were on his mind to his girlfriend, she too betrayed his trust and brought the issues up at times when she became angry at him. Eventually Al's girlfriend began to get the wrong idea about his hesitancy to talk, so she began to accuse him of hiding things from her. She even went so far as to accuse Al of cheating on her. Al was in a serious dilemma and he knew it. On the one hand he desperately needed to get rid of the guilt he was harboring, because not doing so was weighing down his mind and clouding his judgment. Secretly Al used drugs to cope with his feelings. On the other hand, Al needed to be in a safe and supportive atmosphere in which he felt trusting enough to empty his mind without fear of criticism or judgment. His girlfriend was not helping the situation any because she continued to wrongly suspect Al of cheating on her, which caused him to clam up even more. Al felt he was "up against the ropes", always having to unnecessarily defend or justify his actions to his girlfriend.

It was during this period in Al's life when he experienced the repeated incarcerations, usually for minor offenses. Al's indecision to empty the trash of guilt from his mind was costing him both his freedom and the opportunity to participate in a healthy relationship with another person. Al's girlfriend, although on the insensitive side, was not the source of his problems, he was. The turning point in Al's life came when it was suggested to him that before he sought forgiveness from others for whatever he felt guilty or burdened about that he had to first forgive himself. Maybe talk to God, get it all out, forgive himself and never look back.

When Al sincerely made the decision to forgive himself and resolved to let go of his troubles from his past, his thinking changed and so did his life. Al instead found a neutral, more trusting professional to discuss his personal challenges. As Al began to open up about the guilt he felt and why, he began to see remarkable changes in his energy level, his thinking and his attitude towards himself and others. Al's girlfriend was not so quick to be forgiving. After all, his repeated incarcerations cost him several jobs which left his girlfriend to fend for their young child on her own.

But Al reasoned that it was her right to be upset about him not being there but this time he chose not to react emotionally as he had done in the past which would have caused him to experience more guilt. As Al continued to change his way of thinking, so did his life and the people in it. Eventually even Al's girlfriend began to back off and became supportive of his new attitude towards taking responsibility and control of his life. Freeing himself of the trash of guilt freed Al to think and live more productively.

Resentment

Unlike guilt, which are feelings and emotions that rise from things you've done or did not do, resentment centers more upon feelings and emotions that arise from the actions of other people. Becoming resentful towards someone can be linked to something as simple as being looked over for a promotion at your job you felt should have been given. Instead of accepting the outcome, secretly (or openly) you develop resentment towards the co-worker who received the promotion (your promotion) or towards the supervisor who granted it.

Every time you encounter either person (depending upon who you are resentful towards) in some, usually a small way, you make a gesture to let them know how you feel. A friend of mine, Rich Kurdek, told me that *"harboring anger or resentment towards another person is really counterproductive and doesn't make any sense."* The reason is because the other person usually doesn't even know you're angry or have such resentment towards them. They have moved past the situation but we, on the other hand, continue to hold the poisonous feelings towards them. We continue to carry these feelings around like a corpse which eats away at us on the inside and stinks up our attitude, our relationships, and creates an unnecessary loss of energy. It just makes better sense to let the issues go. Forgive the other person, or forgive yourself and move on. Usually the issue that caused the resentment in the first place is small and not worth the pain, drain on emotions and the effort to maintain the resentment anyway.

Fear

Some aspects of fear [8]are necessary and healthy because it keeps us safe and out of harm's way. For example, fear of crossing railroad tracks after you've heard the horn of an approaching train, would be fear caused by an awareness of danger. The kind of fear that I believe is unhealthy and affects the lives of so many African American men is the perception or expectation of an unpleasant or unknown outcome.

---

[8]An unpleasant, often strong emotion caused by experience or awareness of danger (37).

The effect is often a life of self-sabotage played by many started but unfinished projects or a series of missed opportunities. This type of fear reveals its ugly face amongst African American males in two basic forms; 1) Fear of Failure and, 2) Fear of Success.

Fear of Failure

A fear of failure is a condition of the mind in which a mental stronghold has gripped you and convinced you that you do not have what it takes to accomplish something, so you just don't try. You do not want to fail so you avoid taking on the responsibility or placing yourself in situations where you might fail and incur the negative judgment or opinions from others regarding your failure.

Perhaps your older brother was a star athlete in basketball who won many awards and created a high standard in sports in your family. You enjoy playing sports, for example, basketball, but you find that you are constantly reminded of your brother's accomplishments. Fearing that you cannot measure up to your brother or simply not wanting to deal with the pressure, you stop trying because the prospect of failure is too much to bear.

Fear of Success

Unlike a fear of failure, a fear of success is when you have confidence in your abilities, skills or ideas but not your ability to be successful at applying them (or continue to be successful at it) beyond your immediate circumstances. For example, you enjoy cooking, especially baking cakes. Your family, friends and neighbors love your cakes and regularly compliment you and encourage you to take your baking to others by starting your own business. You may have even baked cakes for the mayor of your city who also complimented your cakes beyond your highest expectation. But you continue to make excuses about not having time, your oven is not large enough, others may not like your cakes, and so on. You keep creating or searching for excuses not to do it; your fear causes you to miss opportunities.

In both kinds of fear the underlying issue may be an inferiority complex which is a form of extreme self-doubt or low self-worth. The feelings of self-doubt have created a stronghold or mental barrier of fear in your mind that overrides confidence in your ability to do something. A fear of success or failure may have their origin in some sort of traumatic experiences that occurred in childhood. In either case the traumatic experiences create within the person, patterns of negative thinking that causes them to engage in usually self-sabotaging behaviors.

The mental energy expended to avoid the emotions of fear and the sometimes negative experiences is how the trash is created, in addition to the fact of having to struggle through life more than necessary. Mentally, African American men, in an effort to avoid the feelings and experience of fear may lower their own standards and expectations of themselves, to lessen the experience of fear. You may recall my earlier comments on self-worth and the subconscious tendencies of our behavior and how we "attract" to us people or experiences to confirm our self-valuation of worth.

I have known many African American men, and I have heard of others, who possess artistic, creative, and athletic skills or intelligence end up on a heap of garbage, not because God did not bless them with some gifts and talents or because there did not exist, opportunities to showcase one's talent or gifts. Rather it was because of thinking and acting from a perspective of fear. There are also aspects of institutionalized racism and discrimination that creates fear, for example, in employment.

A lot of brothers forgo the pursuit of their dreams and the use of their gifts and talents just because they assume or fear, that they will be rejected because of their skin color. Instead they take jobs that have lower qualifications, lower pay, and lower career prospects, or they follow their friends into criminal behavior, such as selling drugs or what may currently be popular as we've discussed in *Myths and Misconceptions about Manhood*. The best remedy for fear is to become involved in religious or spiritual worship where you can tap into the strength and power of God. I learned that fear is nothing but *FALSE EVIDENCE APPEARING REAL*. Get the facts, change your mindset and move beyond a life of fear.

Anger

Our last source of trash producing emotion is anger[9]. I have already briefly touched upon anger in another section, but anger tells us something is wrong. Oftentimes guilt, resentment, fear, grief, sadness and other emotions, will be masked behind expressions of

---

[9] "a strong feeling of displeasure."(39).

anger. In a general sense, there is nothing wrong with anger or expressing displeasure about something we don't like.

Anger can, and often is an underlying factor that motivates people to make changes within themselves or to make changes within the larger social, political or economic arena. These are healthy and productive expressions of anger, but the reality of the experience with anger for many of our brothers is often very different. As African American men we sometimes use anger self destructively by lashing out at others who we believe (belief system) are the causes or the sources of what ills us. Quite often, African American males in an effort to appear tough have a tendency to suppress our true feelings beyond what is necessary in order to save face.

As mentioned in Myths and Misconceptions About Manhood, appearing tough by not crying or showing true emotions makes you look stronger and more masculine but it eats you up on the inside. Both African American males and females tell their male children not to cry because it makes them look like a sissy (girl).

We grow up with these images in our mind and do whatever it takes to live up to them, even if it means replacing our true feelings with anger. Many of us brothers would rather stew on the inside, and let our true emotions eat us up, than to let it be known that we are simply hurting, afraid, sad, lonely, or that we miss someone who may no longer be part of our life. This is what employers, the public or others see when they see us; an angry black man. They have no idea that we may be hurting or just miss our lady and they really don't care.

Anger left unsolved or improperly vented is the worse form of trash that is a part of a lot of African American men's' daily existence, although it does not have to be that way. Men let out! Run! Scream! Yell! It's ok to say that you are hurting inside. Holding in unresolved feelings and emotions for extended periods of time is not healthy for anyone. When you carry around a lot of unresolved issues you can become a walking time bomb waiting to explode.

Everything and everyone annoys you and it is usually the simplest issues that can set you off and cause another outburst. "Didn't I tell you to leave me alone? You're not going to be satisfied until I put my foot up your _ss! Stop asking me so many f__ king questions!" When these angry outbursts begin to affect your health, your family or your relationship with others, it's time to get help and take out the emotional trash before it kills you, others or lands you in a hospital, or worse, a jail cell. Drinking or using drugs will not make the anger or the problems go away, either.

If anything, the problem gets progressively worse. In most cases the issues that we unnecessarily carry around can be released from our minds with a little help and by making the choice to do so. Besides, no one wants to be around a hot head which is liable to blow up at any given moment.

"Anger is a depression of the spirit. So much energy is expressed in anger that it is even more depressing because it permits a constant leakage of energy (40)." Unreleased and unresolved anger are often the culprits behind domestic violence issues with African

American men and unreleased and unresolved issues certainly in a key factor when it comes to substance abuse. A lot of us simply just don't understand some the seemingly "psycho-babble" that comes out of the mouths of our wives, girlfriends, fiancés or "baby mommas". Sometimes it just sounds like that they are putting us down or insulting us on the sneak tip, so we react by getting angry.

Anger deceptively makes some of us feel like we are in control of the situation and it certainly can scare the sh_t out of the woman who is on the receiving end, but it does not go very far in solving the issues at hand. Expressing anger in this way can also be very damaging to our relationships with women and it makes it easier for us to get angry the next time that we don't feel understood or if we think that we are being belittled. I know what I'm talking about on this one. I can roar like the biggest and baddest lion in the jungle but I did not like the end result of seeing my lady's eyes open wide with confusion, fear or even terror every time I over-reacted to a perceived putdown or when I couldn't calm myself enough to say what I was really feeling inside.

Unlike the faucet in our kitchen sink or bathroom, which can be controlled and shut off with a valve, our emotions don't quite respond so easily to a little tightening from a valve. When things get out of control during these kinds of occurrences it is not uncommon for the police to get involved or from someone, usually us, to get hauled off to jail. In extreme circumstances someone, usually not us, gets hurt. On top of that there is quite often irreparable emotional damage as well. If this is you, you must do whatever possible to get help fast and learn new and healthier ways of expressing and coping with, anger.

Some things may require professional help like from a counselor or a therapist. Many employers have EAP (Employee Assistance Programs) as part of their health insurance coverage. If you feel that the emotional trash you may be carrying around may be eating at you, do something about it. You may also benefit from support groups such as NA, AA, Al-Anon or a more specialized group particular to your situation when there is substance abuse involved.

Marshall Rosenberg in *The Surprising Purpose of Anger*, suggests that *"anger is the tip of the iceberg of deeper unmet needs that lie beneath the surface (41)"*. In his book, he proposes four steps to effectively handle anger in a non-violent way. The first step, says Rosenberg, is to become conscious that the stimulus, or trigger, of our anger is not the cause of our anger. That is to say that it isn't simply what people do that makes us angry, but it's something within us that responds to what they do that is really the cause of the anger.

The second step involves our being conscious that the stimulus is never the cause of our anger. That is, it isn't simply what people do that makes us angry. It is our evaluation of what has been done that is the cause of our anger. Rosenberg says that the third step involves looking for the need that is the root of our anger....Instead of being directly connected to our need, we go up to our head and start thinking of what's wrong with other people for not meeting our needs. The judgments we make of other people —

which is the cause of our anger — are really alienated expressions of unmet needs.

The fourth step involves what we would actually say out loud to the other person after we have transformed our anger into feelings by getting in touch with the need behind the judgment. The fourth step includes saying to the other person four pieces of information. First we reveal to them the stimulus; what they have done that is in conflict with our needs being fulfilled. Secondly, we express how we are feeling. Notice we are not repressing the anger. The anger has been transformed into a feeling such as, sad, hurt, scared, frustrated, or the like. And then says Rosenberg, we follow our expression of our feeling with the needs of ours that are not being fulfilled.

And now add to those three pieces of information a clear, present request of what we want from the other person in relationship to our feelings and unmet needs. It is this very four step approach that I learned and use to cope with feelings of guilt and resentment that held me in captivity for many years. I now pass these steps on to you in hope that you too, might be liberated from the grips of unhealthy, emotional trash.

Chapter 9
Manage the Karma in Your Life

Let him who thinks he stands take heed lest he fall. (1 Corinthians 10:12)

The next area that must be addressed on your way to becoming a man of vision, purpose and character is to remove and/or transform the many aspects of negativity that are likely to be present in your life as a result of being *"stuck in maleness"*. In its simplest form, Karma is the total effect of our words and actions over a period of time (42). Karma can be negative or it can be positive.

Karma never really goes away, even when you die. But it can be transformed, just like our belief system can be transformed, through changes in our thinking and the way we live. My mother, an intelligent woman, said it to me this way as a little boy; "Russell, you need to stop doing what you're doing. Watch what you do in life because what goes around comes around". At the time, I was young and immature, and didn't know any better. For years I failed to take heed to my mother's wisdom so I ended up learning about Karma the hard way.

You may be experiencing the effects of negative Karma in your life right now. But you do not have to continue dealing with the bad relations and unstable emotions that is caused when it goes unresolved. I decided to include this Chapter on Karma because it is an important aspect to your journey of overcoming being *"stuck in maleness"*. You cannot become the man God created you to be and have, or continue to create, negative Karma in your life or the lives of others. As a matter of fact, men who become *"stuck in maleness"* more often than not are people who have a great deal of negative Karma going on in their life.

Negative Karma is also a form of "trash", because it can take the form of unresolved issues that stink up our minds and create anxiety, worry, stress or barriers in our lives. Low self-worth, thinking errors, and a pattern of successive negative decisions is part of the reason why you to become *"stuck in maleness"* in the first place.

Unpaid traffic tickets, open court cases, unpaid loans to friends, items borrowed but not returned, child support arrears, problems with your "baby's momma" or a bad reputation can cause others to turn away from you because they can actually "see" all of the negative things attached to your life. Your access to needed services and even employment can be blocked or rescinded due to the negative Karma you've created.

Employers and rental agents do it every day when they use credit reports and criminal background checks to make judgments about your credit worthiness for employment or your suitability for certain housing. I have resolved many of the barriers that were created by my own *"stuck in maleness"* challenges, but I continue to encounter people who doubt my sincerity, question my credibility or who simply refuse to change their perception of me despite evidence to the contrary. They'd rather stay stuck in their old perception of me than to resign themselves to the reality that I've finally "got myself together."

I've known entire families that were plagued by negative Karma created by merely one or two of its members. Fair or not, when one family member commits a crime, or does something foolish, the whole family may be viewed as co-defendants. In the minds of other people, "they had to know what he was doing." A scandal for you easily becomes a scandal for your entire family. Quite often opinions are formed and judgments are made about us before we move into a house, enter a courtroom, sit at a desk, or even occupy a jail cell, because of the Karma created by our actions.

When you fail to address the issues created by negative Karma, they do not go away. Karma has a tendency to come back around bigger and more harmful than when it was originally created. Unpaid traffic tickets become warrants for your arrest, unpaid loans become garnishments against your paycheck, unpaid child support become nights in jail and nights in jail can cause you to lose your job. It's quite that simple.

Men coming out of prison or people who are recovering from an adverse situation, such as substance abuse, for example, must be extra mindful of the negative aspects of Karma associated with their environment. For ex-cons or substance abusers, "people, places and things" can become triggers that cause you to relapse into former behaviors, especially if you have not used your time in prison or treatment to reflect on the causes of your behavior and there has not been a positive change in your valuation of your self-worth. Neglecting this very important area of your life will only cause you to continue to self-sabotage your life by engaging in and attracting, negative experiences.

Four of the top influences that cause ex-offenders and substance abusers to relapse are, 1) Anti-social values (thinking); 2) Anti-social peers; 3) Dysfunctional families; and 4) A history of past substance abuse and/or criminal behavior. These are all forms of negative Karma that must be overcome. Now here is the good news and the reason I elected to include the topic of Karma as a part of the process of moving out of maleness into manhood. Remember, Karma can be transformed just like our belief system through successive changes in our thinking and actions. Ok, Russell, what's the catch? The answer is simple, manage it! No longer avoid or run from the negative Karma you've created. Transform its negative energy by managing the issues in the same way you would manage a business.

If you've never operated a business, that's okay but you are already in business for yourself. You are in the "public relations business." Your attitude and how you deal with people and the issues of your everyday life says a lot about you. How you address issues and resolve problems sends out communication (Karma) to others that reflects the kind of person you are (your self-worth). As a public relations business, make a list of the problems or issues (your accounts) such as traffic tickets, unpaid fines, personal loans, unresolved conflict with people, pending court cases, or other issues that may be impacting your life in a negative way. (See Figures 9-1 and 9-2).

Separate them into relevant categories such as legal, financial, personal, social, or employment. List each individual problem or account that falls under that particular heading. These are your individual clients. Rank order your accounts (problems or issues) in order of priority. For example, place your focus on first taking care of issues that can cause you the most harm, such as legal or employment.

The courts have the ability to incarcerate you and/or impose fines. Your physical freedom is always most important. I've learned that the hard way. If you get locked up you can't pay anyone and you could lose your job if you're locked up for an extended period of time. It only takes a week or so to lose a job once you've exhausted sick, personal, and vacation time. If your legal problems are serious you should consider obtaining a lawyer to advocate on your behalf. In the long run it's worth it. Rank order your individual problems or issues (your clients) in the same way. The problem or issues that are more delinquent or pressing should be addressed first.

If you've had problems with tardiness or absenteeism, it's simple; get up and take your butt to work. From your job you can pay your bills, negotiate lower payments, and meet other financial obligations. In some cases having a job can keep you out of jail because maintaining steady employment is always looked upon favorably. This is but one of the many reasons why we as African

American men must make it a priority to always have a job, even if it's mopping floors, flipping burgers, washing dishes, shoveling snow, or mowing lawns. Employment is positive Karma across the board. If you don't have a job, get one.

Figure 9-1 - Outline for Managing & Transforming Negative Karma

Step 1. Make a list of major areas of negative Karma in your life. For example:

- Social – Constant conflict over money with "baby's momma".
- Legal – Unpaid traffic tickets.
- Employment – Late for work three times this week.
- Financial – Cell phone bill is due. If not paid today, they will cut my phone off.

Step 2. Rank order the list of negative Karma in order of what can harm you the most to what is least likely to harm you. For example:

1. **Legal** - Unpaid traffic tickets are the most important because they could cause major legal problems. Failure to pay them could turn into a warrant for my arrest potentially causing me to lose my job and my apartment.
2. **Employment** -- If I continue to be late for work, I could lose my job, which could mean loss of my apartment, my baby's momma should I become unable to pay child support.

3. **Relationship** -- Although not as immediately harmful as getting arrested or losing your job, but conflict with your child's mother can be emotionally draining and distracting, especially if there is a tug of war over children and/or the potential threat of incarceration for unpaid child support.

4. **Financial** – Paying your cell phone bill is the least of your concerns. Although your service may be disrupted and you may incur late fees, service is usually restored as soon as the bill is paid. Temporarily you could use a pay phone, house phone, friends phone or access email to communicate via computer.

Figure 9-2 - Inventory Sheet for Managing Negative Karma

1. Legal	2. Employment
a.	a.
b.	b.
c.	c.
d.	d.

3. Financial	4. Relationships
a.	a.
b.	b.
c.	c.
d.	d.

5. Family	6. Children
a.	a.
b.	b.
c.	c.
d.	d.

7. Other	8. Other
a.	a.
b.	b.
c.	c.
d.	d.

Despite a mostly professional employment background, I had to work on transforming the negative karma in my life as well. At one point I had to work at a supermarket retrieving shopping carts to earn extra money and at another time I worked in a factory assembling heating and air-conditioning units.

Both of those jobs were necessary at that time in my life in order for me to meet my daily expenses and as a stepping stone for me to advance to the next level in life. Life can be a series of beginnings and endings, you may find the need to crawl and work at various junctures in your life. Bill collectors, my landlord, my ex and cashiers at the supermarket were all too happy to accept the fruits of my employment, wherever it was at the time. They didn't care, they just wanted their money.

With relationship or social issues your focus is not any different. Your attitude and your words become the form of payment. Make a sincere effort to repair the relationship by apologizing and being honest about what caused things to go sour. Explain your circumstances and give a little insight to what you may have been going through. Ask for forgiveness, or at least understanding, and explain that you'd like to clear the air and move the relationship in a different, more positive direction. If the person does not accept your apology or effort to mend things be okay with it and keep it moving.

Do not become agitated and send out more negative Karma. People have a right to be angry or less than forgiving when you've wronged them. Explain that you are sorry the issues could not be worked out and move on. Everything cannot be repaired, no matter how you feel. If your apology is accepted, thank the person for understanding and make your best effort t not to reoffend them or make the same mistake again.

When you face up to the issues or problems that caused your negative Karma, you do three important things: 1) You stop the negative issues from building up and becoming bigger problems; 2) You neutralize them so that they can no longer harm you (in most cases), and; 3) You gain a valuable opportunity to transform negative Karma into positive Karma. You will be creating new actions and new experiences that will become the basis for how that person or entity, will view you in the next transaction.

As long as you continue in a positive direction, your credibility (Karma) will continue to go in a positive direction. Everyone makes mistakes but you have to "man up" and show that you have learned from your mistakes. Manhood is about being Response-Able when and where you are required to do so.

When we have fallouts or disagreements with our spouse, partner, or our children's mother ("baby momma drama"), we must take a similar approach as we do with other issues, such as legal problems. Unpaid child support can land you in jail, whether or not you like her, or whatever your opinion may be about what she does with the child support money. The bigger issue is your child, anyway. The Karma between you and your child's mother is transferred to your children. Negative opinions and experiences quite often affect our children, and you and I both know that we sometimes use these comments to manipulate one another. One of you wants to see the child while the other withholds access to the child. Either way, your child(ren) lose out. If your relationship with your spouse/partner or "baby momma" is so bad that you cannot directly communicate with each other, then do it through a neutral party such as a relative or a mutual friend. If that becomes impossible, then it may be necessary to establish visitation and other related rights with your child(ren) through the courts. But at all cost, avoid doing nothing. You do not want to create the kind of Karma that, several years into the future, will become the basis for another male becoming *"stuck in maleness"*, because his father was not there to show them the way. You also do not want your daughter to grow up without her father and seek love and attention in the arms of another messed up male. Every child, no matter their gender or the relationship between parents, deserves the best of both of them.

Managing Karma is really about managing your life and taking responsibility for the things that you do or have done. It also means that you must manage the relationships that you have with other people. When you make mistakes, correct them. When you exercise poor judgment, acknowledge it and make good on things by doing the right thing, no matter how you feel. Feelings are a form of emotions, and emotions can be deceptive. Manhood is about doing the right thing regardless of how you feel. Whatever you do, remember that what goes around comes around, and it comes right back to you.

Chapter 10
Attitude Is Everything

"A merry heart does good, like medicine" (Proverbs 17:22)

Now that you are aware of your power of choice, your tools, and you have been given your blueprint to becoming the man God created you to be, and you are getting rid of trash and negative Karma in your life, you must learn the meaning and importance of how your attitude reflects upon you as a man. The best made plans can only lead to failure if your attitude towards life, sucks! Attitude[10] has made the difference in everything from winning wars, basketball games, selling vacuum cleaners to leading multibillion dollar corporations. Even winning over the heart of the woman of your dreams could slip through your fingers, if she's not feeling your attitude.

Every day, we are bombarded with phrases such as, "He has a nice attitude"; "Why do you have an attitude?" "Change your attitude, Russell" (my mother) or we hear that our "attitude influences our altitude". But why is this often used buzzword so important to becoming the man God created you to be? It's simple,

---

[10] "A mental (mind) position or feeling with regard to a fact or state" (43)

bad thoughts lead to bad attitude and bad behavior. It's Monday morning and you've put on your best suit, shoes and you show up for a job interview 15 minutes early. You've put together a winning resume; your qualifications are impeccable on paper. You seem like the obvious candidate for the job, but you go into the interview with a cocky attitude and become defensive when the interviewer questions your shorter employment at a previous job. By the time you catch yourself, the interviewer stands up and terminates the interview. Unfortunately, your winning resume didn't match up with your poor attitude. Employers want more than a paper qualified applicant; they want someone who can handle pressure and is likeable by both co-workers and customers, someone with a good attitude.

Actor Will Smith, in his starring role as a struggling salesman of home bone density equipment in *The Pursuit of Happiness*, demonstrated a persistent and winning attitude. Hoping to obtain an intern position with Wall Street brokerage house, Dean Witter, Smith did everything he could to capture the attention of someone on the inside of the company who could get him in front of the key decision makers.

Despite enumerable personal problems and the responsibility of raising a son as a single father, Smith overcame his challenges; he never gave up. Barely making it out of jail after suddenly being locked up for unpaid tickets on the morning of his interview, Smith's character made it to the interview wearing the paint-stained clothing and work shoes he had been wearing the night he was arrested.

Stuck In Maleness — Russell A. Ligon, Jr.

The interviewers were stunned at his appearance at the interview and the obvious thought would have been to assume the worst. But it was his enthusiastic and humorous attitude, coupled with obvious intelligence that landed him the internship with the Wall Street giant. Based upon a true story, the real life intern (a black man) eventually made Dean Witter, and later himself, millions of dollars. Despite the odds against him it was his internal motivation, attitude (mental position), and will power that allowed him to see beyond the many obstacles that continued to come his way. He had a vision (mental picture/position) and he refused to let anything deter him from achieving it. You might say that his attitude was more important than the facts of his individual circumstances. As a man, this is how we must approach the circumstances of our lives.

I'm sure if you think about it, you will be able to recall moments in your own life in which your attitude was the deciding factor in your getting something that you really wanted. It does not have to be under such extreme circumstances, but it was a big deal to you at the time. I remember as a kid wanting a pair of Chuck Taylor's, which were made by Converse Sneakers. To my 8 year-old mind there was something magical about the square blue label on the back of the Converse high tops with the big blue star on the inside of the sneaker over the ankle. Back then Chuck Taylor's came in just about every color. I did everything I could to get my mother or step father to buy me a pair for Christmas or my birthday. Instead, I got a green and white pair of P.F. Flyers. In those days (let's just say before Jordan's came out), we considered anything that wasn't

Converses as "Jeepers". Jeepers was a name we gave to any sneaker that was an off brand or fake. I cried and begged but it didn't matter, my mother wasn't changing her mind. I made myself (and my older sisters) miserable for about a week, moping and pouting around the house.

After a while I got over my disappointment and realized that I could stop on a dime just as I thought I would with Converses. The only thing that changed was my attitude. The real difference in performance was between my ears, my attitude and how I chose to view my circumstances. So what does attitude have to do with becoming a better man? I'm glad you asked; *EVERYTHING!*

If you will recall our discussion on the tremendous power our belief system (thought system) has over how we can become stuck in maleness. Of all the components of our belief system our attitude has the most visible effect over how we are perceived as men, and as a person. "But I don't care what another man thinks about me, people either like me or they don't", you might be thinking to yourself. The truth of the matter is that you should care because it does make a difference how we are perceived by other people. No man is an island unto himself. Part of what makes us human is our interaction, our communication with other people. If your purpose is to remain stuck in maleness and continue to act like a boy trapped in a man's body, then don't change; it may not be a big deal how other people view you.

When I was in prison I had the opportunity to observe first hand, hundreds of men with negative attitudes, all in one place, on a daily basis. What stood out more than anything was that most of the men would tell you that they did not care what other people thought about them. Because they did not care what others thought about them, they made no effort to change how they thought about themselves. Daily, I listened to complaints about the physical aspects of being incarcerated, and wanting to get out, and so did I, but many of these men did not make any efforts to free themselves psychologically from the prison they had constructed in their own minds.

God has provided each of us with the power to transcend our environment (mentally and physically), no matter how grim the circumstances or how lowly we become. God gave us the power to think, to love, to will, to laugh, to imagine, to create, to plan, to speak and to pray, to name only a few of the powers of choice that we have at our fingertips. With the attitude that we take on towards life, through our power of choice we can choose failure and despair or success and happiness. The choice is always yours. The choice is exclusively yours. **Stuck In Maleness** is about becoming the man God created you and me to be, by choice. That means changing the negative attitude you may have towards yourself and others. As a man you must wear many hats and you are required to perform just as many roles in the lives of other people.

Husband, father, parent, boyfriend, son, co-worker or brother, are but a few of the shoes you may wear throughout your lifetime. In essence, your life is not about you or how *YOU* feel. It's about leading and directing the people God has placed in your care.

The attitude you take does and will impact others. Many of those people are individuals who love and depend upon you to have correct thoughts and the right attitude as a man. Let's look at some additional areas where our attitudes make a difference for us as men.

Motivation

If you want something out of life you have to do it for yourself, because no one else will. Growing up as children, our parents were responsible for feeding and clothing us and providing for our needs and wants, regardless of our attitude or whatever kind of mood we were in. Sometimes quickly, sometimes slowly, they put food on the table, changed our diapers, bought us clothes and they kept a roof over our heads, no matter how they felt. As men you must provide these things for yourself and your family.

You will be able to provide for yourself and obtain other things you want out of life to the extent your attitude (and your will power) motivates you to do so. Should you constantly allow the challenges of your life or difficult times to overwhelm you, it will become more difficult to find the energy and mental toughness needed to meet the demands of your life. The people in our life either react or respond to the kind of attitude we carry around. When we present a positive and motivating attitude to the world, one of optimism and expectancy of success, we have the potential to transfer that energy to others. When others pick up on our positive energy they are more likely to help us to achieve our goals than they are to hinder us.

Conversely, when your attitude is negative or when you present an attitude of entitlement, that is, when you want things but show an unwillingness to participate in your own success, people will generally react negatively towards you which will likely further depress your attitude. Also, as a husband or parent, for example, you have the responsibility of setting a positive and productive example for the people in your care. When you demonstrate an enthusiastic attitude about yourself, in whatever you're asking others to do, they will see you as more credible and will most likely follow your lead. This is particularly true for your family members who experience your leadership every day. A positive and cheerful disposition will likely translate into your spouse and children feeling safe, loved, motivated, and happy to be a part of your family. So remember, your attitude affects others. It's not all about you. Your family especially, deserves your best motivating attitude.

Along your journey transitioning out of being *"stuck in maleness"* and becoming the man God created you to be, you're going to make mistakes. You will always encounter criticism from different people. To receive criticism is a given, it is virtually impossible to please everyone and you shouldn't try to please everyone anyway, but how to take that criticism and what you do with the information received, can make a world of difference. Whether or not you view the criticism constructively, or become defensive because you didn't like the way someone spoke to you, can help or hinder your maturity and growth as man or an employee of a company. No one likes a person who thinks they know it all, or who can't handle criticism; not employers, wives, girlfriends or friends. How you respond to criticism may be the difference between getting fired and getting another chance, changing your life, or continuing to falter in maleness.

Handling Stress and Obstacles

A friend of mine, an old timer who always spoke words of wisdom whenever we crossed each other's path said, "Another day above ground is another day to make it right." What he meant was that we should always be grateful for each day. We should not become caught up in the obstacles or stressful situations of life as if everything has to be solved all at once. Today is a new day. Try to maintain a level attitude, stay focused on the big picture, keep your eyes on the prize, your children for example, and not what it's costing you. Norman Vincent Peale, founder of Guidepost, said it this way, "Take a hopeful and optimistic attitude, think happy thoughts, say happy things and put joy into people's lives. The more you do this, the more you are sure to keep your own spirit high." (44).

Appearing Angry

In recent years African American men have acquired a reputation in the media of appearing angry and unapproachable. The perception of appearing angry has been conveyed by news coverage of mug shots of African American men with angry expressions on their faces; cop shows with police in pursuit of alleged drug selling and gun-toting African American males who resist arrest and; rap videos featuring foul mouthed rappers chanting anti-authority lyrics who throw up gang signs while booty-shaking, skimpily dressed women dance to the beat of the music. This perception has also been fueled by some African American men who struggle with feelings of disempowerment, disenfranchisement, fear, and frustration while attempting to express their manhood in a society that often looks down upon them.

While these stereotyped images are certainly not representative of all or even most African American men, I believe brothers must learn to be more cognizant of how they project themselves in public. I recommend that African American men monitor their behavior and manage how they communicate to children, to employers and to the public. Here's why:

Children

Let's not forget the challenges you may have faced growing up as a child, how certain experiences with your parents or others influenced your self-esteem, self-worth and your sense of safety and security. As much as we'd like to reverse time and go back into our personal histories and change our parents or experiences, we can't. But as an adult you can make better decisions and choose to be responsible in a way that may not have occurred in your childhood. This is your opportunity to stop any abuse, neglect or dysfunction before it starts by the manner in which you communicate and interact with the children in your life. Children are like sponges, they observe or hear things from us even when we think their little ears and eyes are not focused on us. While we are watching them and monitoring their behavior, they too are watching us and monitoring how we manage our affairs. How we express anger and our feelings of displeasure and disappointment to the children becomes a form of instruction and direction in how to express their feelings. It creates real reactions and feelings in the mind of children and it becomes a form of advertising of who we are as men. Children easily misinterpret inappropriately expressed anger as rejection or punishment, even when you don't mean it that way.

Children need to understand that you are dissatisfied with their behavior but you are not rejecting them as a person. As a man and as a parent, you should be mindful that the expression of your anger never takes the form of disrespect, temper tantrums (yes, temper tantrums) or violence. Intentional or not, your behavior is instructional to children. Your children's safety, sense of self-worth, and healthy feelings of security should always come before your need or desire to show how angry you are.

Employers

I briefly gave an example of the impact of attitude at the beginning of this chapter. But when it comes to anger, how African American men conduct themselves at work is just as important as how they conduct themselves in front of their children. I venture to say that inappropriately expressed anger at your job may be more important. The reason is that as a man, you need your job to provide sustenance and other essential necessities for your child and family. One slip of the tongue or venting of anger in the wrong way is not likely to cost you your relationship with your children. But a bad attitude or outburst of anger with or in front of a co-worker or supervisor could be damaging to an employment relationship.

A suspension or termination is not an unlikely outcome should you make the mistake of going "postal" at work one day. Every negative stereotype from the movies, the evening news or personal experiences will be on the minds of co-workers as a filter to interpret your attitude or behavior. Losing your job because of an anger outburst or an attitude will affect your ability to provide for your children and family.

One of the problems that seem to plague a lot of African American men is the inability to follow directions, take instruction, or criticism while on the job. Many brothers struggle with authority figures and tend to over react to perceived affronts to their manhood. The image our brothers have of themselves as men cannot overshadow the reality of keeping their job.

Jobs are much too hard to come by in the present economy. The last thing you'd want to have to do is walk in the door early from work to report that you've been suspended or terminated because of a bad attitude or because you couldn't control your anger. Identifying the cause of feelings of low self-worth, which is at the root of a lot of anger issues, can provide the insight and awareness to transform anger into more productive expressions and communication.

Image, feelings and emotions can never supersede the requirement for you to be responsible. Experiences with African

American men who've had bad attitudes have left many employers hesitant to hire them, especially younger African American males. At the same time African American men often sense that no one wants to hire them because of stereotypes and racial discrimination. These feelings may be compounded for men who have criminal records, who already are likely to have difficulty finding employment. However, as men you must learn to manage your anger and to express your feelings of dissatisfaction in a healthy way that makes the point but does not alienate those with whom you seek understanding.

If you don't change, change will change you. The loudest voice and the quickest reaction are not always the best way to handle a problem. You cannot intimidate your way through life, certainly not with your employment. When you blow up with a co-worker or supervisor at your job in front of others, you place them in a reactionary position. They may feel compelled to do something in retaliation or to save face. If they are from another racial or ethnic group, this is most likely where the verbal or non-verbal cues of racism and discrimination will arise.

Keep your priorities (and your vision) in order. Learn to express your feelings in a calm and constructive manner. You may just have to let some things slide. If you are without a job, keep looking. There is always a job somewhere even if the job is not something you would normally find yourself doing. I am a college graduate but on more than one occasion, I found it necessary to do temporary work at a factory alongside unskilled workers half my age.

It's what I needed to do at the time. But you should not allow anger or any other self-pitying, or self-defeating emotion overtake the need for common sense. If you are angry because you've been fired, you cannot find a job or no one will hire you, turn your anger into positive motivation and go out and create your own job.

The Public

One of the reasons why Coca Cola is such a successful beverage company, in part, is because of its advertising and marketing campaign. Yeah, it's a great product and millions of people like it and buy it every day. But what drives (sells) Coke are the displays and how it is marketed to the public. Ok, now let's reverse that scenario back to you. You are in business for yourself, the product is you.

Your attitude and the kind of person you are is your advertising and marketing plan. Just like those cans of Coke that we see on display in supermarkets, gas stations or convenience stores, one never knows when an interested, potential customer is going to walk by us to make a "purchase." If your display is unorganized, sloppy, dirty or unattractive, no one will want to engage you.

When you consistently and inappropriately advertise anger, hostility, and dissatisfaction through your facial expressions, tone of voice and your body language, it suggests that you don't want to be bothered; you are killing your sales. The reactions that you will get from the world will be that you are pissed off at the world and you are not open for business. Remember what we discussed in the chapter, "*How African American Men Become Stuck in Maleness*" concerning self-worth. Subconsciously, how you feel about yourself creates tendencies. A part of the effect of how you feel about yourself is that you attract to you the kind of people and the kinds of reactions that confirm your self-evaluation. In the public's mind, regardless of their race or ethnicity, you look just like the guys on television in the mug shots, cop shows and the rap videos.

Take heed and do what is necessary to make needed changes within you. Take responsibility for you and actively participate in your own success. You don't have to walk around with a fake smile plastered on your face. People would likely think you are high on something or you're suffering from mental illness. But you can and should learn to manage your attitude, feelings, and how people see you.

Success and Failure

I think that it is safe to say that most men enjoy the feeling of winning, but dislike how it feels when they lose. It may be a quirk in the male personality. I'm ok with losing when I know I've done my best, but I'd much rather win. But in order to become the man that God created you to be, you must learn to become comfortable with both winning and losing. The attitude that you display when you lose is just as important as the attitude you take on when you've won. The reason is because life is not based entirely upon winning and losing or our successes and failures; rather a combination of experiences in between that produces its own highs and lows that become a better indication of who we are as men. Remember, as a man, your life is not all about you and how many notches you have on your belt on any given day. It's about keeping yourself "Response-Able", balancing your attitude so you can remain motivated to meet your personal needs and the needs of your family.

Maintain a positive attitude when you become stressed, angry, face obstacles, or defeat. You can win with excitement while still maintaining a humble demeanor and not humiliate or discourage those whom you've defeated. You can see by now there are distinct differences in attitude (mental position) that influence males who become stuck in behaviors or life styles that negatively impact their ability to mature into full manhood.

Nothing distinguishes a man from a male more than the attitude he exudes towards himself, his family and his life. Men, as opposed to men stuck in maleness, are focused in life; they live intentionally and demonstrate a willing attitude to learn. They go out and provoke change, achieve their goals and are adaptable to change when it knocks at their door. Several years ago I lost my cell phone and like a lot of people, I couldn't remember all of the numbers in my phone, nor had I a back list.

I was still able to retrieve messages by calling my telephone number and accessing my voicemail, which is separate from the phone itself. In an effort not to miss any important calls and to rebuild my phone list, I left the following message on my voicemail: "Hi, this is Russ. Unfortunately I've dropped my phone in the rain and it washed down into the sewer. Please leave your full name and telephone number and I'll get back to you as soon as possible".

Amongst all of the messages I received after that incident, one particular message from my friend Gary stood out and I've never forgotten it. "Beep, hey Rou this is Gary. I heard about your phone, just dive in and get it! Give me a call when you get this message...." I have never forgotten those words from Gary and they illustrate the importance of a positive attitude, especially when things seem to be going wrong. The attitude you take in life is more important than the facts of your life, good or bad. As a man you must monitor your inner voice and manage the real impact it has for you and for others. Nelson Mandela, former president of South Africa, spent 27 years in a South African prison cell. He could have succumbed to negativity and self-pity, but he did not. He changed his attitude and provoked change in others as well. So with an open mind and a new attitude you are positioned to transform your old attitude and move your life into a new direction, from being stuck in maleness into full manhood.

Chapter 11
Men, Come Forth And Lead!

This chapter could have been included as a part of Chapter 7, "*What It Means to Be a Man*", under the subtitle of "Purpose". Purpose is one of the areas of lack for African American men. Two of man's important roles alongside of purpose are to lead and to teach his family. Due to the harmful effects posed by the absence of leadership within the African American family, I have elected to spend more time discussing the leadership and teaching roles in more detail here in Chapter 11.

I've attempted to argue that a part of the ongoing crisis within the African American family can be abated and made less harmful as African American men become healthier. As African American men come into awareness of their true purpose as men, coupled with a vision for themselves and their families, they will increasingly develop the ability to respond in a healthy and stable manner to the circumstances of their life. The more African American men look for solutions to their problems outside of themselves, the longer they (and their families) will remain stagnant and held in a state of dysfunction and bondage to the interference of outside forces operating against them.

In the same way, the longer the African American community looks for solutions to the crisis of the African American family outside of African American men stepping up to the plate, the longer it too, will remain a state of dysfunction and dependence upon others as well. I believe that there is no amount of money or government aid that can solve social problems such as crime, substance abuse, gang affiliation, child abuse, and so on, within African American communities, if African American men do not become willing and able to make change themselves. Manhood and leadership are a condition of a man's mind.

Stuck In Maleness has been about providing African American men with the awareness of your powers, the tools and the blueprint to change the condition of your own mind. The time for change is now and long overdue. The practice of blaming others for our condition and making excuses about what we don't have is no longer the way to achieve personal freedom.

You must now step up to the plate of life and lead yourself, lead your children, and you must lead your family. History is replete with examples, i.e. kings, princes, writers, philosophers, generals, inventors, teachers, sports figures, parents, and a new president, that clearly demonstrate the potential and divinity, within you. No one can give you your value, self-worth or self-respect, but you.

We have discussed in detail the illusory images of manhood, what it means to be *"stuck in maleness"*. You have been shown the tools God has provided us through our belief system, the blueprint for manhood and our religious and spiritual sourcebooks such as the

Bible, the Koran and the Torah. All of these resources, coupled with intelligence and awareness of your power of choice, and a belief in God are all that you need to lead you, your children and your family towards the vision that you desire n life. So how do you lead you?

Yourself

You lead yourself by first knowing when and how to follow. Up to this point in your life, you may have misused and abused your power of choice by following images, doctrines or people that undermined your role as a man. An excellent starting point from this point on is to base your personal leadership upon principles, values, and strategies that have already been proven to work for others.

The mistake that many of our brothers make is to try and create what has already been made available for our use by other people. In an effort to appear different from others or to align ourselves with what seems to be popular, we place ourselves in situations or in the company of people that even a blind man (sorry Stevie) can see are not good for us. Men, real men, know and understand their purpose, do what is right, not what is popular. Remember, diseased thinking is only going to produce unhealthy, counterproductive and dysfunctional behavior. The values and principles that I use, which are the basis for the tools and blueprint to cure the various areas of lack, are contained within the Bible.

If you choose to, you may substitute the values and principles taught by your own religious good book, because there is only one God. The Bible, Koran, Torah or whatever your source book, should be become the place that you go to for direction and guidance on correct living. For many of us the starting point may be as simple as falling back on the values and lessons taught by our parents or taking the time to listen to the observations and insights of the people around you, like a supportive wife or girlfriend who has your back and really wants to see you prosper. You do not need to reinvent what often has already been made available to you as an aid to leadership and making maximum use of your power of choice. You may also choose, as I do, to attend religious services at your local church, mosque or house of worship on a regular basis. Consult with your church's pastor or spiritual leader for further leadership or guidance.

Men, you lead yourself by establishing and committing to a vision plan and the goals and objectives necessary to make your vision plan become a reality. Think outside of the box. Do not allow fear, friends, immediate gratification, adversity or what's convenient hinder your decisions on the direction you take your life, or how you get there. You must make sacrifices in order to be successful. If achieving all or part of your vision requires you to obtain a diploma, certificate, college degree or a license, make the sacrifice and give up your present life style to achieve your future vision. Your boys on the block, the guys at the bar, the chicks at the strip club (don't make me tell your business) can wait. You are responsible for your *OWN* prosperity. Do what is necessary to achieve your vision because if you don't, no one else will.

Your dream is your dream, and your vision is the light that you will see in your mind's eye that will propel you forward when you feel like quitting, so go and get it. A good leader is aware of his weaknesses. He places himself in a position of learning so that he can be taught the concepts (thoughts) or skills that he needs to continue to transform his mind and behavior in order to lead effectively and efficiently.

If you have personal challenges that require counseling, therapy or treatment, get the help that you need. Use the resources as suggested or required. A wise man can always play the fool but the fool can never play a wise man. Being a man is not always about you.

The degree of positive Karma that you create is in direct relation to the company you keep and the way in which you use your time (power of choice). If you are in recovery from drugs or alcohol or some other form of addiction, get into a support group, obtain a sponsor and stick with them both. It is ok to need help. Your sponsor is likely to have gone through some of the problems you are facing. He/she can be a valuable source of information, lifesaving information.

If you are not in recovery from an addiction, you should consider getting a mentor (if you have a sponsor you can also have a mentor). A mentor is a person with spiritual or specialized knowledge in a particular area. It can be someone from your profession of interest, such as law, finance, music, etc., or just someone that you admire. Either way, he/she should be someone of good character and reputation who is in a position to advise you in the direction in which you would like to take your life. Remember, to always keep yourself Response–Able, using your tools (your mind, power of choice) and relying on all the components of your blueprint; 1) Awareness, 2) Purpose, 3) Vision, and 4) Responsibility.

Children

I have chosen to speak about leading and teaching children separate from the family for men who have children, but may not presently be in a committed relationship with their lady or spouse. No matter the circumstances, all children need the direction (leadership) and guidance that come from the involvement of both parents. Both parents are in a better position to teach their children correct values and appropriate behaviors in a way that cannot be accomplished with just one parent. This is why African American men must look beyond the confusion of "baby mama drama" and look to the needs of their children instead. It's not about you or her. What is more, parents should not look for other people or government agencies to do what they must do as parents, unless they really cannot do it. In addition, pre-school programs, daycare centers, elementary schools and after school programs cannot be expected to perform your job as a parent. Children get their cues on correct living and acceptable conduct from you. Programs (or school) can only supplement and reinforce what you are already teaching your children at home. A personal friend of mine, Pastor Victor Hudson in his book, "*Fathers, Come Forth: The Journey of*

Family Leadership", stated the importance of leading your family this way:

> "The essence of leadership is the ability to encourage others to do something they normally would have never thought to do on their own accord. A leader takes no interest in his title, position, or status but exists to serve and influence others....Manhood is not about the man, it is a spiritual position and journey. As a father, you are called to serve. To lead is to serve. One of your primary roles is to place your family's needs above your own selfish desires. Your family is your first ministry, your primary responsibility. Their needs should be your first priority before anything else including your career, your friends, even your parents, or siblings." (37)

It is your job to send your children to school and to select programs that support and compliment the values that you are teaching them at home. Here are several suggestions to help you in your leader/teacher role as a parent.

As early as possible, structure your children's behavior by structuring their time. You structure their time by structuring your time. Establish a regular schedule for meals, sleep, play and other activities. Obviously, this will be set up according to the hours of programs, school schedules and the work schedules for you and your child's mother.

Make an effort to stick to your routine and deviate as little as possible. As often as possible, speak to your child in a normal tone of voice. With good intentions, one of the mistakes that many African American parents make is yelling at their children, especially in public, usually out of frustration or anger.

Many parents believe that speaking in a loud voice and hostile or threatening language (profanity) will get the desired message across to their child better than speaking in a normal tone of voice. I see this most often with younger parents. This is a thinking error and continuing to do so could also be the beginning of your child developing issues with anxiety, fear or anger.

      Parenting is a patient process. You cannot have a club, party or entertainment mindset when you are in your parent mode. That is often where the frustration sets in. Subconsciously, your child is interfering with the "other you", the person that still wants to be childless and do things that single parents do. Not really intending any harm, you yell at your child because their behavior reminds you that you are no longer single and free. Instead, verbalize instruction to your child in a normal tone (unless there is danger) and make sure to speak to your child in a way that relates values to the behaviors that you desire for them to learn. Repetition and consistency on your part and monitoring your own thinking and behavior, will speak louder than any words.

      Involve your children in activities with you where they can learn, especially as they get older. Simultaneously, you should monitor the verbal and non-verbal gender cues that you are communicating to your children. Our children begin to imitate our facial expressions, body language and other non-verbal cues at an early age. My 20 year-old daughter Symone, who was ten at the time, embarrassed me at a family gathering one evening when I returned from a trip to the restroom only to find her in the middle of the floor imitating me in front of others on various things she'd learned about me over the years from as far back as when she was strapped in car seat as I drove from place to place. More than embarrassed, I was amazed at her memory and attention to detail since some of the things she related occurred while she was still young enough to be in diapers.

Continue to teach your children in an age appropriate manner as they enter structured programs outside of the home, such as daycare, pre-school, or grade school, in a way consistent with the environment. Speak to them in ways that will help to improve their thinking and aid them in developing problem solving skills and improve their ability to make better decisions.

By the way, do not make the mistake of bribing your child to do what he/she must eventually learn to do anyway. Bribing your child with 'things' in particular surrenders your power as a parent and sets the stage for you to be manipulated later, as your child gets older and smarter. You have to be both diligent and patient in your instruction. Love must be demonstrated in your instruction and respect and responsibility by what you require of them.

Provide them with age appropriate tasks so they can learn responsibility. Help them with their homework but do not do it for them. Make sure they grasp concepts properly and help them to develop and practice good study habits.

Monitor your children's understanding of correct values by monitoring their performance in school and their behavior with friends. Attend parent/teacher conferences to obtain information on how to adjust or reinforce instruction at home. Many parents dislike it when their kids want to bring other children into the home, some out of privacy while others fear the mess that can be made. Instead, welcome these requests as an opportunity to observe your children's choice of friends and how they interact together. The same goes when your children become involved in sports or other activities outside the home.

Drive your children and their friends so you can observe behaviors and monitor what your children are learning and from whom. Getting prior permission before other children come to your home or before offering to drive them anywhere can also be an opportunity to meet other parents and to monitor their attitude and conduct as well. Occasionally, accept invitations by other parents to their homes so you can determine if their home will be a safe place for your child should they go there to play or sleep over.

Family

Families create Karma (Chapter 9) just like individuals do. Families that have more positive Karma associated with them (and in them) are led by parents who usually have a vision for their family. The parents, along with personal goals, have set family goals and have clear standards by which the family's vision is to be achieved.

Along with your wife or partner, discuss with your children the plans you have for your family as a whole, and how their individual conduct and achievement contributes to the overall success of the family. Discuss your children's behavior, successes or challenges, and compliment or reprimand them as appropriate but speak to them, do not yell. You always want your children to feel valued and worthy. Dinnertime or other regularly scheduled meals are best.

You should discuss your goals and achievement and those of your spouse/partner, and prompt them to share their goals and achievements as well. Freely complement each other in a manner befitting the setting but never reprimand or show disapproval of your lady in front of your children. Remember, you are also teaching appropriate attitudes and behavior towards the opposite gender.

Show your children that good leaders can also follow by deferring leadership when appropriate. At times your spouse or partner may clearly have more knowledge, expertise or understanding of a situation than you do and be the best to lead the family on a particular task. The reality of life is that everyone is good at some things and bad at others. You do not want to send the wrong message or any negative cues to your children about your spouse/partner's abilities. You also do not want to discourage your children from respecting or admiring your lady's competency.

I grew up with my stepfather who was very good at many things, but my siblings and I also clearly knew that my mother was the brains behind many things in our household. I am not talking about just cooking but finances and the purchase of real estate as well. My mother knew how to make the eagle on a dollar crow. Furthermore, you are the leader of your family, not the boss. Bosses are to be found at our places of employment. They also used to be found on the plantation during slavery but slavery is over. While men tend to be the disciplinarians in relationships, you and your spouse/partner are a team and should govern your household with a united front and work together as such. Lead with a firm but gentle hand.

Whenever possible take your children to places or events that provide insight into the vision you have for them individually or the family as a whole. Visit your old college alma mater, the college you or they would like to attend, or places you'd like to consider living as a family. Encourage optimism, hard work and focus, along with honesty, integrity, trust, a belief in their abilities and belief in God.

Attend your children's school functions and sporting events. Encourage them and show support for their endeavors. Children need to know that they are important to their parents. When a child looks out in the audience or crowd and sees their parents, (win, lose or draw) it makes a world of difference in their heart and in their mind.

Set your children's imaginations aflame by exploring possibilities beyond their immediate environment by taking family trips to places outside your community, city and state. Re-enforce community, cultural and racial pride by emphasizing respect for themselves and respect for the views, values and culture of other people.

Teach your children about your family history and whenever possible, include grandparents from both sides of the family, in celebrations, special occasions or school functions. It will become an opportunity for your children to participate in family history and to place the value that you seek to teach them into the larger context of the family beyond the walls of your immediate household. Let politicians and government officials run the city, state and the country. You must lead your family. Lead by example.

Chapter 12
What Women Want

"Two are better than one....for if they fall, one will lift up his companion" (Ecclesiastes 4:9-10)

Up to this point we have discussed men, myths and misconceptions about manhood, what it means to be *"stuck in maleness"*, how you become *"stuck in maleness"*, what it really means to be a man, the importance of leadership and the importance of modeling and teaching correct values to your children. But to discuss men without also touching upon the man's relationship to women would be analogous to discussing what it mean to be human without talking about people.

One of the major side effects of African American men who are *"stuck in maleness"* is their dysfunctional way of relating to women, especially to the mothers of their children. Because the minds of African American men have been filled with so many myths, misconceptions and distorted imagery about manhood, African American men have misunderstood, mistreated and even missed the mark in their relationship with African American women.

I believe that the foundation for the unhealthy interaction between African American men and women was laid during slavery, but the more immediate cause for the challenges between our brothers and sisters is due to bad programming about what it means to be a man and how we should relate to our women.

God created women as a helpmate and companion to men, but African American men seem to do everything in their power to negate help and companionship from their women. They negate African American women and push them away because they don't understand how to relate to them and they don't know and understand what a woman wants and needs from them as men and fathers of their children.

The relationship between African American men and women is where the most harm has occurred to the African American family. I do not believe that either African American men or African American women should look down upon each other with contempt as the source of our problems. It was the larger historical forces of the institution of slavery and its offspring, institutionalized racism, coupled with poor personal choices that have set many of the maladapted attitudes within the African American family and to each other in motion in the first place.

However, today in 2014, both African American men and women are culpable and must share in the responsibility to reverse these negative and deadly trends within our communities. In recent years, advances in education, employment and income by many African American women has, indirectly, exacerbated existing tensions between African American men and women. Some of our brothers are intimidated by these advances on the part of African

American women and others avoid sisters altogether, whom they perceive are too "uppity" because they feel unworthy and less needed as men.

Stuck In Maleness has been about creating the awareness and the opportunity for African American men to heal in their relationship with African American women. I have provided as a guide, 10 insights into what I believe African American women want from African American men regardless of their education level, profession, social or economic status, or their income. It is my hope and goal, that these 10 insights will open the door to better understanding, more effective communication and create more positive Karma between African American men and women that will become a healthy force for the African American family.

Respect

The precursor to any relationship with another human being is respect. You must respect a woman as a human being, an individual and as a person, and, you must have self-respect as well. Respect is a basic obligation that you have towards other people, and self-respect is a right that you have as a human being. Before you consider becoming friends with a woman you got to respect her as a human being. The problem with African American men who are *"stuck in maleness"* is that they have a tendency to disrespect African American women. They use African American women as objects or things, including using them for sex, money, drugs, or other forms of gratification. African American men tend to abuse women when they feel a woman has "stepped out of her place" or when they perceive she has challenged the distorted imagery they have of themselves. African American men who disrespect women do not respect themselves. They are suffering from a diseased mind because of lack (self-awareness, purpose, vision, responsibility), and low self-worth.

When you don't value yourself, you will not see value in your woman and you will also be disrespectful towards your family. The lack of respect (value) for African American women is one of the reasons there is such a large number of baby mamas, baby daddy's and single female headed households in the United States. African American men don't respect their women because they don't respect themselves.

Men, never let a disagreement, argument, falling out, or any amount of finger waving in your face (you know how some of our women can be), cause you to disrespect your lady.

African American women want and deserve to be respected as women and as the mothers of our children. It is safe to say that most men will not disrespect their own mother. Your lady, whether she is your wife, finance, girlfriend, or baby's mama, should be given the same regard. Our mothers are a reflection of our past family, while our lady is a reflection of our future. Women want to be respected.

Honesty and Trust

In the same way that women want men to respect them, they also want men to be honest with them, no matter what. Honesty is the quality or condition (condition of the mind) of showing truthfulness, and integrity, in your relations with others (38). In other words, if you tell a woman that you are single or divorced, that should be the truth. If you tell her that you have a job or you are not in a committed relationship that should be the truth as well. And if you tell your wife or lady that you are going to the gym to work out every Thursday evening, that had better be where you go on Thursday nights. Two times a day, five days a week, the show *Cheaters* captures the lives of men and women in relationships filled with dishonesty and lies. In most cases the lies that are told can be avoided by communication and honesty.

When you have not been honest with someone or you strategically leave out certain parts of key information, you are being both dishonest and deceptive. Relationships built upon lies and deceptions are not really relationships at all because the telling of the lie will have denied your partner with information they have a right to know. The lie denies them with the opportunity to make an informed decision about your character and credibility as a man.

Everyone has right to know the truth. How they use or interpret that information is their choice. It could be that you have a criminal record, a child you fathered out of wedlock, or even the existence of another family altogether. Either way, she has a right to know the truth. Everyone makes mistakes or exercises poor judgment in life, including you. Again, it is low self-worth and a poor valuation of yourself that causes you to want to misrepresent who you really are as a person. But if you lie and she finds out the truth later, then she will be forced to look at you from the perspective of the lie anyway, because her trust in you will have been breached.

Real men pick themselves up from their mistakes in life, they learn from them and go on to form new patterns of behavior; they create new Karma (Chapter 9). They change but they are honest about their past mistakes. For example, a criminal record can be overcome with new thinking, new values, hard work, respect, honesty and responsibility. But if you lie about it, no matter what your fears might be, then you are still thinking deceptively, like a criminal, and when your lady (or others) find out about your deception they may see you just as that, a criminal. If the relationship is meant to be, it will be. It would be better to lose her by being honest than it would to lose her by deceiving her to believe you are someone that you are not. I knew that my decision to write **Stuck In Maleness** would involve becoming transparent and publicly coming clean about my own criminal background but I chose to write it anyway. I must keep emphasizing this point because some of the most successful and well respected men in history didn't start out that way.

Once you lose trust in a relationship with your lady or others everything, I mean EVERYTHING, becomes an uphill battle. If you are half the man that you believe (belief system) you are, be honest with yourself and be honest with others about who you really are. You do not have to take your lady on the Jerry Springer Show to come clean with her, but she does deserve your respect and honesty. The problem with lying is that you can't tell just one. One lie leads to another and another….. to the point where you will start believing your own lies, and that is where you get caught and will probably lose her and everything else, anyway. Men, do damage control and be honest. Women want you to be honest with them.

Women Want To Be Listened To

Women like to talk about how they feel and want to know how you feel too. Take the time to actively listen without speaking shows your wife or lady that you value what she is saying. Women are looking for an emotional connection and need to know that you are really listening to them. Brothers, be patient; women are not asking for you to solve a problem or to help them with an issue (unless it's stated), at times they just want to vent or to share. If it's not a good time to talk, let her know that you are interested, but give you a few minutes to relax or take care of something first.

Friendship

The importance of friendship in romantic relationships is grossly underrated and relegated to a lower priority level in relationships than should be the case. Friendship is the foundation material upon which long term and lasting relationships are made. When you've taken the time to cultivate the friendship of your wife or lady, you are better equipped to weather the relationship storms of life and you have the proper foundation for your romantic relationship to grow. One of the mistakes that a lot of black men make is they place a disproportionate amount of emphasis on a woman's looks, her physical appearance and "things."

Don't get me wrong, there is absolutely nothing wrong with pursuing a woman whom you are drawn to because she is attractive or has a nice body. In reality, looks and nice figures are usually the first qualities we notice about a woman we become interested in. We even record songs about it, "She's a bad mamma jamma, just as fine as she can be." At the same time, appearances are deceptive and are not an indication of as person's true character or worth. The deceptiveness of appearance is one of the key reasons why relationships falter, especially if there is nothing else to keep the parties interested. When the initial attraction wears off, many couples find that other than bills and children, below the surface they really do not have anything in common. Paying bills and rearing children have proven not to be the best ingredients for a lasting relationship, but many couples stay together out of an obligation to the children and the convenience of making ends meet.

But what happens when there's an argument, or when her body is stretched beyond recognition during childbirth or due to lifestyle changes? Will the two of you continue to see each other the same should one of you lose his or her job? These are the kinds of challenges that will come up once the initial attraction has faded. Changes occur all the time in relationships, but when you have taken the time to get to know your lady you have something to stand on for endurance and support.

You have more of a motivation to clear the air and make up after an argument with your lady when she is also your friend. When her outer beauty begins to change (as may yours), it really will not matter because you have taken the time to find out who your lady is on the inside. Also, when neither of you is no longer impressed by or has the ability to produce material things, and your intimate desires fade, you can look past the balding head, the sagging breasts, the teeth in the jar or the crooked wig on her head, and you can still look across the room and see your friend.

Take the time to get to know your lady. Find out who she is as a person and as a woman. Learn about her hopes, dreams, goals, aspirations, fears, hang-ups and what she desires out of a relationship with you and out of life in general. Ask about her childhood, her family, and listen for things that you may have in common and what makes you different. Most importantly, listen to her and make a consistent effort to try and understand her point of view, even if you don't agree with her. In the same way, share information about yourself. Be honest, be open, and be informative as you would want her to be with you.

This is what friends do. And when the seasons of life change and the storms come to bore on your relationship, you will have something to stand on because you took the time to become her friend. Women want a friend.

Love

When I first began compiling notes for this chapter, I made the mistake like most people would, I believe, of placing love as the first quality that women want out of a relationship with a man. I don't know; there may be women or men who feel that way. But I know that you can't legitimately love your woman, and at the same time deny her the first three qualities listed above. The reason is because in a romantic relationship respect, honesty, and friendship are the pillars that love is based upon. Yes, love is about having compassion and understanding for her as a person. It is about that feeling she gets in the pit of her stomach when you have to go away or the longing she feels in her heart when you've been away for too long.

Those are real inner feelings of love that your lady may have for you. But disrespect her in front her friends, lie to her, or betray your friendship by confiding in another woman and you will immediately be made aware of what your lady really thinks about love. "If you loved me, then you wouldn't have disrespected me in front of my friends," "If you loved me, then you wouldn't have lied to about how the car got banged up" and "If you loved me, you wouldn't have confided in that other woman what you should have been telling me." So men, if you didn't understand this before, consider yourself on notice; love has "conditions" that go with it. Do not violate love's condition.

When you love your lady you should avoid doing or saying things that piss her off, or make her sad. You got to learn to "play out the tape" and think beyond your feelings and the initial impact your words or actions may have on her. Consider the long-term impact your words have, and the message about you that you will convey to her. When you love your lady, you extend yourself beyond the usual realm of actions and do things that will make her happy.

When you love your lady, you give her encouragement and support in times of need, and you do whatever it takes to help her achieve her goals and aspirations. When you love your lady, compromise becomes more of a viable option to solve problems than does conflict or competition. When you love her, you become more willing to say "I'm sorry" or "I forgive you" because your love for her has become more important than the mistake. When you love your woman, you tell her as often as she needs to hear it, and when you love her, you do whatever it may take to show your love so she can feel it. Women want to be loved.

Commitment

Under normal circumstances a commitment is an agreement, through words, actions or both, to participate in some type of endeavor with or for another person. When a man and a woman discover they have a lot in common with each other, they will often take the relationship farther and become romantically involved. They date, then date each other exclusively, live with each other, become engaged or even get married, all differing degrees of commitment. In a general sense, it has been my experience that a woman's level of expectation for commitment is greater than that of a man because women have a greater need for commitment.

This is a point that I believe so many African American men fail to understand or they just refuse to consider. It is not because African American men have a problem with commitment; to the contrary, brothers have a high degree of commitment. The problem is that they are just committed to saying and doing the wrong things when it comes to our women.

The primary reason women have a greater need for commitment from African American men is because of their ability to become pregnant and to bear children. Once a woman becomes pregnant, and has made the informed decision to follow through with her pregnancy, changes begin. Every couple of weeks her body, appetite, moods, clothes, looks, goals, finances, and so on, undergo change for the next nine months and beyond. This does not happen in the same way for men.

So men, when a woman becomes involved with you, she has a desire and a need to know what to expect from you. She needs to know that you are going to be there for her, preferably as her husband or partner, to share in the changes that she may go through and the responsibilities that come with those changes. If she already has children certain aspects of the relationship may be different but the need for commitment will still be present.

African American men *"stuck in maleness"*, who suffer from lack of vision and purpose in particular, are more prone to enter into a relationship with the wrong woman for the wrong reasons. The reason is because men who lack vision and purpose are not likely to know what they want from a relationship in the first place. Their focus is likely to be centered on sex and immediate gratification. So it is no wonder that many of our brothers run or abandon relationships with African American women at the first sign change is on the horizon, especially pregnancy.

What I am getting at is that a man who doesn't know and understand who he is as a man, why he is here on earth, where he is going in life or how he is going to get there, is a liability to everyone, including himself. Our sisters need more from African American men.

African American women need to know if you are going to be there for them and commit as a partner or potential mate. If you are not going to commit to them, then they want to know so they can move on with their lives and seek their dreams somewhere else, preferably before there are children involved. It is not uncommon amongst African American couples for there to be children from a previous relationship or for some partners to be involved in multiple relationships at one time.

While children from a previous relationship are an increasing reality for couples, and they do pose real financial and emotional challenges, they can be worked out in a healthy way. I can tell you from experience that a failed relationship involving children is challenging. And a relationship with a woman involving children from her failed relationship with another man is both challenging and, complicated. This is especially the case when the emotional ties have not been fully severed and when children are old enough to harbor dreams of their parents getting back together. Difficult as it can be, the relationship still can work, and there is nothing more rewarding than when a plan comes together.

But many of these kinds of issues can be avoided if we did more thinking before acting. With an increasing number of African American men coming out of the closet and brothers operating on the "down low", compounded by risky behaviors associated with substance abuse, African American women have a greater need for commitment from African American men. This has been a major part of the problem with the relationship between African American men and women, the tension that arises because they are thinking and behaving from different value structures. Men, use your tools, blueprint for manhood, and your power of choice to better navigate the direction of your life. African American women want and need commitment.

A Provider

Men, women want and need you to provide financial support for your family. Providing financial support is a part of what it means to be a man. Financial responsibility is also a part of your overall purpose as a man. This is where many African American couples become unstable and unnecessary strain is placed on the relationship. Men, and sometimes the women, use issues that may arise within the intimate and personal aspects of the relationship to manipulate (or disrupt) the financial requirements of managing the household. Men do not let anger, a bruised ego, denial of sexual intimacy or any of these things interfere with your responsibility as a provider. No matter how you "feel", do the right thing. A part of being a man is doing the right thing regardless of how you feel. Bills still have to be paid whether you "got some" the night before or not. Your children and your lady still have to eat because the food is not going to buy itself.

If you can afford to support your family by yourself, and you lady does not have to work, fine. But if you are like most people, both you and your lady will have to bring home the bacon to support the family's financial needs. But let me say this, it doesn't matter who makes more money, you or she. Provider means provider. I say this because many African American men take issue when their lady earns more money than they do. Being a man, a good man is more than the value of a dollar, although we have a tendency to see things that way. Your lady just may be employed in a higher paying profession than you, or she may simply may have been at her job longer and worked her way up in the company to where she has earned a higher salary. If that's the case in your relationship celebrate her success; stop hating.

What is more, don't get it twisted, making more money doesn't necessarily make you more of man. Your provider role coupled with your attitude in your other roles as a leader, protector, teacher and companion/helpmate to your lady and your family as a whole, is what makes you "the man".

In addition, there are other things that you can do to enhance your role as a provider. The house must be painted, the lawn mowed, the car washed, the children fed, or the leaky faucet fixed, so don't get this important role twisted. You got to feel better about yourself as a man than to limit yourself to an hourly wage; you are worth so much more. You must stop thinking about yourself one dimensionally; think outside of the box, and realize that your value as a man is more than the difference between you and your lady's paycheck. If your lady makes more than you and it really gets under your skin, don't hate her for her success and good fortune. You can always go out and look for a better job, get a second job or simply go back to school to improve your skills by getting more training so you can earn more. When you cannot obtain employment in your regular line of work, get a job doing something else. The grocery man, the utility woman, or the landlord will take your money regardless of whether you work for Corporate America or for McDonald's flipping hamburgers. Your lady and your children need to depend upon you to be responsible and keep a roof over their heads and keep the household running smoothly. It's your duty and responsibility as a man. Women want a dependable provider.

Co-Parent

When I was a kid attending elementary school, one of the games we played was kickball. During kickball, if a player kicked the ball out of bounds on their first try or if the pitcher rolled the ball and you were not ready, you got a "do-over", or another try at kicking the ball. Men, this is your do-over and a chance to kick again and make things right in your life.

One of the major causes of African American men who become *"stuck in maleness"* is that at some point in their lifetime, they were not exposed to either positive or correct information about how to conduct themselves, usually in their childhood. Those incorrect and negative experiences in childhood shaped and formed how they feel about themselves today and may also influence their present day interpretation of parenting. It has been proven that dysfunctional behavior in adults is linked to traumatic, negative and dysfunctional experiences in childhood.

Men, many of you as you are reading **Stuck in Maleness** will be able to recall experiences in your childhood that affected how you feel about yourself today. You may already see a connection to how you parent (if you have children) and how your parents treated you as a child, so I approach the subject of parenting and co-parenting with extreme caution and mindfulness to its long term implications.

African American women don't want an adult child who sits at home where they have to give out instructions to him like one of the children; they want a responsible co-parent and partner. This is a do-over for African American men for two reasons: 1) Being in a relationship can become an opportunity, if you choose to view it that way and I hope you will, to correct the areas of lack in your life (awareness, purpose, vision, responsibility); and, 2) Parenting can be an opportunity to learn from your mistakes by "doing better" for your own children as a parent. Your parents and mine did the best they could as parents under the circumstances at the time, good or bad. Thank them or forgive them, but move on. You are now an adult man, in a relationship with an adult woman, so now you must be held accountable and responsible for your own actions.

Parenthood is a tough job at best and raising children becomes more challenging as your children get older. Under the best circumstances two parent households struggle to properly care for and raise children. They do this while also juggling the demands of work, running a household and while still trying to make time for themselves. Simply performing in your provider role is not enough. Both your lady and your children need you to step up to the plate and perform the other functions of your purpose as a man (leader, teacher, protector and companion/helpmate) as well.

Take time to share in the daily responsibilities with your lady. Help bathe or feed your children, offer to take the children to the park, daycare, school or other activities. These simple tasks can take a load of time off your lady and provide an opportunity for you to bond more with your children. Take turns attending school functions and other activities to lessen the burden on any one parent. Doing so will also enable you to become familiar with your child's adjustment in those areas and familiarize you with the other adult authority figures who are participating in your child's life.

When your children do well, compliment them and let them know how proud you are of their performance or behavior. When they don't do so well, discuss their behavior or performance, and suggest alternative ways of problem solving. Let your children know what you expect of them and remind them that you are there to help them. Discuss your children with your lady and make sure the both of you are modeling the behaviors you expect of your children. Make adjustments to your parenting style, add to your parenting repertoire and keep the focus on what's best for your children, not what's convenient. What you and your lady will be doing, men, is leading your children, teaching them correct values and helping them to develop emotionally and responsibly. You will be functioning as a co-parent. There is a saying that states "If you fail to learn from the past you are doomed to repeat it." Men, this is your do-over. Women want a co-parent.

Loyalty

When two people are in a committed relationship there is an expectation that both partners will be loyal to each other. To be loyal to your partner means to be faithful to her by not having sexual relations with other people, and to show allegiance to them in non-sexual matters as well. As simple as this statement seems, failure to adhere to it by misunderstanding the responsibility placed on each partner has been the source of arguments, infidelity, breakups, divorce and even wars. But it doesn't have to be that way.

It has been my experience that when loyalty is based entirely on feelings towards your partner, the chances of disloyalty are increased because feelings are subject to change. In the best of relationships, ups and downs occur that affect how we feel about ourselves and our partner, if only temporarily. When you are not feeling each other at the time, it can become easier to step in the wrong direction and say or do something inappropriate to another woman.

Men, when you properly use your power of choice, your tool belt and your blueprint for living, doing the right thing by your lady becomes the more obvious decision to make. Loyalty to your lady should be based upon sound principles, as well as your love and respect for her as a woman. Be loyal and respectful to her because you understand your purpose as a man and the reasons God created you. You chose your lady because she is a part of the larger vision that you have for your life. What I'm saying, is to give her respect and loyalty because God says that's what we must do as men. What God says does not change, although our feelings and emotions towards our wife or lady might change, if only temporarily. This is even more reason why it is important to base your choice of a woman and the way you interact with her on sound principles such as found in the Bible, Torah, Karma, for example, and not just because she looks good and has a big butt.

Remember men, a good leader knows when and how to follow first. The religious and spiritual source books above can become an invaluable tool to your relationship by providing guidance and answers to dilemmas that we face every day. As men we like to do our own thing, create new things or modify existing ones, but when it comes to loyalty you simply just have to use your power of choice, and do what's right.

Loyalty also involves the allegiance to your wife or lady in non-sexual matters. Jaheim, the R&B singer recorded a song several years ago that warned men "you better put that woman first" and he was right. When you are in a committed relationship, especially when you become engaged or married, you have declared that you are now one with your lady or your intention to become one. What one person does will affect the other person so what you do should be done with thoughts of how it is going to affect your partner.

When your brother asks you to borrow $200 dollars to get his car fixed, you should discuss it with your lady, even if you have the money. There could be a bill or something pressing that needs to be taken care of or purchased. Even if you have the money, it would be wise to at least mention the request to your lady because your brother's failure to repay the money could cause friction later.

The same goes in your relationship with people from your past such as ex-girlfriends, buddies, and so on, who may not be aware of the changes that have occurred in your life. When we run into people at the supermarket or at a public event, we have a tendency to pick up where we left off, or try to, anyway. It's best to be open and honest with people about the changes that have occurred in your life and keep it moving. Let the past stay in the past. Should some of those chance meetings take place when your lady is present, respect your relationship first and respect any feelings of concern that she might have concerning the unknown person. In your mind things may be ok but she may not have the same perspective as you do and want to put a little more distance between you and the other person. Be the bigger person and respect her feelings and desire for this display of loyalty.

There is one final topic related to loyalty that has been the catalyst for many arguments, breakups and divorce. In the previous section on respect I stated that our mother is a reflection of the past and our wife or lady is a reflection of our future. With that statement in mind, it should become clear where I am going with this point. Men, especially men who are "mamma's boys", have got to let go when you commit to another woman. Many years ago my mother, sensing that I had not made the full emotional transition from being single to having recently gotten married, saw an opportunity to educate me on loyalty.

In private, I had agreed to do some much needed painting for my mother. I showed up at my mom's and painted late into the evening but had not shared with my ex-wife what I was doing or when I'd be coming home. Later, this lapse in judgment caused friction between my ex-wife and me. After painting for several hours into the evening, my mother said to me, "Russell, although I really want my house painted and for you to clean up this mess, I'm sure your wife is expecting you home. Did you call to let her know where you were and when you'd be coming home? I'm your mother but you're married now, your wife comes first."

Men, this does not mean that we don't do things for our mothers or family members. We do not have to divorce them because we've gotten married or become involved in a serious relationship. But it does mean that we must show respect, consideration and loyalty to our wife or lady first. The same loyalty and consideration should be afforded to you by her family members.

When you become committed to another person both partners must sever the emotional umbilical cord from the past and give 100% to each other. In most cases communication, consideration, forethought about these issues will do just fine. But you better put that woman first. Women want loyalty from their men.

Stability

One of the most important qualities that you can bring to a relationship with a woman, and what the African American family disparately needs, is stability. When two people come together there is an implied expectation that life for them together will be better for them than it was when they were separate. When you come together you are now sharing, for example, rent, food, time, daily tasks, etc., that used to be handled separately.

Since 2007 the economic downturn has caused everyone to look for ways to cut cost and save money. High unemployment and an unstable housing market, rising costs in education, including childcare, and fluctuations in gas and oil prices, are choking the life out of even the savviest saver. These are all factors in why some people stay in relationships and the reason others come together in the first place. Two heads and incomes are supposed to be better than one.

Make no mistake about it, living together and raising a family is like running a small business. The owner and shareholders are supposed to do what is best for the long term stability and success of the business. I'm sure that you have heard of the popular phase, "I can do bad all by myself". *"I Can Do Bad All By Myself"* was also the title to a popular stage play, written by Tyler Perry. The play gave a peek inside the comedic side of relationships. While the play was funny, a lot of African American women were not laughing in real life in their relationships with African American men. As a matter of fact, the title of the play vividly captures the inner sentiment and attitude many African American women have towards their relationships with brothers.

Some women desire "swinging from the chandelier" type sex, others want to have a good time out on the town, and they want you to have a good paying job so you can pick up the tab. Still others just want you to buy them "things" so they can talk about what their man buys for them. But the fact of the matter is that all African American women (all women really) want you to be stable. They want you to have a stable job, a stable attitude, stable emotions, stability in the bedroom, stability in dealing with the children and consistently stable to meet your provider responsibilities.

I have emphasized throughout **Stuck In Maleness** that manhood is a condition of male's mind. If you cannot, at a minimum, bring a stable mind and a healthy attitude to your relationship, you are increasing your chances of failure because many women feel that they don't need you anyway. Women need a certain amount of predictability in a relationship with you, and African American women are no different. They need to trust that you are who you say you are, have the qualities you say you have, be where you're supposed to be, and at the right times, without second guessing you.

Past studies have revealed that women mature earlier and at a faster rate than men and women also show a capacity for more complex reasoning and brain activity. I could never understand how my mother could be at the stove cooking with one hand, hold my baby brother with the other arm, talk on the telephone while simultaneously carry on a conversation with my stepfather who was sitting at the kitchen table. Yet, she still heard me sneaking out the back door; "Russell get your butt back in here. Nobody told you, you could go outside. Go and find something to do with yourself."

The ability to multitask may be because of a woman's God given capacity to bear children and to take care of her family. So, a woman's brain is already programmed and set for handling business. When you come along she is already scanning you and evaluating your swagger to determine if getting into a relationship with you is going to be a good or bad decision, and what the impact getting into a relationship with you is going to have on her life. I'm providing this information not to intimidate you but to inform you of the reality of some of the factors that may act as a filter when African American women look at you. What I am saying is that African American women don't need you in order to survive as they did in the past. Instead, today they want to be in a relationship but they need you to be stable, and to come to the table with something else to offer other than sex.

So, don't show up at her door with your I-Phone, Xbox 360, PlayStation, 50 pairs of jeans, 25 pairs of different colored Tims and a couple of dollars in your pocket straight from your mother's sofa, professing to be ready for a relationship when you know damn well you are not ready because you're not stable. It doesn't and shouldn't work that way. Even if you have a great paying job, a late model Benz and your own crib, it really doesn't matter; if you throw a few back at the club, come home drunk. cuss your lady out, and then beat her, then it doesn't matter; you got issues.

Men, neither does it matter if you shower your lady with clothes, jewelry or a new car from your drug dealing proceeds for six months, but then go to jail for three years because you're not stable. I've made the mistake of stepping on the wrong side of the law for short-term gratification and ended up with long-term incarceration. I know the fear, disappointment and financial instability that can disrupt a household and a relationship, when you and your lady are living in two different worlds, one of you is rowing north and the other is rowing south, but thinks she doesn't notice it.

Finally, when you enter a new relationship with someone but you have not fully resolved issues with your old one, you are asking for trouble as well. No one, certainly not your wife or lady, wants to have to hear about or have to deal with baggage from the past. When you carry around unresolved issues from the past and drag them into your relationship with your new love, you bring the trash (Chapter 8) and the negative Karma (Chapter 9) that comes along with it.

This is not fair to your wife or lady, your ex, and any children that may be involved. Be a man and properly close old doors before you open new ones, even if it hurts. Otherwise your new lady and your new life will become unstable. Address your areas of lack (awareness, purpose, vision, responsibility) so you can come to the table prepared and equipped to deliver and stay there. Manhood is the condition of a stable mind. Women want you to be stable.

Adventure & Romance

Every woman wants to feel special in her relationship with her man; your lady is not any different. You can be the best provider, husband, leader, boyfriend or friend and discover that your lady wants more. What makes your relationship with your lady more than two people caught up in the daily grind, is when you bring a sense of adventure and romance into the picture. Doing exciting and interesting things with your lady will keep her thinking about you in a positive way and make her feel special. When you can make your relationship with your lady adventurous (without drama) and take the time to romance her, you have the ingredients for a lifelong love affair with her that will last and last. Here's how:

- _Listen_ to her to find out what she finds interesting and important in life. Learn how she communicates her wants and needs. Use those cues to get a better understanding of what makes her happy, sad or excited about different things. Don't be too quick to silence her when she rambles on, there's valuable information about her in there somewhere.

- If you have not done so already, _commit_ to her by showing your exclusive interest in her by giving her a friendship ring or proposing for marriage. Do something special to mark the occasion. Take her out to dinner, put on the apron and prepare a meal yourself or take her to a place she will find both special and memorable.

- Take the time to _explore_ with her and find out about her hopes, dreams, wishes and establish a vision of how the two of you would like to spend your life together as a couple. Be specific about details such as location, timeframe, benchmarks and cost so that achievement of your shared vision can become a part of your daily lives. This can become a part of the planning stage for future activities and travel.

- _Remember_ special occasions like her birthday, anniversary, graduation, promotions or success at overcoming obstacles by sending cards, planning surprise parties with friends and family, or taking her out to dinner. Order cakes or treats with her favorite filling and purchase a gift, such as jewelry to make it more memorable.

- *Honor* her by doing something special, just because, to let her know how much you appreciate her as a woman, parent, and friend. Recognize her achievement at work, in education or a special interest of hers. Involve other people from her profession, family, or friends.

- *Travel* with her by planning trips to destinations and places the two of you will find interesting and exciting. Start with short overnight trips to nearby locations or states. Plan more extensive travel as time, interest and financial resources, become available.

- *Ask* her opinion or input on a project that you may be working on at home or part of your employment responsibilities. Women often have a lot more knowledge and experience than we give them credit for; finances, budgeting, sports, home repair, employee relations or how to fix your car. Times have changed. Just be prepared to listen.

- *Reverse* the roles sometimes and take over for a day (or weekend) the tasks and others that she is normally responsible for. Volunteering to do the shopping, cooking, laundry, run errands or related things may provide her with needed relief and rest.

- It is the *little things* that you do that really count. Now and then, without asking, run her bath water after the children have gone to bed. Place candles around the tub and pour her a glass of wine or her favorite beverage as an added treat. Ask her to close her eyes while you ease around behind her and wash her back or massage her in all the right places.

- Sometimes *surprise* her with special gifts, treats, lunch or toys, just because. Send her flowers, chocolate covered strawberries or buy her personal items such as lingerie that you like on her but you know she will like as well.
- *Stay fit* by walking together, riding bikes, roller skating, going dancing, hiking or joining a local fitness club. Exercise will keep the two of you fit and stimulate your endurance and interest in other areas.
- Be *spontaneous* and do things out of the ordinary. Jump on a bus, train and take a day trip to the downtown area or a neighboring city for shopping, attend the theatre or just walk around and sight-see.
- Share a hotdog, ice cream or beverage and stroll through the park. When you really want to be spontaneous just take her into the bedroom, the bathroom, the basement, the closet or wherever your imagination takes you, and wear her out until the both of you collapse from exciting adventurous and romantic lovemaking together. Women want adventure and romance from their men.

Chapter 13
One Size Doesn't Fit All

I personally believe that all women have goodness in them and there is a woman for every man. At the same time, every woman is not good for every man. Let me repeat that; "Every Woman Is Not Good For Every Man." But somewhere in the recesses in the mind of men, brothers think that they gotta have every woman that crosses their pathway. Some of us act like children unleashed in a candy store full of sweets when we see a woman that we think we like. We may not know one iota of information about the woman or what she's about, but what we see physically sends the message to our brain that we have to have *HER* without any further explanation. But is the woman we see with our physical eyes good for us? When we look at her for the first time what is the image that appears in our mind's eye? Do we see her body? Do we see ourselves making love to her in our bed? Do we see her in a big house, in a nice a car, as our wife or as the woman of our dreams or how she would be as the mother of our children? The reason I ask this very important question is because as African American men we tend to have a lot of issues with the women we choose to align ourselves with in romantic relationships. I think that the main problem is that we tend to hook up with the wrong women for the wrong reasons. The assumption many of us men bring to the table is just because she looks like a woman, talks like a woman, smells like a woman, does womanly things, and for all intents and purposes is a woman, then she is open game. But we seem to have a high divorce rate, couples are shacking up longer and getting married less, there's an increasing incidence of single female headed households, fatherless children, domestic violence and everyone seems to already have a baby daddy or a baby momma attached to them when they go into the relationship. Either we may need to get our eyes checked or cupid is sending the wrong messages to our brains.

When I was growing up as a child and began to experience puberty around age 11, my friends and I talked about the things we liked or disliked about girls. We talked about actresses we liked, such as, Pam Grier and other female celebrities and compared them to the girls in our school. Later we advanced to comparing ourselves to African American men on the big screen and sports figures, and the girls in our school to the women in dirty magazines when they were available. We'd do these comparisons with interest and enthusiasm because in our young minds what we were doing was fun and innocent.

By the time I turned 13, most of us were equipped with an arsenal of assumptions, stereotypes, misconceptions, bad language, and opinions about African American women that could rival those of most adult men. As innocent and harmless as those behaviors were at the time, many of us seemed to have carried those same assumptions into adulthood. And many of us continue to relate to adult women based upon the same assumptions we had as immature boys. At the time, little did we know that continuing to think in the same way would later get us into a lot of trouble with our wives, girlfriends and other women. Some of us quickly learned that those stereotypes we had about women were just that, stereotypes, but many of us didn't.

All women with big butts or large breasts and a pretty smile are not waiting for you to come along and grab or gawk at them. Neither is the lady with the sexy walk usually doing so because she is trying to entice you to go to bed with her. That's just the way she walks in heels. A lot of us continue to make these immature stereotyped observations despite our age and what women themselves are telling us. All women are not the same, certainly not all African American women. They range from the hooker on the street corner selling her body for money, to the hands on hips, eye and neck rolling "Sapphire" sista', to the professional mother who juggles job and family, to the Barbara "B" Smith restaurateur, to the daytime talk show hostess and media mogul Oprah, to a first lady named Michelle Obama, and every women in between. None of these women are the same, except that someone loves them and they all are deserving of respect, and some honor, in their own way.

We were born with two heads, the head on our shoulders and the head of our penis. The problem that a lot of us men have is that our version of manhood causes us to rely heavily upon the head of our penis. Sexual prowess has been a part of African American folklore and mythology for years. That's part of what I touched upon in an earlier chapter about the misconceptions and myths about manhood. The problem with relying so heavily upon the head of the penis is that the penis just has two gears, first and second. The penis has no real purpose other than sexual gratification and urination. That's it! Once the blood leaves the penis after sexual gratification it becomes flaccid, or soft. It's purpose has been fulfilled so it goes back to having no other usefulness beyond taking a leak. Men *"stuck in maleness"* tend to rely heavily, sometimes exclusively, on the head of their penis to make what are often life-changing decisions when it comes to which woman they choose to align themselves with, which woman they have sexual intercourse with, why they have sexual intercourse with her, and whether or not they use protection against disease and pregnancy. I can personally tell you that this way of thinking is not the most effective way of aligning yourself with a woman. This type of practice is what creates the bulk of the "baby daddy" and "baby momma" drama, along with the large numbers of fatherless African American children. Both "baby momma" drama and fatherless children are mostly victims of lower head thinking.

But when you know and understand your purpose as a man (leader, provider, protector, teacher and helpmate/companion), you have the "Response-Ability" to process cues from your smaller head from a completely different perspective. Your mind becomes equipped to understand that one size doesn't fit all, and you're able to move on past those casual encounters with women. Although her looks and her body may arouse your groin, you have a system "override" mechanism that lets you know she does not fit the long term purpose and vision that you've established for your life. God created a man for and with a purpose, not merely the practice of screwing every woman that we can. Don't get me wrong, I'm aware of the compulsion to pounce on every women that passes your nose but there are long term consequences for thinking with your groin instead of the head on your shoulders.

The Bible (you may substitute principles from your own religious source book) says that we shouldn't be unevenly yoked with unbelievers (Corinthians 6:14). I believe it's safe to say that the same reasoning also applies to women in our everyday life that may not be meant for us; it's not simply a religious concept. When you have your head together, i.e., vision, purpose, job, goals, car, home, etc., your internal navigation system provides you with the foresight to re-navigate your attention beyond the pretty face, the nice figure, the seductive walk (Lord have mercy!) and to keep it moving to wherever you were going before you laid eyes on her. There may not be anything wrong with a particular woman but she simply is not the right one for you. The purpose that you have established for your life can and should be one of the main tools that you use to determine a woman's suitability. The other tool should be her character and whether or not she has established a vision for her life. I cannot emphasize enough the importance of making sound choices in your relationships with women.

Aligning with the wrong woman can also be toxic. Households, just like individuals, have Karma. I am sure you will be able to recall interacting with a family or a friend whereby everyone in the house seemed to act the same way or exhibit similar tendencies towards certain types of attitudes and behaviors. Those attitudes and behaviors might be towards being argumentative, fighting, substance abuse, stealing, creating confusion or exhibiting disrespectful behavior towards self and others. If the Karma surrounding the woman you are seeking to align yourself with is not positive and healthy it may suggest that she is not positive and healthy herself. This may not always be the case because we are not merely products of our environment, rather the choices we make in relation to that environment. But here is an example that can apply to a woman you are considering regardless of her environment. If you have a vision for your life and you are working towards goals that you have set for yourself and she doesn't work, go to school, and wants to hang out and party every time she hooks up with you then she may not be a fit. If she's messy and you're into cleaning, or her child rearing style leaves much to be desired and you find yourself constantly in conflict with her about her children's behavior, or she allows her family to constantly interfere in your relationship, in the long run such an environment could not only become toxic to the relationship but to you as well.

When individuals come together one of three things will happen: 1) The Karma you introduce will be accepted; 2) The Karma you introduce to her will be rejected or, 3) The Karma between you and her will form new Karma and you and her will develop a healthy system of co-existing together. Making these kinds of prudent observations and decisions about a potential relationship and delaying your quest for immediate gratification is expression of manly maturity and character. That *IS* manly maturity and character. One of the main consequences of not understanding how to use your powers, your tool kit and your blueprint for manhood is that you cannot properly navigate through the bad neighborhoods and streets of life and avoid obvious pothole-type situations of casual relationships. Men, gratification without navigation produces a lot of babies but fewer and fewer of those babies will have a chance to be a part of healthy relationships and healthy families if you continue to abuse your powers, especially your power of choice.

The most important point I'd like to leave you with about this chapter is that you will spend a lot more time standing up in an intimate relationship with a woman than you will lying down in a sexual/intimate position with her. Before you hook up with her or before you continue just spending time in the bed with her, you really need to spend more time observing who she is and gathering data (dating) and evaluating the woman that you have an interest in to find out if she is the right fit for you. It only take a few moments to have sexual intercourse, make love, "get it in" or whatever you want to call it, but the consequences of not putting more focus on the "stand up time" can and will last a lifetime for you and others. You gotta learn how to be a better "standup guy."

Finally, I'd like to suggest that should you already have a good woman in your life, do not make the mistake of stereotyping her or comparing her to someone else from your past life. She is not your mother, although she may do or say things that remind you of your mother. She certainly is not your ex, and never make the mistake of calling her by your ex's name, or dragging the trash from your ex to her doorstep. She is not the woman in the dirty magazine you've been looking at, nor the woman you see on television, in a movie or soap opera. But she is or may become your lady or wife and you should take the time and opportunity to find out who she really is. Take the time to discover who she is as an individual, her inner beauty, and intelligence despite whatever her profession may be.

Appreciate the way she keeps herself together despite the many pressures and challenges she contends with daily. Reflect on why you laugh at her jokes and how she always finds a way to boost your spirits when you're down and feeling less than a man. And although she may not do things exactly the way you want them done, or exactly at the time you want them done, you will see that she is a good mother to your children and you can understand why they call her mommy. It doesn't take much to see these things when you understand yourself, your purpose and vision as a man and your responsibilities, because then you will be in a position to see hers.

Chapter 14
Marriage Or Shacking, Which Way Do You Go?

"One who asks a question is a fool for five minutes. One who does not ask a question remains a fool forever." ~ *Chinese Proverb*

In Chapter 12, "*What Women Want*", I introduced you to qualities and expectations that I believe women want and look for in a romantic relationship with African American men. One of the qualities and expectations is the ability to make an exclusive commitment to them in a relationship. This is not surprising with an increasing number of brothers operating on the down low and the risk of contracting sexually transmitted diseases, especially HIV/AIDS, where the highest percentage of those infected are heterosexual African American women. But many brothers misinterpret the urgency to commit as an attempt by African American women to control them or put them on lockdown. While some of those concerns may be true, far more is at stake for women than handcuffing you to the bed at home while she goes about her day. A casual encounter on your part or a tryst with your secret lover could mean an encounter with infection or even death.

At the same time, your decision to commit to a woman by living with her, especially the bigger commitment of marriage has implications and responsibilities that extend to others. I've tried to impress upon you throughout **Stuck In Maleness**, that manhood is not about you, there are others tied to your purpose as a man. No book can or should purport to have the magical formula to replace what ultimately is a decision that involves many variables and unforeseen circumstances. When making the decision to live with someone or the more serious commitment to marry, there are many questions to be asked before going to the alter and many more that will arise long after the initial euphoria of a wedding ceremony has worn off.

In more traditional times, a man and woman remained with their parents until either was ready for marriage. When the man became gainfully employed and was in the position to support his bride to be, he proposed and sought the permission and blessings of her parents and then they got married. Eager to begin their new life together, the man and his new bride would move into their new home, sometimes with the help of either of their parents.

However, since traditional times, the nature of society and how men and women relate to each other has changed and so has the nature of relationships and how couples come together. The social, political and financial issues that most African American men and women face in their relationships has undergone tremendous change. Women as a whole, are now more educated, competent in the workplace, have more social, political and economic clout than was the case just 60 years ago. Many African American women openly compete with men in the workplace and, in some cases, they have surpassed African American men in education, political acumen and in earning power. While African Americans as a whole have benefited from these changes, in recent times it has been African American women who have become the major catalyst of change in African American communities nationwide. In the late 60's and early 70's, as African American men began to drop the leadership ball, African American women silently but consistently picked it up and made inroads into education, politics, industry, professional occupations, and socially.

In the 70's, African American women saw brothers lose focus, motivation, and begin the precipitous decline in self-worth and leadership that led many brothers to become *"stuck in maleness"* long before they knew it themselves. When anger and frustration towards society and its racist institutions began to be turned inward by African American men in self-destructive ways, African American women regrouped and changed their focus. Sisters realized that in order for them to survive they had to change how they lived and how they treated themselves. They realized that they could no longer merely rely on benevolent treatment from others, including African American men. It was during this period when African American women began to shift their thinking from waiting to be rescued by marriage to how they could become independent and self-reliant through their own efforts. Brothers were under attack by white society, messing up the rent money, going to jail and providing nothing but excuses to why they were not handling their responsibilities. In response, African American women began squirreling away money in the bank instead of leaving it under the mattress or in the sock drawer where they knew brothers would find it. They also started taking classes and pursuing higher education degrees to get ahead while many brothers were hanging out on the corner, getting high, or sitting in a jail cell blaming others for the problems they mostly created for themselves.

African American women have their jobs, apartments, houses, luxury cars, positions in government, education, businesses, and many have become politically and financially savvy. What I am saying to you my brothers, is this: African American women don't need you to come and rescue them anymore. Most African American women have the vision, purpose, and ability to rescue themselves. Instead, African American women want you to be a part of their life but not like in the past. Some brothers may take my words to be harsh or even offensive, but that is not my intention. Instead, my intention is to provide you with insight into yourselves, information on relationship dynamics you may not be aware of (or have neglected to use) and inspiration….I feel like preaching….to transform your life on your own terms. If you do not provoke change, change will provoke you.

The fact of the matter is, African American men and women need each other and we must work together in order to solve the problems that we jointly face in our relationships and in our communities. If you are a brother who has his own place, big or small, and you are paying your own way with a steady job, fine, that is a beautiful and responsible thing. Should you connect with a woman who also has her own place and a joint decision is made to live together, go for it. I would just caution you to think things through ahead of time before your final decision is made, especially to give up your place for hers. Consider how you will share the rent, will you buy a new place or remain in the old? How much will each contribute to the fixed expenses and how will you handle the variable expenses such as gas and electric? Will you both be on the lease or mortgage and be jointly responsible and if not, why not? It's a business transaction so it should be handled as such and put in writing outlining all terms and conditions <u>BEFORE</u> you move in.

Now if you've never had your own place but are considering moving in with a woman, I will suggest that you <u>NOT</u> do so until you learn to live on your own for a while, even if only a room, and live on your own for at least six months to a year and then revisit the idea later. Here's why:

<u>Why You Should First Live On Your Own</u>

- God bless the child (man) who has his own. Always demonstrate that you have what it takes to take care of you first, <u>*Before*</u> you try to participate in a joint effort with another person, especially a woman. You are not going to understand or appreciate the importance of maintaining employment, budgeting, paying bills on time, and learning to sacrifice what you want for what is needed, if you have never had to do it before. Don't be in a rush to play house before taking the time to learn how to take care of you.

- Remember our discussion from Chapter 10, *One Size Does Not Fit All*; if the woman you aim to move in with does not fit within the purpose you have for your life, don't try to fit into hers by moving in with her just because it may be sexually or financially convenient. The convenience you get today may very well become a major obstacle for you as you grow or begin to experience the difficulty of sharing close quarters with someone you already know had an agenda or lifestyle different than yours. If you are pressured to move or you are being forced to leave another living arrangement, again, it would be better to delay and live on your own than to live in an arrangement you already know is unfavorable.

- Never go into a living arrangement where you will be totally dependent upon another person, especially a woman. If you do not have a job, or financial resources, you do not have any leverage or power to participate as an equal partner. You have to be ready to give your 100% at all times. With nothing to contribute in the areas where it really counts (expenses) you are likely to find yourself being controlled or manipulated to do things you may not otherwise like to do. You would become an adult child to her because you lacked the purpose, vision, self-discipline, responsibility, and financial means to act upon things on your own.

- Respect. She is not going to respect you if you do not respect yourself enough not to place yourself in an inferior position. You will most likely become defensive and/or try to justify your position every time an issue of responsibility or bill paying arises in the relationship. In a living situation, a woman will respect your actions, not your words.

Finally, there could be potential problems because the woman/your lady will be living and functioning at a level and living in a lifestyle that is consistent with the purpose and vision she already has for *her life*, especially if she has children from a previous relationship. Here you come with your cell phone, PlayStation, XBox and some clothes trying to fit into a situation that was not created with you in mind. It's possible for this type of arrangement to work but not if you are not Response-Able and not if this type of scenario is already inconsistent with the vision you have for your own life. Achieving your vision requires maturity and patience.

If you already have your own place and are considering for your lady moving in with you, still keep focus on your purpose and vision, use your power of choice and think with your head closet to your shoulders rather than the one closer to your feet. Either way both you and your lady must consider your motivations for wanting to live together and discuss the opportunities and challenges that may arise.

Thoughts to Consider Before Moving In With Her

- What is it about your present living arrangement that you desire to change? Why? How will moving in with your lady solve the problem? Is it cost? Space? Increased intimacy? What is your motivation?

- Why do you wish to move in or share space with her? Can the needs you're seeking to satisfy be delayed until you are in a better position? Is the move desirable on both sides?

- What are the pros and cons of moving in? Can you get along with her 24/7? Is she stable? Will she be a negative influence on you?

- What are you bringing to the table; money, a steady job, furniture, a car, leadership? What about her? Will you bring enough to the table to have an equitable say in the overall affairs of the arrangement or will you become a dependent?

- Will you consistently be able to handle your portion of the bills and expenses, both fixed and variable? Is this move going to become an opportunity to move up to another level, and become more responsible, or will it become a move from the usual *"stuck in maleness"* playbook?

- Is she (or you) going to remain the primary lease holder? Will you/she provide towards any security deposit or equity in the home?

- Will the two of you have a written agreement separate from the lease on how you will share expenses and pay bills? You've seen the Judge Mathis Show; if it isn't in writing it doesn't exist, unless it's admitted by the other party. Moving in with someone is sort of a business arrangement that can become legally binding with monetary, credit and legal implications. You need to discuss these issues prior to moving in so that these issues will be spelled out ahead of time clearly and legally. The reason is some bills or expenses are steady while others fluctuate with increased usage, especially should friends or relatives frequent the premises. Jobs are lost; emergencies arise, so these payments and expense scenarios should be considered. Many friendships and marriages are destroyed over issues related to money.

- Is there or will there be any credit cards or loans involved? If so, what are the terms of repayment?

- How does existing or potential move-in relate to the vision you have for your life? Will the move-in be consistent with the direction you seek to take your life? Is she a part of your vision, plan?

- What does your heart say about the move-in? What does your head say (the one on your shoulders) Are they in agreement? If not, why not?

Some couples, however, continue to shack up for years to where it appears to everyone else that they are married anyway. But they never fully commit to each other and they never provide their partner with the emotional, financial or social benefits that go along with marriage. In addition, unless your lady actually agrees with not wanting to get married herself, continuing to live with her but not loving her enough to go the extra step and propose marriage speaks volumes about how you feel about her as a person and as a woman.

It may also mean that you are with the wrong woman for the right reasons or you are with the right woman but for the wrong reasons. Every woman has within her the characteristics to become a queen of royalty whether her castle is in the projects, suburbs, a trailer park, or at the end of a long winding dirt road. Marriage may not be the ultimate goal for every relationship; you have to decide what's best for you. But I do believe that marriage is and should be a form of relationship royalty that has a higher status and calling than mere dating or friends with benefits, whether you are living together or not. Living with your lady for an extended period of time (three or more years) but at the same time denying her the respect, dignity, honor and the right (personally and publicly) that she deserves, is like playing the king of the castle but choosing not to share the throne with a queen. Instead you have a concubine that you have around for your personal pleasure and convenience. You have to make the decision for yourself. But a man *"stuck in maleness"* will let his relationship dictate his purpose, while a real man will allow his purpose as a man and his vision for his life to dictate his relationships. The casual attitude that many of our brothers have towards hooking up with women, from strictly a male perspective, certainly has its benefits. It requires less "leg work" between the time that you meet someone and the time that you may end up in bed with her, but without the formal courtship and the commitment that naturally may evolve over time. Besides, men *"stuck in maleness"* have a tendency to want to "hit it and quit it" because it suits their lifestyle and immature way of thinking. I certainly understand because during my more entrenched *"stuck in maleness"* days, I've been there and done that, but not without cost to myself and harm to many unsuspecting women. But let me share a different perspective with you. While there are many factors, such as age, education, income, occupation, and even the cultural norms of various racial groups that may influence both marital and divorce practices, research conducted by the National Survey of Family Growth, a subdivision of the Center for Disease Control and Prevention (CDC), suggest that there may be a link to cohabitation (shacking up) before marriage and the increased chances for divorce.

> *"One of the factors related to the likelihood of divorce from a first marriage is whether or not a person lives with a partner before marrying. It has been well documented that women and men who cohabit with their future spouse before first marriage are more likely to divorce than those who do not cohabit with their spouse before marriage"(41).*

These findings are inconclusive and certainly cannot be assumed across any and all age groups or racial, cultural or ethnic groups, but again marriage is not for everyone.

According to the Pew Research Center, in 1960, 72% of all adults ages 18 and older were married; today just 51% are. If current trends continue, the share of adults who are currently married will drop to below half within a few years. The Pew Research analysis also finds that the number of new marriages in the U.S. declined by 5% between 2009 and 2010, a sharp one-year drop that may or may not be related to the sour economy. In the United States, the declines have occurred among all age groups, but are most dramatic among young adults. Today, just 20% of adults ages 18 to 29 are married, compared with 59% in 1960. Over the course of the past 50 years, the median age at first marriage has risen by about six years for both men and women. It is not yet known whether today's young adults are abandoning marriage or merely delaying it. Even at a time when barely half of the adult population is married, a much higher share—72%—have been married at least once. However, this "ever married" share is down from 85% in 1960 (42).

During this same period, the divorce rate in the United States has fluctuated from a high of 5.3 divorces per 1,000 people in 1981 to its current rate of about 3.6 per 1,000 in 2009. Also, in 2009, 14 states had divorce rates for men that were significantly above the U.S. average (9.2 per 1,000 men), ranging from 10.0 to 13.5. In contrast, nine states had divorce rates for men significantly below the U.S. average, ranging from 6.1 to 8.5. Of the nine states with below average divorce rates for men, five states were located in the Northeast (New Jersey, New York, Connecticut, Pennsylvania)(43).

The current divorce rate percentage averages between 40%-50%. This is actually misleading because it refers to the divorce rate for first time marriages. When you compare first marriages to second marriages and third marriages the divorce rate becomes even more dismal. Fifty percent of first marriages, 67% of second marriages and 74% of third marriages end in divorce, according to Jennifer Baker of the Forest Institute of Professional Psychology in Springfield, Missouri (44). The top age category for divorce for both men and women is in the 20 to 24 year old range at 36.6% for women and 38.8% for men, respectively (45).

In addition to the above research, the reason I chose to include the above data on marriage applications and divorce was not to discourage you from getting married or from moving in with your lady. Statistics are just that, data on groups of people, large or small, which are not an indication of what will take place in your individual circumstances. But if there is any value to be gained from the information on marriage and divorce, is that you should take your decision to be in a relationship with someone seriously, especially when your relationship begins to move in the direction of becoming emotionally, financially and legally interconnected. In the absence of sounding like the marriage counselor, religious or spiritual advisor I am not, I have compiled a list of observations and questions as food for thought from my own experiences to help you work through your own relationship dilemma.

Thoughts To Consider Before Marriage

1. Do not marry unless you know and understand your purpose as a man and are willing to commit to it BEFORE you commit to the woman you're seeking to marry. Why? As a man you must always remain Response-Able regardless of the changes that may occur in your marriage or how you "feel." She may become ill, pregnant, disabled or you may decide that she is no longer for you. But as a man, you will still need to provide for her (or with her) until such time as you are no longer married because that is a part of your purpose.

2. Do not move in unless you have a clear and definable vision for your life. Why? Because as a man, a part of your purpose is to provide leadership for your wife and family. Where will you lead them to if you do not have a vision, goals, and plans on how you propose to get there? You must have a sense of direction to offer your present or future family.

3. Do not marry a woman who has not taken the time to learn and understand her purpose as a woman. If your lady does not have an idea of her purpose as a woman she will not likely be capable of participating in a relationship with you, certainly not a marriage relationship. While not all roles in a marriage are gender specific, she should not be attempting to be both mother and father to children,

for example. Having made needed changes in your thinking and now understanding your purpose as a man, the last thing you need is a female version of a purposeless, visionless woman, stuck in …… femaleness.

4. Do not marry a woman who does not have a vision for her life. Why? If she does not know where she wants to go in life and how she is going to get there she will likely resist or be disagreeable to whatever vision you have.

5. Do not marry unless or until you are already capable of providing food, clothing and shelter for yourself. Why? How will you provide for the both of you should she become ill, pregnant or lose her job if you can't even take care of you? Marriage is more than about love and romance, it's also about business.

6. Do not marry a woman you do not respect as a human being or as a woman. Why? When you do not respect someone, you are more likely to look at them as an object or a possession, less human. People have a tendency to abuse things or people when they no longer like them or no longer have any use for. Everyone deserves respect so if you do not respect her, leave her alone. It may also be an indication that you do not respect yourself.

7. Do not marry a woman you have not taken the time to befriend as a person. Why? With marriage come both, opportunities and challenges that may place strain on your relationship such as arguments, fights or un-

resolvable disagreements. You will be in a better position to withstand these challenges and makeup with someone whom you really love and appreciate as a friend in addition to her being your wife.

8. Do not marry a woman just because she looks good or because you are physically attracted to her. Why? Looks are deceiving, plenty of women look good but do not work, cook, clean and believes that you should just be happy that you have them. Re-read Chapter 11, *"One Size Doesn't Fit All"*, for additional insight.

9. Do not marry a woman that you cannot totally be honest with about who you are, who you were, or want to become as a man. Why? A relationship not built on honesty is built upon lies. If you are not truthful and comfortable with yourself, neither will she. Embellishing your personal attributes or hiding your faults will not really change who you are but it can permanently damage your relationship and/or marriage later. Eventually the truth will come out and so will your deception. You build upon the truth but telling lies will sink you into a bottomless pit. Trying to maintain a false image of who you are is one of the attributes of being *"stuck in maleness"*. Avoid it.

10. Do not marry a woman whom you feel you have to change. This is the flip side of the coin of number 9 above. Women are not like chickens that can be stuffed, garnished or fattened up to our liking. They have

personalities, character and physical attributes that are specific to them and may not change, at least not in the way we'd want them to. No one is perfect. If you can't accept her the way she is, good or bad, then certainly do not marry her. Do damage control and follow both your heart and your head. One size does not fit all. You can only change you.

When you make the decision to live with your lady (or any woman) and/or the more serious decision to get married, your decision should not be made without considerable introspection and forethought. Your motivation, your ability to handle financial and emotional responsibilities, and your purpose as a man are but a few of the factors you must consider before moving in with her or her with you. Is she the one for you and is living together or marriage the way for you to uncover the answer to that very important question? Relationships, moving in, or marriage should be about more than immediate gratification but also about purpose, vision and where you want to take your life.

Chapter 15
The Spirit of Manhood

"Our strength grows out of our weakness. The indignation which arms itself with secret forces does not awaken until we are pricked and stung and sorely assaulted. When man is pushed, tormented, defeated he has a chance to learn something; he has been put on his wit, on his manhood, he has gained facts, learns his ignorance, is cured of the insanity of conceit, has got moderation and real skill." ~Ralph Waldo Emerson

When I was *"stuck in maleness"*, before I began to change the way I thought about manhood, I thought I was "all that and a bag of chips." In my mind, life was about women, cars, clothes, drinking, drugging, hanging out with the boys and the pursuit of "things" I thought would make my life happy. I was very anti-spiritual because the more I thought about and pursued things, the less I thought about and cared for the people in my life. Spiritual men understand their connection to others and they do things to improve and nurture their connection and relationships with others. When I pursued things I became extremely selfish and self-centered. Everything was about me; what *I* felt, what *I* liked, what *I* wanted, when *I* wanted it, and what was convenient for me. Others, including my lady and children were secondary; at least that is what I believed. I was stuck in my maleness game.

I behaved sort of like an ostrich and I kept my head buried in a hole, in the sands of my own pleasure or problems while at the same time I gave the world my ass to kiss, figuratively speaking. I disregarded all that was going on around me; I shunned responsibility and I could care less about the impact my thinking and behavior was having on others. I was like a modern day Jonah, from biblical times. If you are not into church or reading the Bible, that's ok; you don't have to be in order to benefit from the meaning of the story so please bear with me for a few lines. In the story, God places a purpose on Jonah's life by telling him to go to the people of Nineveh to change their wicked ways (Jonah, 1:2). Jonah did not want to carry out the purpose God had given him so he fled and boarded a ship to a faraway land hoping to avoid his calling, his purpose. But God was not to be shunned and caused a great wind to blow against the ship on which Jonah was traveling. The tempest beat against the ship so hard and forcibly that it caused fear and discomfort to the unsuspecting crew members of the ship. What made this short but powerful biblical significant to me is that unlike Jonah, I had not been made aware of the real purpose God had for my life, but just like Jonah, God disciplined me and made it uncomfortable for the unsuspecting people in my life (or the unsuspecting people in your life), who were also connected to my purpose as a man. I ran away from my purpose through the use of drugs, alcohol, women, hanging with the boys and the pursuit of things, while Jonah simply slept the time away in the bowels of a ship headed for a foreign land.

Because of the intensity of the storm that beat about the ship, fearing for their lives, the crew members woke Jonah up from his sleep and confronted him as to his real purpose for being on their ship. They reasoned that Jonah seemed to be a little too comfortable in the midst of the storm while others feared for their lives. Men, you may be able to relate to some aspects of this story through experiences in your own life. While *"stuck in maleness"*, you may have pulled people in your life into the bowels of your selfish thinking and destructive behaviors. You may have placed their lives at risk by the negative things that you were doing. But when they confronted you about your behavior out of love, concern or friendship, your ego got in the way. "I'm alright!" "I'm good." "I'm a grown ass man! I can take care of myself!" "Why don't you mind your own business?" But there you were, in the depths of despair, addiction, alcoholism, negativity, denial, unemployed, or even without a penny to your name, stuck into your maleness game, but there is always a way out, you have to be willing to change and take it. God, through the very same friends, family members, loved ones, or others (God works through our relationships) that you have pushed away decided there needed to be a change in your life and He sent those same people to help you. You may need to be fired from your job, kicked out the house by your lady, locked up in a jail cell....or thrown overboard, like the crew did to Jonah, so you can get the real impact of what is taking place in your life. This is my testimony. Without those sudden changes you would continue to live stuck in your maleness game, messing up your life and everyone in it.

After being thrown overboard, God placed Jonah in captivity by causing him to be swallowed up by a big fish (a whale) for three days and three nights until he repented and resumed the calling of his purpose. Where are you now? Are you in captivity? What has been your form of captivity? What does it take for you to recognize, understand, and to use the disciplines of life that God has been providing for you so you too can become aware of your real purpose as a man? Be honest with yourself and think these things through.

After three days and three nights, Jonah had plenty of time to reflect upon his purpose and decided (he used his power of choice) to repent. It was during this time that Jonah received his second commission from God to go unto the city of Nineveh and preach the word to the people about their wicked ways. It was then that God (stay with me) spoke to the big fish and caused the fish to vomit Jonah out onto the shores of dry land. Once Jonah did as God commissioned him, despite the long and arduous journey before him, he preaches to the people of Nineveh; they repent from their wickedness and are granted mercy.

What have you learned from your moments of captivity (jail, prison, drug addiction, homelessness, sleeping on someone's sofa, or being shunned by family and friends)? What have you learned from the disciplines of your life? When we go through things in life and are faced with adversities we have two choices; we can either let it help *Design* who we are or *Destroy* who we are. How long do you intend to remain *"stuck in maleness"* of your own making, deceptively blaming others for the circumstances only *YOU* can make the decision to change? What will it take for you to accept your purpose and responsibility as a man so the people in your life....your wife, lady, children, parents, siblings....can experience God's mercy, blessings and prosperity? As a man you have to learn to be resilient, which is the process of adapting well in the face of adversity. Resilient means "bouncing back" from difficult experiences. In the words of Dr. Martin Luther King, Jr:

> *"The ultimate measure of a man is not where he stands in moments of comfort and convenience, but where he stands at times of challenge and controversy."*

Dear brothers, you have been made aware of your powers, the tools at your disposal and you have been given your Blueprint for Manhood so that you can navigate your way (with God's help) out of being *"stuck in maleness"*. There is no shortcut or easy way but the way you and only you need to go. You do not have to continue aimlessly and purposely meandering about your life. Drinking, drugging, abusing, freeloading, screwing everything that moves or standing on every street corner in America with other purposeless and anti-spirited males who also act and think like life is all about them. You now know that that kind of thinking is false; it's a thinking error. Men, real men, understand that there is more to life than themselves. So get off the sofa, get a job, stop being defensive and insecure about your manhood. Take on God as a partner; take on the mind of the One who created you.

Manhood, a Condition of Your Mind

Now, let's get back to our friend, Jonah. Once Jonah received his second commission from God, he preached to the people of Nineveh as instructed and all of them, led by their King, repented and changed their ways and worshipped God. But Jonah, not happy with his purpose and the way things turned out, lost focus. He became disgruntled with God and he did not continue to follow his purpose and lead the people as his purpose required. In a sense, Jonah relapsed back into selfishness, self-centeredness and became *"stuck in maleness"*, again. Men, in order to remain a good leader, you got to know how to follow instructions, the right values and principles of which good leadership is based. Manhood is a condition of your mind so you must always remain "plugged in" to the mind transforming power of the One who created you and the principles on which good leadership is based. You see, your disease, *"stuck in maleness"*, will always be there waiting for you (just like Jonah) to become selfish again. It will be there waiting for you to resume operating your mind based upon thinking errors, myths and misconceptions about manhood and for the strongholds of your past to re-take hold of your mind, so you must stay plugged into your purpose as a man.

The nature of your *"stuck in maleness"* disease may be different from the next man. It's origins; drugs, alcohol, childhood trauma, abuse, materialistic, momma's boy mentality, attitude of entitlement, and so on, may reveal itself in different ways and cause you to act out in different ways. But remember, the man who sits in a jail cell because he sold drugs on a street corner is no different than the man who, after removing his business suit or uniform at the end of the day and lies in bed next to the woman he beats before going to sleep, are not really different from each other. They both lack knowledge of self, self-respect, respect for others or an understanding of what it means to be a man. They both are *"stuck in maleness"* and suffer from the same disease. They both fell down, so to speak, and they both need to get back up again.

Men, real men, get back up when they fall or falter. Every time you fall should be an opportunity to learn (OTL). Every time you fall, reflect, check your swagger, your tool kit (your choices and belief system) and review your Blueprint for Manhood. Review your purpose and make the adjustments in the way you are navigating your life. Stay focused on your vision.

In Chapters 2, 3, and 4, I introduced you to seven African American men who suffered from thinking errors that, in varying degrees, caused them to become *"stuck in maleness"* as I've defined it throughout the chapters of this book. Thinking errors are an attempt to reason or draw logical conclusions based upon faulty or incomplete information that becomes a part of one's belief system, thinking and behavior patterns. African American men (males) are particularly at risk of engaging in thinking errors and becoming *"stuck in maleness"* due to latent psychological effects from slavery and the social, political, economic and educational influences of racial discrimination. These influences have either hindered African American men's access to meaningful experiences as a part of their development into manhood or, most importantly, have had the psychologically crippling effect of deceiving African American men into believing they lack motivation or the power within themselves to achieve success and to overcome their own marginal position within American society. I beg to differ. The reality is that African American men have always possessed within themselves the inherent God-given abilities to survive difficult challenges, to be creative and to effectuate change. What African American men lacked was a blueprint for manhood that addressed the issues of racism, and the barriers it creates, while also providing direction and viable tools and solutions to solving daily living issues. The good news is that change is at your fingertips; you can overcome the limiting disease of being *"stuck in maleness"*.

All of the men I introduced in the beginning Chapters have in different ways, been able to extricate themselves from being *"stuck in maleness"* and, so can you. Charles, the husband and father of two boys, thought that referring to himself as a "grown ass man," while pounding on his chest with an open hand, was sufficient to proclaim his manhood to his wife but he later learned that manhood involves much more than mere words. Through a mentoring relationship with his boss he became aware of his self-centered and immature attitude towards his family and his job. Charles began to understand that his life was no longer just about him and what he wanted. He changed his attitude about responsibility and what it required of him, and he was later promoted into a supervisory position within the company. Charles continues to hang out with his friends but only on weekends. Charles made the decision to include his wife and children in activities that now involve his friends and their families. He has placed less emphasis on drinking and spends more time doing things that involve his wife and boys.

Nick, the 25 year-old drug dealer who lived on top of the furniture store with his mother and sold drugs mostly as a way to appease his demanding and manipulating girlfriend, made the decision to stop selling drugs and get a job. Nick enrolled part-time in community college to study graphic arts, an interest he's had since high school. Nick moved out of his mother's apartment and now shares an apartment near the college with another student. Nick left his girlfriend and told her he needed to be on his own more than he needed to risk his freedom just to get sex from someone who really didn't care about him anyway. He reasoned that his freedom wasn't worth the risk of incarceration or toxic relationship that he and his girlfriend had.

Clarence, the 47 year-old government employee married to the pediatrician, whose feelings of inferiority towards his wife caused him to become abusive towards her whenever he drank alcohol, has stopped drinking. Clarence stopped drinking because he realized that he still felt the same way about himself when the alcohol wore off. He's now a regular attendee at an AA (Alcoholics Anonymous) group meeting composed mostly of professionals where he openly discusses his feelings of low self-worth and inferiority. Clarence has learned that there are other people who drink for similar reasons as he does, even doctors and lawyers, who make lots of money. Prior to his marriage, Clarence enjoyed cooking and he often entertained and cooked for friends, which is how he met his wife nearly 20 years ago.

Urged by several members of his AA group, who have become his friends, Clarence decided to take up cooking again. He now invites friends over for dinner parties and luncheons instead of going out to restaurants where he'd feel uncomfortable whenever his wife paid the bill. Clarence's wife really likes the change in his attitude and how he treats her. She sees a new self-confidence and gentleness in Clarence that she never knew existed. Some of Clarence's wife's professional colleagues have even paid Clarence for hosting and catering professional events and some of their own dinner parties where Clarence makes a sizeable fee for doing what he enjoys. Clarence's wife likes to sit and plan these events with Clarence but she is mindful not to take over and respects and enjoys his need to take the lead in these events.

Frank, my 51 year-old friend who lived with his mother and was obsessed with the image that expensive cars and the appearance of success the cars provided, still lives with his mother. But Frank has now become his mother's caregiver instead of being a care receiver. Within the past 18 months, Frank's mother became ill and could no longer drive and care entirely for herself without assistance. Frank made the decision to sell his Mercedes Benz and bought a 5 year-old Ford pickup truck and an enclosed trailer. Frank continues to work at his job of 18 years and has also started a lawn care business which he operates mostly on the weekend. Every Sunday morning Frank picks up his boys for church and Sunday school. On days when Frank mows lawns, the boys hang out with their grandmother, who appreciates their company and the extra help on days when she is not feeling well. Frank's change in behavior has caught the attention of his children's mother, who is not seeing anyone and has invited him over for dinner on both Thanksgiving and Christmas. Frank has his eye on a duplex in his neighborhood as an investment and a source of income to pay for the private school he wants his sons to attend next year.

Change for Jamal, the 32 year-old former football star athlete, whose competitive nature and zeal for winning placed a strain on his relationship with his son and wife came from an unlikely source; his son. One evening while walking past the open door to his son's bedroom, Jamal overheard his son talking to his best friend about his much he enjoys coming over to his house because his father takes the time to show him how to do things and lets him win at checkers. Jamal was crushed; he adored his son but was unaware that his behavior was pushing his son towards another man who, according to his son, was a better father. Jamal wondered if his wife was having similar thoughts about their relationship as well. He feared the worst.

Jamal moped around the house after work for days, avoiding eye contact with both his wife and his son. But after some soul searching and the realization that his addiction to winning was costing him his family, Jamal made the decision that it was time he started acting like a coach and leader instead of the egotistical star football player who garnered all of the praise and attention. He came to realize that his role as a father and husband was not about him at all, but his family, and he wasn't going to lose them just so he could win at another silly game.

G-Money, the drug dealer and womanizer on Section 8, who prided himself on his ability to get over on the "system", has undergone the most significant changes in his life. While serving 14 months of a 3 year sentence for drug possession, G-Money, now known as brother Lateef, became a Muslim and enrolled in a program to become a licensed barber. Upon release from prison, G-Money (Lateef) obtained a job in a popular unisex hair salon. Six months later, Lateef, along with another former inmate turned Muslim, opened their own barbershop on a busy street in an urban downtown district. Lateef's favorite activity is to pick up his 8 year-old daughter every Friday and watch as she takes gymnastics classes at a nearby gymnastics studio. Lateef mentors ex-cons returning from prison at the mosque he attends. He wants to sponsor a boy's little league baseball team in the future.

Darryl, the 30 year-old lab tech who slept on his parent's sofa for nearly a year after breaking up with his fiancé Tiana, has been the most resistant to change. After another six months on his parent's sofa, and a nasty blow up with his father, Darryl continued to drag his feet about getting his own place. Darryl mistakenly thought the issue to be money and began to give his parents money every month for room and board but simply didn't think that the money could be used to pay for his own apartment. It wasn't until returning home from work late one Saturday evening did Darryl see the "For Sale" sign firmly stuck into the front lawn near the sidewalk, did he finally get the message that his parents wanted him out.

Darryl's parents wanted their privacy back but observed how resistant (*"stuck in maleness"*) Darryl was to doing things on his own, so they decided to give him a push. They were selling their home and moving into an adult community for people aged 55 and over. Darryl's mother had just turned 55 and wanted her life back. Darryl got the message and now lives on his own in a one bedroom apartment. He has begun to date an energetic insurance executive from a nearby community but continues to struggle with doing things on his own.

Big Tank ended up going to prison for violating a restraining order and assaulting one of his many girlfriends. Although incarcerated, Big Tank took advantage of counseling and an educational support group for inmates who have a history of domestic violence. Occasionally, Big Tank is asked to co-facilitate the support group by the instructor which he enjoys doing.

To my brothers in prison who may be reading this book, you have not been forgotten. You must use your time wisely and reflect on the cause of your incarceration. No, I am not referring to your physical imprisonment. Your incarceration is not to be blamed upon your parents, the "white man", racism, discrimination, a "snitch", or because you may be poor. These are excuses and you must abandon them if you are truly to be free. Your incarceration is first and foremost psychological; it is a condition of your mind. Only a transformation of your mind (belief system) and the spirit within you, can free you. Your freedom begins and ends in your mind. Reflect back to that day, that moment when you confused manhood with violence, theft, selling drugs, rape, robbery, or even murder. I have been there with you. If you do not reflect, you will not begin to understand why you sit, stand and peer out of a jail cell onto the walkway like a caged animal. Use your time to reflect upon the people you've left behind, the babies, the woman you rely on for a letter, visit, or to accept your collect phone call. Think about them and what your version of manhood has done for them, done to them.

If you reflect, you will realize that you are not the man you thought yourself to be, not because you do not have a good man within you; rather, you have been misled by others that manhood, your manhood, is outside of you.

And if you listen to the voices of the other inmates and the stories being told by them, you will realize that you are not alone. They too have been tricked, deceived, bamboozled and lured into believing the lies told to them by the larger societal forces and other men *"stuck in maleness"* as well. But do not be dismayed, because some of the greatest men, real men, in history did not start out that way. They became great because they learned to reflect, learn from their mistakes and rose up to break the cycle of deception and mediocrity. They kept getting up when they fell down, again and again. They refused to be relegated to a cell, mentally or physically, because they came to understand their purpose in life and that manhood was a condition of their mind and they refused to continue wasting their minds, stuck on stupid.

Chapter 16
Final Thoughts and Our Responsibility as Men

Because of the unwritten but omnipresent racial policies operating within the United States, and changes in the social, political, and economic playing field (driven by fear and the quest for more profits), African Americans must re-think former outdated ways of doing things. The racial clocks of history have been turned back against African Americans, although they operate in a sleeker and more sophisticated manner.

African Americans must re-think and revise what is needed and what will be needed to progressively move forward if we are to remain an integral part of American society, lest the entire African American male species risk banishment into jail cells and prisons of profit warehoused on the outskirts of every rural and small town community in American society.

The nature of American society has undergone a great deal of change for the vast majority of African Americans. The most far reaching of those changes is being played daily in the lives of tens of thousands of African American men in a way that can only be described as epidemic. Daily, a silent but devastating war is being waged against African Americans in their homes, neighborhoods, communities, and in major institutions across the American landscape. As with any war, there are opposing enemy forces (African American males), defending troops, attack strategies, collateral casualties, and artillery. The artillery used in this war are weapons of mass destruction, but not the kind of weapons of mass destruction used as political jargon to distract the American people from the real issues at hand. These weapons of mass destruction are deceptively and furtively used against targeted citizens of this country under the disguise of making our country better, greater, and more secure by rooting out the presumed "undesirable elements" of society but instead it has and is creating a caste of emasculated African American men. African American men must re-think and re-define what it means to be a man and, the best ways to pursue and realize that manhood under the current system of operation, not an elusive and imaginary society of times past. The Bible in Proverbs 29:18 states, *"A people without a vision will perish."* African American men are perishing physically, socially and symbolically within American society for pursuing a vision that is not our own. We must revise our vision of what it means to be a man, as black men in American society in order for our manhood to be functional, for it to mean something to ourselves, to our families and to other men and women in this country.

Despite the election of President Barack Obama to a second term in office, the lens by which we presently look at our place within the present society is no longer functional, adequate or applicable. The present state of affairs in education, employment, housing, industry, and the disproportionate number of African American (and Latino) men who are being herded up like human cattle within the criminal justice system for profit continues to harm us in many ways. Daily, tens of thousands of black and brown African American elementary and high school children across this country are being arrested and taken from classrooms of learning and placed in jail cells and holding pens destined for a later social death while being warehoused and incarcerated in prisons for acts that are anything but criminal, but they are made criminal by the perspective of overzealous quota-driven law enforcement officials anxious to save their jobs. The only crime these innocent black and brown children can be found guilty of is that someone views them as being born the wrong color, the wrong race, attending the wrong schools and living in the wrong part of town. Like other children, little black and brown African American boys and girls aspire to become doctors, lawyers, teachers, writers, policemen (and women), computer professionals, nurses or engineers.

But unlike other children African American children daily are subjected to systemic forces beyond their perception or control that operate to snub out their dreams, hopes, and aspirations, to rob them of their innocence, like a thief in the night. The invisible but omnipresent forces of men and women eager to turn a profit and to maintain the status quo, continues to operate even if it means that the precious youth and lives of these innocent African American children will be sacrificed. So we as African American men, and the fathers, uncles, brothers, cousins, and grandfathers of those children, must develop a new vision for the future and re-define what it means to be a man, an a African American, black or brown man, in American society. We must "let go of the old and reach for a new thing" (Isaiah 43:18-20) and become new men of the new millennium.

African American men must unify and no longer allow ourselves, our children or our families to fall victim to the old tactics of divide and conquer. African American men must come together and no longer allow outside forces, the opinions of others or insecurities, dysfunctional ideas about manhood or poor choices to deceive us into behaving in selfish and self-serving ways of thinking that pit us against our women or against ourselves because self-hate is terminal.

As African American men, continuing to think in the old ways drives a wedge in our ability to move forward and continues to divide our households and our communities. Anger, self-hate, self-recrimination, hate for others and the "me-me" syndrome can longer be the driving force behind our thoughts or our actions. Along with the larger emasculating forces that operate against us within society, our self-sabotaging behaviors keeps African American men in a perpetual state of inertia *"stuck in maleness"* and hinders our ability to experience our manhood as we can and should be. Thinking in these ways keeps us blind and impotent to the needs of our families, the responsibilities of manhood as men within American society. It keeps African American men as a whole in a perpetual state of "acting like" men instead of living as men. **Stuck In Maleness** was written with the purpose of meeting the call for a new vision and blueprint for

African American men as a starting point to begin the mind-transforming process of becoming vision and purpose-driven men of healthy character who actively meet the needs of our children, our families, our communities, as the men God created us to be.

"Our strength grows out of our weakness. The indignation which arms itself with secret forces does not awaken until we are pricked and stung and sorely assaulted. When man is pushed, tormented, defeated he has a chance to learn something; he has been put on his wit, on his manhood, he has gained facts, learns his ignorance, is cured of the insanity of conceit, has got moderation and real skill."
~Ralph Waldo Emerson

Russ Ligon
2014

Summary of What You Learned In Chapter 1

1. There is a crisis growing within the United States that threatens to destroy the African American family that is manifesting it's most visible and destructive effects on a systemic "institutional" level and on an individual "mental" level amongst African American men.

2. African American men embrace corrupted and dysfunctional images about manhood that are self-sabotaging and unhealthy expressions of manhood.

3. As was the case during the former institution of slavery, the purpose of the existing system is to break the will and spirit of African American men by treating them like animals by creating pool of outcasts through incarceration and creating dependence on the "system."

4. Violence, substance abuse, gang membership, chronic unemployment, incarceration, and the expectation of an early death have become the constant but unwanted bedfellows in the daily life of many African American men.

5. Some African American men may begin to question their manhood and engage in unhealthy lifestyles when they are unable to obtain viable employment.

6. Having women or others take care of you, such as a governmental agency, is not a healthy expression of manhood. Both hinders and cripples healthy maturity into manhood.

7. Conducting oneself as a man does not only assume knowledge of correct manly values and principles but also consistent opportunities in mainstream society to experience the many roles and demands that manhood implies.

8. As men, when we lack the proper understanding of manhood, we tend to act out in self-centered and self-destructive ways towards ourselves, our families and our communities.

9. During childhood and the early teenage years, males have the opportunity to observe impressionable interaction between their parents and learn what is expected of them as males, members of a family unit and as men.

10. Manhood or becoming a man is not really about the man, it is about responding with your God-given and learned skills and abilities towards the people and circumstances that God places in your life.

11. African American women sometimes participate in the self-sabotaging and crippling thinking and behavior demonstrated by African American men.

12. In order for African American men to become healthy, and for the African American family to survive as a viable social unit, there must be a transforming and renewing experience in the minds of African American men.

Summary of What You Learned In Chapter 2

1. Domestic violence is a pattern of abusive behavior in any relationship that is used to gain or maintain power and control over another intimate partner.
2. Domestic violence and abuse are learned behaviors that usually evolve out of a history of either being abused or witnessing the abuse of others. There are many additional factors that can exacerbate the tendency towards abusive such as exposure to social violence, poverty, unemployment/underemployment and personal feelings of inadequacy.
3. All African American men are at risk of committing domestic violence because of our history of the social, political, economic and physical abuse that is regularly directed towards us within American society.
4. It's deceptive to think that putting down a woman and/or seeking to control her can elevate you as a man because it can't.
5. Many men displace their insecurities, weaknesses, addictions, and money problems onto the people closest to them, mainly a woman.
6. Your sense of impotence and lack of personal control must be addressed within and not violently and abusively towards a woman.
7. The tendency towards domestic violence and abuse are sometimes the unfortunate outcome of choosing to align ourselves with the wrong woman for the wrong reasons.
8. Women are not other men and should not be treated that way.
9. There is nothing unmanly about getting help for abusive and controlling behavior; domestic violence often has multiple victims.

10. Abusive and controlling behavior is one the many signs of being *"stuck in maleness"*.

Summary of What You Learned in Chapter 3

1. There is a person inside of every man or woman. Sometimes we hide the real person that we are inside behind "faces" or images to protect us so that people will not see who we really are on the inside. Usually these protective faces or images are developed in childhood when society, usually our parents, relatives or close friends, try and shape us into who they think we should be and/or we become fearful and do not want to take the risk of revealing who we really are. Either way a face is developed that covers up who we really are on the inside.

2. A pattern of not revealing who we really are may cause us to begin to develop more entrenched behaviors towards ourselves and others by interacting with them from the outside-in versus the inside-out where living up to the image or face takes the place of who we really are on the inside.

3. In order to move from relying on the many faces that we may have developed as a shield to hide who we really are on the inside, we have to make change, i.e., go inside and look at who we really are and sort through the various parts of us. We have positive and good qualities but we also may have parts of us that need to be changed. Some of the changes that we make can come about through our own efforts, while others parts may need to involve the help of a support group, counselor or even a therapist.

4. You are not your environment. Instead, you may have developed reactions or response patterns to the people, places and things within your environment. No matter what, you are still in control of you. You always have the power within you to think, reflect, plan and to make choices and decisions about the course of your life.

5. Oftentimes the faces or images that we develop are in response to efforts to please our friends so that they will find us more acceptable or so that we can retain their friendship. Real friends should accept you for who and whatever you are and not try and change you. If your friends don't support the *REAL* you, get new ones!

In order for you to take control of your life and begin expression the real you, you gotta set boundaries. Boundaries are like property lines that define who you are and who you are not, and influence all areas of your life. Physical boundaries help you determine who may touch you and under what circumstances. Mental boundaries give the freedom to have your own thoughts and opinions. Emotional boundaries help you deal with your own emotions and disengage from the harmful, manipulative emotions of others.

Summary of What You Learned In Chapter 4

1. Manhood is the condition of being an adult male (18 years of age or older) and possessing the qualities (intellectual, behavioral, physical, character) associated with manliness.
2. An image is a mental (mind) picture or conception, the ability of the mind to call up mental pictures; the power to imagine.
3. Our belief system is an individual or institutional set of attitudes, behaviors and practices.
4. A misconception or to misconceive is to interpret information incorrectly.
5. Myths are usually legendary narratives that present part of the beliefs of a people or explains a practice or natural phenomena; an imaginary (mental) or unverifiable person or thing.
6. Thinking errors are an attempt to reason or draw logical conclusions about yourself or others, based upon faulty or incomplete information.
7. Three areas that exert tremendous negative influences on the concept of manhood amongst African American males (and others) are: 1) movies; 2) rap music and, 3) gangs.
8. Rap music is a form of artistic expression and communication that can be negative or positive, empowering or destructive.
9. Edutainment is a term coined by KRS-One of Boogie Down Productions, which refers to using the entertaining aspect of

rap to also educate its listeners about social problems, politics or economic issues that affect them.

10. Rap music can, if used positively, be used to empower youth, people and others such as with voter registration during 2008 with President Barack Obama's presidential campaign.

11. Black males who base their manhood primarily on the pursuit of things or imitating others are more likely to imitate negative behavior or lifestyles than positive.

12. Collectively, movies, rap music and gangs create a form of domination culture and exert tremendous influence over the thinking and behavior of African American males.

13. African American males join gangs because they lack a father or strong male figure at home that can provide structure, discipline, proper role modeling and a sense of belonging.

14. Some of the negative influences of rap music on the attitudes and behaviors of young people and other listeners, including African American men are:

- Promotes disrespectful, rebellious and anti-authority attitudes through its lyrics and videos.
- Promotes a false male bravado that black males (and others) feel that they have to live up to in order to be accepted.
- Enforces negative and degrading stereotypes about both African American people and women in general.

- It has become a negative form of domination culture for millions of young people, primarily African American males.
- Through its lyrics and videos it has become a primary gateway to substance abuse, gang affiliation and violent behavior.

Summary Of What You Learned In Chapter 5

1. To be *"stuck in maleness"* means that you have not, cannot, or will not, make the full maturational transition from boyhood or the actions of a boy or teen, into the thinking, actions and attitude required and expected of a man.

2. Manhood is a state of being that directs and influences the attitude, behavior and thinking patterns of men (adult males) to engage in actions that are proactive and productive towards himself and/or the people that he is responsible for.

3. Manhood is the condition of a man's mind.

4. Thinking errors are attempts to draw logical conclusions based upon faulty or illusory thinking.

5. The imagery and pictures behind our thoughts produces real outcomes on out attitudes and behavior.

Summary Of What You Learned In Chapter 6

1. To be *"stuck in maleness"* means that you have not, cannot or will not, make the full maturational transition from boyhood or the actions and behaviors of a boy or teen into the thinking and behavior required and expected of a mature man.

2. Men are more left brain oriented than women. The left brain houses the brain's logical, analytical and aggressive components. Self-worth is the overall sense of value, deservedness, and self-respect that we have for ourselves.

3. Self-worth is a self-imposed value rating of ourselves that we subconsciously carry around everywhere we go.

4. Tendencies are your subconscious mind's inclination toward certain types of behavior.

5. Self-esteem (associated with self-confidence) refers to liking or feeling good about yourself, your appearance, or your abilities.

6. Imagination is the power of our mind to form mental images or concepts of something that is unreal or not present.

7. Our imagination is a part of a larger system called our belief system. Our belief system is an individual or institutional set of values, principles, practices and attitudes.

8. Our belief system contains "maps" that give direction to our attitudes, thinking and our behavior.

9. Traumatic and/or negative experiences in life, particularly in childhood, may have caused the development of strongholds in our mind which influenced us to become *"stuck in maleness"* and/or harmful and counterproductive behaviors.

10. A stronghold is a psychological barrier in our mind that hinders our ability to think clearly and rationally.

11. Becoming *"stuck in maleness"* is a learned behavior.

12. The institution of slavery and it's offspring, racial discrimination has produced "cultural strongholds" in the minds of many African American men.

13. A thinking error is an attempt to draw logical conclusions based upon faulty or incomplete information.

14. How we feel about ourselves, especially when our self-worth is low, can create a tendency in us towards self-sabotaging behavior.

15. The issue with our self-worth is that we subconsciously choose or attract into our life those people and experiences we believe we deserve based upon our inner sense of value.

16. Many of the thinking errors and behaviors associated with being *"stuck in maleness"* began or were leaned in childhood.

17. Remnants of slavery and racism have and continue to the growth and development of African American males into manhood and play a part in some African American men who become *"stuck in maleness"*.

18. A syndrome is a group or series of behaviors, thinking patterns or attitudes with a common cause or conditions.

19. Low self-worth, low self-esteem, inferiority complexes, attitudes of entitlement, displaced anger and reverse racism are some of the mindsets that exacerbate the tendency of African American men to become stuck in maleness.

20. Being *"stuck in maleness"* is a condition of a man's mind that can be overcome.

Summary Of What You Learned In Chapter 7

1. Being *"stuck in maleness"* is when we think and act in ways that hinder or prevent us from maturing into manhood or that keeps us from reaching our full potential as a men.

2. If you are not already a spiritual man, you will become one.

3. Your imagination is the headlight of your belief system.

4. Your belief system must become your system of thought discipline to transform your thinking from maleness into manhood.

5. The main issues that keep African American men *"stuck in maleness"* are problems of lack. Lack means to be without what is needed, required or essential.

6. The areas of lack that black struggle with are: 1) Awareness; 2) Purpose; 3) Vision; and, 4) Responsibility.

7. Awareness is when you have knowledge and understanding of yourself in what's going on in your life.

8. Purpose is your reason for being as a man. The main purposes of a man are to: 1) Lead; 2) Provide; 3) Teach; 4) Protect; and, 5) to be a companion/helpmate.

9. Vision means to have a mental image of something. The vision you have for yourself and your family helps to act as a guide for living and decision-making.

10. Responsibility or Responding with Ability is when you possess ALL of the areas of lack: 1) Awareness; 2) Purpose; 3) Vision; and, 4) Responsibility in your roles as a man. You

then know and possess the tools and the blueprint to think and act responsibly.

11. Responsibility without acceptance, commitment, sacrifice and discipline can cause you to fall back into being *"stuck in maleness"*.

12. Manhood is the condition of a man's mind.

Summary Of What You Learned In Chapter 8

1. Trash is unresolved guilt, grief, resentment, anger, or other emotions that accumulates in your mind and keep you stuck in the past. Trash can sap your energy, cloud your judgment, and can cause health problems.
2. Anger is a great feeling of displeasure, hostility, indignation, or exasperation. Anger tells us something is wrong.
3. Resentment is indignation or ill will felt as a result of a real or imagined offense by someone. When you have resentment towards someone you actually hold the poison.
4. Grief is a deep mental anguish over the loss of something or someone.
5. Guilt is a feeling of responsibility for wrongdoing.
6. Fear is alarm caused by the expectation or realization of anger.
7. Fear and other emotional trash can be overcome by faith and a belief in God.
8. Most issues that we carry around as trash can be resolved by our choice to do so.
9. Counseling, therapy and support groups are another way to get help to release the stress and pressures on the mind associated with trash.
10. Anger is really an expression of unmet needs that, when identified, can be fulfilled and give us power over our emotions.

Summary Of What You Learned In Chapter 9

1. Karma is the total effect of our words and actions over a period of time.
2. Karma can be negative or positive.
3. Karma never really goes away but it can be transformed.
4. Failing to "man up" and address negative Karma that you've created can cause it to return to you in a bigger and more harmful way.
5. Karma has material forms such as unpaid traffic tickets, fines, bad credit, warrants, loss of employment, or incarceration.
6. When unresolved, negative Karma becomes a form of "trash" that weights upon us emotionally, psychologically, financially, or socially.
7. Men who are *"stuck in maleness"* more often than not, have accumulated a lot of negative Karma.
8. Karma can be managed and transformed in the same way that our belief system (thoughts) can be transformed.
9. You can manage Karma just like you can manage a business. Rank order your problems or issues (accounts) in order of priority by category. Rank order the individual problems or issues within that category (your clients) in priority order as well.
10. Entire families have Karma, negative or positive.
11. Ex-offenders and substance abusers are at high risk for relapse or re-incarceration by returning to negative Karma

such as anti-social values, anti-social peers, dysfunctional families, and previous abusive or criminal behaviors.

12. When you address negative Karma you:
    - Stop it from building up or becoming worse.
    - You neutralize it so it can no longer harm you.
    - You gain a valuable opportunity to transform negative Karma into new patterns of thinking and behavior.

13. Men must face up to negative Karma that may exist between them and their children's mother(s) because our children deserve the best of both of their parents.

A Summary Of What You Learned In Chapter 10

1. Attitude is a mental position. It is an outward expression of how you feel about others.
2. Attitude is more important than facts.
3. Our attitude is one of the components of our belief system. Other than our behavior it is the most visible aspect of how we are perceived as men.
4. Your life is not about you and how you feel. It's about leading and directing others who are in your care. The attitude you take has a real impact on the people who love and depend upon you.
5. If you want something done in life you must be self-motivated to do it.
6. People can either react or respond to attitude. Choose to respond.
7. Our attitude affects how we handle criticism, stress, obstacles, anger, success and failure.
8. Because African American men have a negative image of being angry, they should both monitor and manage their feelings and emotions and how they communicate to children, employers and to the public.
9. Children may misinterpret inappropriately expressed anger as rejection or punishment.

10. As parents, our children are more prone to imitate and emulate our attitude and how we express our feelings and emotions.
11. Some African American men struggle with authority figures and tend to overact to perceived threats to their manhood.
12. Some employers are hesitant to hire African American men because of negative experiences or because of negative portraits of African American men in the media.
13. Your desire to express anger should never outweigh the reality of the need to maintain employment to support yourself and your family.
14. You are in business for yourself and your attitude is a form of advertising and marketing of who you are as a man.
15. As African American men, you must be mindful not to feed into stereotypes.
16. Whether you win or lose, succeed or fail in life, you must maintain a balanced attitude.
17. Some African American men have an attitude of entitlement. They look for others to do for them what they should do for themselves. They refuse to participate in their own success and then walk around with a negative attitude about it. We have within us the ability to change our attitude toward ourselves and others.

Summary Of What You Learned In Chapter 11

1. Two of your roles as a man are to lead and teach your children and family.
2. Before you can lead others you must know how to lead yourself.
3. A good leader knows when and how to follow.
4. Leadership should be based upon values and principles that have already been proven to work for others.
5. Lack of leadership and responsibility is part of the problem within the African American family.
6. Share the vision you have for your family and set individual goals and expectations for each family member.
7. Parents should never look for other people or government entities to do what they are responsible for as parents.
8. Be your child/children's first and primary leader and teacher.
9. Families create Karma in the same way that individuals do.
10. Show your children that good leaders also follow by deferring leadership to your spouse/partner whenever appropriate.
11. Lead your children to explore possibilities beyond their immediate environment. Take them on trips outside of your community, city or state.
12. Leaders always keep themselves "Response-Able" by using their tools and relying on all the components of their blueprint for manhood; 1) Awareness, 2) Purpose, 3) Vision, and 4) Responsibility.
13. Lead by example.

Summary Of What You Learned In Chapter 12

1. African American women want to be respected by you as a human being, a woman and as an individual, regardless of how you "feel" about them.
2. Men who disrespect women often also do not respect themselves.
3. African American women want brothers to be honest with them about what and who they say they are. They don't want to be denied their right of making an informed decision regarding your character as a man.
4. African American women want to be able to trust that you are who you say you are and that you actually have the ability to do what you say you can do as a man.
5. Breaching trust on a relationship can cause irreparable damage and may cause the relationship to falter.
6. Take the time to get to know your lady as a friend first before you become romantically involved.
7. Friendship can become the glue that holds your relationship together with your lady during tough times or when the initial attraction that brought you together begins to fade.
8. Respect, honesty, trust, and friendship are the pillars that support a loving relationship with your lady.
9. Love is more than a giddy feeling in your stomach, it also involves having compassion and understanding for her wants and needs as a person.

10. Disrespect, dishonesty and mistrust are opposing forces against love.

11. Commitment is an agreement, through words, actions, or both, to jointly participate in an endeavor with another person.

12. African American women want brothers to commit to them exclusively and to discontinue their romantic or sexual relations with other people (that includes brothers on the down low).

13. Women have a greater expectation for commitment from men because they have a greater need for commitment.

14. African American women want brothers to be able to financially provide for the household and for the children (family) in a relationship with them.

15. African American women want a co-parent to lead, teach, protect and discipline children in a relationship with them. They do not want an adult child.

16. African American women want your emotional and sexual loyalty to them in a relationship.

17. African American women want and expect loyalty to them, especially if married, even over your mother, friends and family members.

18. African American women want brothers to be mentally, physically, emotionally, financially and spiritually stable in a relationship with them.

19. African American women want their relationship with you to be romantic and an adventure and kept exciting and interesting.
20. African American women want brothers to keep the romance in their relationship with them by doing things with them to make them feel special, like sending flowers, making dinner for them and keeping them interested sexually.

Summary Of What You Learned In Chapter 13

1. The intention (purpose, vision) you have when you meet a woman influences how you see, interact with and treat her.

2. Every woman that we see or meet, no matter how attractive, is not good for you. One size does not fit all.

3. When you operate without your powers, your tool kit and your blueprint for living, you are more likely to think with your smaller head (penis) whose only purpose is gratification and urination.

4. When you know and understand your purpose as a man and have a vision for your life, you are better equipped to avoid the bad neighborhoods, streets and potholes of life.

5. Men *"stuck in maleness"* are more prone to think and act one dimensionally.

6. Not all women are the same, certainly not all African American women.

7. Stereotypes about African American women can cause you to look at them in negative and degrading ways.

8. Take the time to discover your lady's individual qualities and attributes that make her unique.

9. Never make the mistake of comparing your lady to your mother, ex, or another woman.

10. When you understand your purpose as a man and you have vision for your life, you will be in the position to understand and appreciate your lady's purpose and vision for life.

Summary Of What You Learned In Chapter 14

1. African American women have a higher level of expectation for commitment from men because they have a greater need for commitment.

2. Some African American women may no longer need to be rescued by black men but they still desire to be in a healthy relationship with them.

3. African American men need to be able to take care of themselves <u>BEFORE</u> they move in with or be a part of a relationship with a woman. Men, always demonstrate that you have what it takes to take care of yourself first, before you try to participate in a joint effort with a woman.

4. Men, let your purpose and vision for life be your guide as to whether you move in with or decide to marry a woman, not for convenience, gratification or physical attributes.

5. Moving in with a woman (or her with you) is a form of a business transaction so it should be handled as such. The terms should be put in writing outlining the terms, conditions and responsibilities of each party, <u>BEFORE</u> you move in.

6. A woman (or anyone) is not going to respect you if you do not first respect yourself, especially if you place yourself in an inferior position to where she has to tell you what to do, or where you do not have leverage or reasonable decision making in your living arrangement.

7. Marriage is a form of relationship royalty and should be treated as such. If you are not prepared to share the throne with your Queen, don't do it.

8. As of 2010, 50% of first marriages, 67% of second marriages and 79% of third marriages ended in divorce. Let your decision to marry be based primarily upon your purpose as a man, your vision for life and not merely as a convenient next step. There are emotional, financial and legal consequences of marriage.

9. Do not marry a woman unless you know and understand your purpose as a man, and you are willing to commit to your purpose <u>BEFORE</u> you commit to the woman you are seeking to marry. As a man you must always aim to remain Response-Able regardless of the changes that may occur in your marriage, or how you may feel about her.

10. Do not marry a woman who does not know and understand her purpose as a woman. Having made needed changes in your purpose and vision as a man, the last thing you need is to be aligned with a female version of a purpose-less and visionless woman …. stuck in femaleness as your lady or wife.

Summary Of What You Learned In Chapter 15

1. Men who are *"stuck in maleness"* are often selfish, self-centered, and only think about themselves.
2. Being *"stuck in maleness"* and being spiritual are polar opposites.
3. Anti-spiritual men often pursue and surround themselves with material things.
4. As you become more of a man, you will become more spiritual.
5. When you do not know and understand your purpose as a man, you place your family and others at risk of suffering from your purposeless mindset as well.
6. God sometimes "disciplines" us and places us in "captivity" as a way to get our attention so we can reflect upon our real purpose as men.
7. You have been made aware of your toolkit, i.e., your power of choice and your belief system, and your Blueprint for Manhood (awareness, purpose, vision and responsibility) that can be used to navigate out of being *"stuck in maleness"*.
8. God has given all men gifts, talents, skills and the power of choice to help us to achieve our purpose as men.
9. In order to be a good leader, you must know how to follow the right values and principles of which good leadership is based.

10. *"Stuck in maleness"* is a "disease" of a man's mind that can re-occur whenever he stops being Response-Able.

11. *"Stuck in maleness"* is a condition of a man's mind. It affects men of all ages, races, professions, income levels, and levels of education.

12. Men who are in prison must reflect upon what caused them to being incarcerated. First and foremost your incarceration is psychological; it is a condition of your mind. Your freedom begins and ends in your mind.

Bibliography

1. *(A Brief History of Jamestown,The Association for the Preservation of Virginia Antiquities,* Richmond, VA 23220,email: apva@apva.org, Web published February, 2000)

2. Freeman, Elsie, Wynell Burroughs Schamel, and Jean West. "The Fight for Equal Rights: A Recruiting Poster for Black Soldiers in the Civil *War."*SOCIAL EDUCATION56, 2 (February 1992): 118-120. [Revised and updated in 1999 by Budge Weidman.]

3. http://black-face.com/ Also see http://www.black-face.com/Bill-Bojangles-Robinson.htm

4. *Slave in a Box: The Strange Career of Aunt Jemima,* M. M. Manning, University of Virginia Press, Charlottesville, Virginia, 1998,ISBN 0-8139-1811-1

5. http://www.ferris.edu/jimcrow/origins.htm

6. Children-our investment.org

7. Children-our investment.org

8. Sources: "Survey of Recent Statistics, "ABA Commission on Domestic Violence.

9. http://www.abanet.org/domviol/statistics.html; "Fact Sheet, "Institute on Domestic Violence in the African American Community, University of Minnesota School of Social Workhttp://www.dvinstitute.org/media/publications/FactSheet.IDVAACAAPCFV-Community%2OInsights.pdf.

10. Africana Voices Against Violence, Tufts University, Statistics, 2002.www.ase.tufts.edu/womenscenter//peace/Africana/newsite/statistics.htm

11. Goldsmith, T. (2006). Who Are the Victims of Domestic Violence? *Psych Central.* Retrieved on March 2, 2014, from http://psychcentral.com/lib/who-are-the-victims-of-domestic-violence/000356

12. Sources: National Domestic Violence Hotline, National Center for Victims of Crime, and WomensLaw.org.

13. http://www.mchenrycountyturningpoint.org/causes.html

14. Table adopted from HelpGuide.org, A Trusted Non-Profit Organization. "Signs That You're in An Abusive Relationship"*Authors: Melinda Smith, M.A., and Jeanne Segal, Ph.D. Last updated: February 2014.*

15. Tournier, Paul, *To Understand Each Other* (Atlanta, GA; John Knox Press, 1962), p.30

16. Cloud, Henry and Townsend, John, *Boundaries: When ToSay Yes, How ToSay No To Take Control of Your Life*, (Zondervan, Grand Rapids, Michigan, 1992).

17. Swets, Paul W., *The Art Of Talking so That People Will Listen*, (Fireside, N.Y. N.Y, 1983), p.22

18. Webster's New World College Dictionary.2006 Wiley Publishing, Inc., Cleveland Ohio

19. Webster's New World College Dictionary.2006 Wiley Publishing, Inc., Cleveland Ohio

20. Webster's New World College Dictionary.2006 Wiley Publishing, Inc., Cleveland Ohio

21. Allen, James. *As A Man Thinketh*, DeVorss& Company, Publisher, P.O. Bod 1389, Camarillo, CA 93011-1389.www.devorss.com

22. Webster's New World College Dictionary.2006 Wiley Publishing, Inc., Cleveland Ohio.

23. Webster's New World College Dictionary.2006 Wiley Publishing, Inc., Cleveland Ohio.

24. Dyson, Michael Eric. *Reflecting Black, African American Cultural Criticism*, 1995, University of Minnesota Press.

25. National Youth Gang Center, 2009, see*Percent Change in Estimated Number of Gang-Problem Jurisdictions*. National Gang Center Institute for Intergovernmental Research Post Office Box 12729, Tallahassee, FL 32317. information@nationalgangcenter.gov

26. NATIONAL YOUTH GANG SURVEY ANALYSIS. Demographic Race/Ethnicity of Gang Members.National Gang Center Institute for Intergovernmental Research Post Office Box 12729, Tallahassee, FL 32317. information@nationalgangcenter.gov

27. NATIONAL YOUTH GANG SURVEY ANALYSIS. Demographic Gender of Gang Members, 199 to 2010.National Gang Center Institute for Intergovernmental Research Post Office Box 12729, Tallahassee, FL 32317. information@nationalgangcenter.gov

28. NATIONAL YOUTH GANG SURVEY ANALYSIS. Demographic Age of Gang Members, 1996 to 2011. National Gang Center Institute for Intergovernmental Research Post Office Box 12729, Tallahassee, FL 32317. **information@nationalgangcenter.gov**

29. Smalley, Gary and John Trent, Ph D., *The Language of Love* (Panoma, CA.: Focus on the Family Publishing, 1988) First Edition

30. Millman, Dan, 1998 / *Everyday Enlighten: The Twelve Gateways to Personal Growth*. Warner Book, Inc.

31. Gills, James P.,*Imaginations: More Than You Think*, 2000. Love Press, 19 N, P.O. Box 5000, Tarpoon Springs, FL 34688-5000.

32. Covey, Stephen R.,*The 7 Habits of Highly Effective People:Powerful Lessons in Personal Change*. New York: **Stuck In Maleness**on & Schuster, 1990. p 24

33. Meyer, Joyce. *Battlefields of The Mind*, 1995. Faith Words, Hachette Book Group, New York, NY.

34. Woodson, Carter G.,*The Miseducation of the Negro*. Africa World Press, Inc. 1990.pxiii

35. Africans in America, Historical Document. The Dred Scott case: the Supreme Court Decision1857.

36. http://www.pbs.org/wgbh/aia/part4/4h2933.html

37. Mandingo, Og. *The Greatest Miracle In The World*, 1975. A Bantam Book/ published by arrangement with Frederick Fell Publishers, Inc. 886 Park Avenue South, NY, NY 10016.

38. Webster's New World College Dictionary, 2006 Wiley Publishing, Inc., Cleveland Ohio.

39. Munroe, Dr. Myles. *The Principles and Power of Vision: Keys To Achieving Personal And Corporate Destiny*. New Kensington, PA. Whittaker House, 2003. p 28

40. Webster's New World College Dictionary, 2006 Wiley Publishing, Inc., Cleveland Ohio

41. Webster's New World College Dictionary. 2006 Wiley Publishing, Inc., Cleveland Ohio

42. Peale, Norman Vincent. The Power of Positive Thinking. Fireside Rockefeller Center, New York, N.Y. 2003

43. Rosenberg, Marshall. The Surprising Purpose of Anger. Puddle Dancer Press. 2010.**www.nonviolentcommunication.com**

44. Zukav, Gary. *Seat of the Soul*. New York, N.Y., Fireside, 1989. p 33

45. Webster's New World College Dictionary, 2006 Wiley Publishing, Inc., Cleveland Ohio

46. Peale, Norman Vincent. *The Power of Positive Thinking*. Fireside Rockefeller Center, New York, N.Y. 2003

47. Hudson, Victor. Fathers Come Forth: The Journey of Family Leadership. Lincoln, Nebraska. Writers Club Press, 2003.p58

48. Webster's New World College Dictionary. 2006 Wiley Publishing, Inc., Cleveland Ohio

49. U.S. Census Bureau, 1983

50. U.S. Census Bureau, 2012

51. CDC/NCHS, National Survey of Family Growth, 2006-2010

52. Pew Research Social and Demographic Trends. Barely Half of U.S. Adults Are Married – A Record Low. New Marriages

Down 5% from 2009 to 2010. By D'Vera Cohn, Jeffrey Passel, Wendy Wang and Gretchen Livingston.

53. The Census 2000 Summary File 3 data are available from theAmerican FactFinder on the Internet (*factfinder.census.gov*).They were released on a state-by-state basis during 2002. For informationon confidentiality protection, onsampling error, sampling error, and definitions, also see. ***www.census.gov/prod/cen2000*** */doc/ sf3.pdf* or contact theCustomer Services Center at 301-763-INFO (4636).

54. Baker, Jennifer. Director of the Post-Graduate Program in Marriage and Family Therapy. Marriage & Divorce in America. Forest Institute of Professional Psychology in Springfield, MO

55. Baker, Jennifer. Director of the Post-Graduate Program in Marriage and Family Therapy. Marriage & Divorce in America. Forest Institute of Professional Psychology in Springfield, MO

Appendix

The following information is meant to provide a snapshot view of some of the more common challenges facing African American men and their impact on the African American family as well. For a more detailed picture of the state of conditions among African American men and the African American family in the United States go to ***Stuckinmaleness.com*** and click on ***African American Men Under Siege*** and you will find links to many informative and useful websites.

Education

Table A-1. Annual High School Dropout Rates of 15 to 24 Year Olds by Sex, Race, Grade, and Black Origin: October 1967 to 2011									
(Numbers in thousands. Civilian non-institutionalized population)									
	Total			Male			Female		
	Total students	Dropouts	Dropout rate	Total students	Dropouts	Dropout rate	Total students	Dropouts	Dropout rate
Black - Grades 10-12									
2011	1,944	78	4.0	911	54	5.6	954	24	2.4
2010	1,898	62	3.2	946	36	3.8	952	26	2.7
2009	1,797	81	4.5	870	38	4.4	927	42	4.6
2008	1,868	114	6.1	925	42	4.6	943	72	7.6
2007	1,781	76	4.3	914	45	4.9	867	31	3.6
2006	1,767	65	3.7	902	29	3.2	864	37	4.3
2005	1,763	122	6.9	943	71	7.5	820	51	6.2
2004	1,716	90	5.2	833	40	4.8	883	50	5.7
2003	1,698	76	4.5	812	33	4.1	886	43	4.9
2002	1,664	73	4.4	782	40	5.1	882	33	3.8
2001	1,655	95	5.7	828	51	6.2	827	45	5.4
2000	1,706	96	5.6	819	62	7.6	888	34	3.8
1999	1,794	107	6.0	925	48	5.2	870	59	6.8
1998	1,759	88	5.0	918	42	4.6	841	46	5.5
1997	1,678	80	4.8	813	33	4.1	866	49	5.7
1996	1,704	107	6.3	803	37	4.6	901	70	7.8
1995	1,598	97	6.1	797	63	7.9	802	35	4.4
1994	1,559	96	6.1	763	50	6.5	795	45	5.7
1993	1,499	80	5.3	740	43	5.8	758	37	4.9
1993	1,447	78	5.4	724	41	5.7	722	36	5.0
1992	1,422	70	4.9	702	23	3.3	720	48	6.7
1991	1,366	85	6.2	685	38	5.5	683	48	7.0
1990	1,303	66	5.1	636	26	4.1	666	40	6.0
1989	1,384	106	7.7	684	47	6.9	701	60	8.6
1988	1,468	93	6.3	751	50	6.7	717	43	6.0
1987	1,463	93	6.4	730	45	6.2	732	47	6.4

Grade, and Black Origin: October 1967 to 2011									
(Numbers in thousands. Civilian non-institutionalized population)									
	Total			Male			Female		
	Total students	Dropouts	Dropout rate	Total students	Dropouts	Dropout rate	Total students	Dropouts	Dropout rate
1986	1,449	68	4.7	711	34	4.8	737	34	4.6
1985	1,422	110	7.7	703	58	8.3	719	52	7.2
1984	1,524	88	5.8	711	44	6.2	813	43	5.3
1983	1,498	103	6.9	687	48	7.0	810	55	6.8
1982	1,553	121	7.8	786	71	9.0	767	50	6.5
1981	1,516	146	9.6	704	66	9.4	815	83	10.2
1980	1,496	124	8.3	714	57	8.0	781	66	8.5
1979	1,479	142	9.6	679	51	7.5	802	92	11.5
1978	1,542	160	10.4	706	78	11.0	835	81	9.7
1977	1,588	133	8.4	746	62	8.3	789	71	9.0
1976	1,449	105	7.2	729	62	8.5	721	45	6.2
1975	1,416	123	8.7	673	56	8.3	743	67	9.0
1974	1,441	167	11.6	679	73	10.8	761	93	12.2
1973	1,372	138	10.1	650	78	12.0	725	61	8.4
1972	1,373	133	9.7	644	65	10.1	756	68	9.0
1971	1,195	87	7.3	552	51	9.2	643	37	5.8
1970	1,192	133	11.2	587	74	12.6	606	60	9.9
1969	1,209	113	9.3	562	58	10.3	646	55	8.5
1968	1,123	113	10.1	523	52	9.9	600	61	10.2
1967	1,066	106	9.9	485	47	9.7	578	58	10.0

- Represents zero or rounds to zero.
r = Revised, controlled to 1990 census based population estimates; previous 1993 data controlled to 1980 census based estimates.
Source: U. S. Census Bureau, Current Population Survey, 1967 to 2010.

Table A-2. Annual High School and College Enrollment Rates of 18 to 19 Year Olds by Sex, Race, Grade, and Black Origin: October 1967 to 2011									
Year, race, and Hispanic origin	Total	Population 18 and 19 years old							
		Still in high school	Percent	Dropped out	Percent	High school graduate only	Percent	In college	Percent
Male									
2011	645	226	35.0	39	6.0	138	21.4	242	37.6
2010	654	159	24.4	83	12.6	174	26.5	238	36.4
2009	659	174	26.4	102	15.5	158	24.0	225	34.1
2008	653	173	26.5	53	8.1	222	34.0	205	31.4
2007	628	161	25.7	54	8.6	186	29.6	227	36.2
2006	600	210	35.0	42	7.0	174	29.0	174	28.9
2005	552	178	32.2	60	10.9	121	21.9	193	35.0
2004	519	137	26.4	91	17.6	126	24.3	165	31.7
2003	502	143	28.5	77	15.3	116	23.1	166	33.1
2002	608	155	25.5	123	20.2	151	24.8	179	29.4
2001	624	179	28.7	97	15.5	169	27.1	179	28.7
2000	593	148	25.0	105	17.7	177	29.8	163	27.5
1999	586	144	24.6	97	16.6	136	23.2	209	35.7
1998	613	163	26.6	128	20.9	128	20.9	194	31.6
1997	554	172	31.0	90	16.2	150	27.1	142	25.6
1996	564	167	29.6	90	16.0	162	28.7	145	25.7
1995	519	162	31.2	94	18.1	118	22.7	145	27.9
1994	497	134	27.0	116	23.3	115	23.1	132	26.6
1993	517	181	35.0	53	10.3	135	26.1	148	28.6
1992	499	180	36.1	82	16.4	114	22.8	123	24.6
1991	504	176	34.9	62	12.3	129	25.6	137	27.2
1990	520	152	29.2	80	15.4	124	23.8	164	31.5
1989	516	137	26.6	90	17.4	163	31.6	126	24.4
1988	510	145	28.4	92	18.0	165	32.4	108	21.2
1987	501	140	27.9	80	16.0	127	25.3	154	30.7
1986	506	149	29.4	74	14.6	165	32.6	118	23.3
1985	518	135	26.1	92	17.8	170	32.8	121	23.4
1984	524	143	27.3	103	19.7	166	31.7	112	21.4
1983	539	158	29.3	106	19.7	182	33.8	93	17.3
1982	549	132	24.0	145	26.4	148	27.0	124	22.6
1981	538	145	27.0	102	19.0	158	29.4	133	24.7
1980	503	118	23.5	114	22.7	173	34.4	98	19.5
1979	497	128	25.8	122	24.5	137	27.6	110	22.1
1978	493	135	27.4	127	25.8	117	23.7	114	23.1
1977	496	161	32.5	118	23.8	127	25.6	90	18.1
1976	499	153	30.7	96	19.2	129	25.9	121	24.2
1975	476	127	26.7	132	27.7	106	22.3	111	23.3
1974	474	116	24.5	128	27.0	128	27.0	102	21.5
1973	467	106	22.7	130	27.8	135	28.9	96	20.6
1972	445	110	24.7	121	27.2	112	25.2	102	22.9
1971	423	120	28.4	110	26.0	99	23.4	94	22.2
1970	414	98	23.7	151	36.5	92	22.2	73	17.6
1969	394	109	27.7	124	31.5	75	19.0	86	21.8
1968	390	124	31.8	93	23.8	90	23.1	83	21.3
1967	356	95	26.7	109	30.6	74	20.8	78	21.9
Female									
2011	671	170	25.4	21	3.1	143	21.3	337	50.3
2010	682	111	16.3	61	9.0	181	26.5	329	48.2
2009	687	145	21.1	78	11.3	130	19.0	334	48.6

Table A-2. Annual High School and College Enrollment Rates of 18 to 19 Year Olds by Sex, Race, Grade, and Black Origin: October 1967 to 2011

Year, race, and Hispanic origin	Total	Population 18 and 19 years old							
		Still in high school	Percent	Dropped out	Percent	High school graduate only	Percent	In college	Percent
2008	681	138	20.3	92	13.5	178	26.1	274	40.2
2007	655	139	21.2	58	8.8	194	29.6	265	40.4
2006	631	122	19.3	60	9.6	158	25.0	291	46.1
2005	574	78	13.6	49	8.6	189	32.9	258	44.9
2004	593	81	13.7	70	11.9	167	28.2	275	46.5
2003	550	133	24.2	51	9.3	157	28.5	209	38.0
2002	574	97	16.9	57	9.9	169	29.4	251	43.7
2001	623	122	19.6	54	8.7	182	29.2	265	42.5
2000	658	113	17.2	82	12.5	172	26.1	291	44.2
1999	613	114	18.6	94	15.3	184	30.0	221	36.1
1998	633	127	20.1	96	15.2	143	22.6	267	42.2
1997	579	107	18.5	82	14.2	152	26.3	238	41.1
1996	597	102	17.1	85	14.2	211	35.3	199	33.3
1995	581	126	21.7	83	14.3	173	29.8	199	34.3
1994	520	105	20.2	83	16.0	154	29.6	178	34.2
1993	523	108	20.7	80	15.3	172	32.9	163	31.2
1992	508	95	18.7	84	16.5	161	31.7	168	33.1
1991	537	99	18.4	85	15.8	187	34.8	166	30.9
1990	559	95	17.0	98	17.5	181	32.4	185	33.1
1989	562	102	18.1	104	18.5	180	32.0	176	31.3
1988	547	105	19.2	97	17.7	172	31.4	173	31.6
1987	542	75	13.8	85	15.7	196	36.2	186	34.3
1986	542	62	11.4	83	15.3	209	38.6	188	34.7
1985	554	78	14.1	94	17.0	244	44.0	138	24.9
1984	568	76	13.4	82	14.4	257	45.2	153	26.9
1983	595	108	18.2	93	15.6	230	38.7	164	27.6
1982	597	95	15.9	108	18.1	244	40.9	150	25.1
1981	590	93	15.8	116	19.7	209	35.4	172	29.2
1980	578	93	16.1	115	19.9	185	32.0	185	32.0
1979	576	93	16.1	125	21.7	189	32.8	169	29.3
1978	572	88	15.4	130	22.7	199	34.8	155	27.1
1977	576	88	15.3	117	20.3	192	33.3	179	31.1
1976	556	77	13.8	115	20.7	183	32.9	181	32.6
1975	553	97	17.5	130	23.5	176	31.8	150	27.1
1974	530	92	17.4	107	20.2	200	37.7	131	24.7
1973	530	77	14.5	122	23.0	234	44.2	97	18.3
1972	513	71	13.8	108	21.1	207	40.4	127	24.8
1971	485	100	20.6	109	22.5	167	34.4	109	22.5
1970	464	62	13.4	124	26.7	160	34.5	118	25.4
1969	443	70	15.8	102	23.0	163	36.8	108	24.4
1968	439	69	15.7	109	24.8	161	36.7	100	22.8
1967	424	81	19.1	93	21.9	187	44.1	63	14.9

- Represents zero or rounds to zero.
1 Starting in 2003 respondents could identify more than one race. Except as noted, the race data in this table from 2003 onward represent those respondents who indicated only one race category.
2 The data shown prior to 2003 consists of those identifying themselves as "Asian or Pacific Islanders."
Hispanics may be of any race.
High school graduates are people who have completed 4 years of high school or more, for 1967 to 1991. Beginning in 1992, they were people whose highest degree was a high school diploma (including equivalency) or higher.
Source: U. S. Census Bureau, Current Population Survey, 1967 to 2011.

Black Employment and Unemployment in 2011

During 2011 the economy grew by over 1.6 million jobs, and for the second half of the year job growth exceeded 100,000 each month. This was the first time the economy had experienced such robust job growth since before the official beginning of the Great Recession in December 2007. However, results for Black workers in the labor market were more mixed. When we examine 2011 employment data, three important trends stand out:

- There was virtually no movement in the official Black unemployment rate from January to December 2011. However, when black women and black men are examined separately, black female unemployment rates rose, while Black male unemployment rates fell.
- While the basic black unemployment rate remained constant during the year, there was movement in the underlying components of the official unemployment rate: employment level, unemployment level, and number of persons not in the labor force.
- In December 2011, the black unemployment rate was still higher than the rate in June 2009 when the recession officially ended.

Unemployment Rates: January 2011–December 2011

In January 2011, the unemployment rate for blacks, 16–64 years of age, was 15.7%. By the end of the year, unemployment was virtually identical at 15.8%. This situation was markedly different than that of the rest of the population. For whites and Latinos, the unemployment rate fell from January to December 2011.

Unemployment Rate for January and December 2011 by Race

January – December
Black 15.7%   15.8%
White 8.1%   7.5%
Latino 12.0%   11.0%

Male Unemployment Rate for January and December 2011 by Race

January – December
Black 17.9%   17.1%
White 8.5%   7.6%

Female Unemployment Rate for January and December 2011 by Race

January – December
Black 13.8%   14.6%
White 7.5%   7.2%

Comparison of December 2011 Unemployment Rates to December 2007 and June 2009

In addition to the racially-differentiated pattern of changes in employment and unemployment levels during 2011, also striking are the racially-differentiated patterns in unemployment rates when comparing December 2011 to the Great Recession's official starting and ending months (December 2007 and June 2009). Unemployment rates rose dramatically during the recession for all black workers, more so for black men compared to black women. Since the end of the recession, the black male unemployment rate has fallen slightly, while the black female unemployment rate has risen.

University of California, Berkeley Center for Labor Research and Education, January 17, 2012.

http://laborcenter.berkeley.edu/blackworkers/Black_Employment_and_Unemployment_2011.pdf

Occupations of African American Men and Women

Black women have made the greatest strides recently. In 2011, **33% of employed black women have jobs in management or professional occupations,** compared to 23% of employed black men. As a matter of fact, **64% of working African American women hold "white collar" occupations compared to 50% of African American men**. Thirty-six percent of employed black men hold "blue collar" occupations compared to 8% of black women.

Source:

http://blackdemographics.com/economics/employment/
Source: All household data in this report is from the Bureau of Labor Statistics' Current Population Survey and is seasonally adjusted.

Incarceration

Today, people of color continue to be disproportionately incarcerated, policed, and sentenced to death at significantly higher rates than their white counterparts. Further, racial disparities in the criminal-justice system threaten communities of color— disenfranchising thousands by limiting voting rights and denying equal access to employment, housing, public benefits, and education to millions more. In light of these disparities, it is imperative that criminal-justice reform evolves as the Civil Rights issue of the 21st century.

Outlined Below shows some facts pertaining to the criminal-justice system's impact on communities of color.

- **While people of color make up about 30 percent of the United States' population, they account for 60 percent of those imprisoned.** The prison population grew by 700 percent from 1970 to 2005, a rate that is outpacing crime and population rates. The incarceration rates **disproportionately impact men of color**: 1 in every 15 African American men and 1 in every 36 Hispanic men are incarcerated in comparison to 1 in every 106 white men.

- **According to the Bureau of Justice Statistics, one in three black men can expect to go to prison in their lifetime.** Individuals of color have a disproportionate number of encounters with law enforcement, indicating that racial profiling continues to be a problem. A report by the Department of Justice found that blacks and Hispanics were approximately **three times more likely to be searched** during a traffic stop than white motorists. African Americans were twice as likely to be arrested and almost **four times as likely** to experience the use of force during encounters with the police.

- **Students of color face harsher punishments in school than their white peers, leading to a higher number of youth of color incarcerated.** Black and Hispanic students represent more than **70 percent** of those involved in school-related arrests or referrals to law enforcement. Currently,

African Americans make up **two-fifths** and Hispanics **one-fifth** of confined youth today.

- **According to recent data by the Department of Education, African American students are arrested far more often than their white classmates.** The data showed that **96,000** students were arrested and 242,000 referred to law enforcement by schools during the 2009-10 school year. Of those students, black and Hispanic students made up more than **70 percent** of arrested or referred students. Harsh school punishments, from suspensions to arrests, have led to high numbers of youth of color coming into contact with the juvenile-justice system and at an earlier age.
- **African American youth have higher rates of juvenile incarceration and are more likely to be sentenced to adult prison.** According to the **Sentencing Project**, even though African American juvenile youth are about 16 percent of the youth population, 37 percent of their cases are moved to criminal court and 58 percent of African American youth are sent to adult prisons.
- **The war on drugs has been waged primarily in communities of color where people of color are more likely to receive higher offenses.** According to the **Human Rights Watch**, people of color are no more likely to use or sell illegal drugs than whites, but they have higher rate of arrests. Americans comprise **14 percent** of regular drug users but are 37 percent of those arrested for drug offenses. From 1980 to 2007 about **one in three** of the 25.4 million adults arrested for drugs was African American.

- **Once convicted, black offenders receive longer sentences compared to white offenders.** The U.S. Sentencing Commission stated that in the federal system black offenders **receive sentences that are 10 percent** longer than white offenders for the same crimes. **The Sentencing Project** reports that African Americans are 21 percent more likely to receive mandatory-minimum sentences than white defendants and are 20 percent more like to be sentenced to prison.

- **Voter laws that prohibit people with felony convictions to vote disproportionately impact men of color.** An estimated 5.3 million Americans are denied the right to vote based on a past felony conviction. Felony disenfranchisement is exaggerated by racial disparities in the criminal-justice system, ultimately denying **13 percent** of African American men the right to vote. Felony-disenfranchisement policies have led to 11 states denying the right to vote to more than **10 percent** of their African American population.

- **Studies have shown that people of color face disparities in wage trajectory following release from prison.** Evidence shows that spending time in prison affects wage trajectories with a disproportionate impact on black men and women. The results show no evidence of racial divergence in wages prior to incarceration; however, following release from prison, wages grow at a **21 percent slower rate** for black former inmates compared to white ex-convicts. A number of states have bans on people with certain convictions working in domestic health-service industries such as nursing, child care, and home health care—areas in which many poor women and **women of color** are disproportionately concentrated.

Theses racial disparities have deprived people of color of their most basic civil rights, making criminal-justice reform the civil rights issue of our time. Through mass imprisonment and the overrepresentation of individuals of color within the criminal justice and prison system, people of color have experienced an adverse impact on themselves and on their communities from barriers to reintegrating into society to engaging in the democratic process. Eliminating the racial disparities inherent to our nation's criminal-justice policies and practices must be at the heart of a renewed, refocused, and reenergized movement for racial justice in America.

There have been a number of initiatives on the state and federal level to address the racial disparities in youth incarceration. Last summer Secretary of Education Arne Duncan announced the **Schools Discipline Initiative** to bring increased awareness of effective policies and practices to ultimately dismantle the school-to-prison pipeline. States like California and Massachusetts are considering **legislation** to address the disproportionate suspensions among students of color. And in Clayton County, Georgia, **collaborative local reforms** have resulted in a **47 percent reduction** in juvenile-court referrals and a **51 percent** decrease in juvenile felony rates. These initiatives could serve as models of success for lessening the disparities in incarceration rates.

http://www.americanprogress.org/issues/race/news/2012/03/13/11351/the-top-10-most-startling-facts-about-people-of-color-and-criminal-justice-in-the-united-states/

Mortality

Black men run a much higher risk of illness and death compared to the rest of the U.S. population. In many cases black men are 2 to 10 times as likely to fall victim to the same diseases that afflict their white counterparts. The following chart lists the top 10 killers of African American men along with the percentage of occurrence. This information was obtained from the latest available reports from the Center for Disease Control (CDC)

Top 10 Causes of Death Among African American Males

1.	Heart Disease (24%)	6.	Diabetes (3.9%)
2.	Cancer (21.9%)	7.	HIV/AIDS (3.0%)
3.	Injury, Violence and Safety (6.5%)	8.	Chronic Bronchitis, Emphysema (2.8%)
4.	Homicide (5.2%)	9.	Kidney Disease (2.6%)
5.	Stroke (5.0%)	10.	Conditions Perinatal/Newborn (1.9%)

Notes: "INJURY, VIOLENCE AND SAFETY" includes: car crashes, domestic abuse, child abuse, youth violence and other various injuries.

"CONDITIONS PERINATAL/NEWBORN" includes issues related to HIV-infected mothers giving birth and pregnancy care.

http://afrodaddy.com/health/top-10-killers-black-men
To learn more, visit Mortality Tables at
http://www.cdc.gov/nchs/nvss/mortality_tables.htm or
http://www.cdc.gov/nchs/deaths.htm (HHS, CDC, NCHS).

Black Men and Sexual Transmitted Disease Syphilis: Young Black Men Hardest Hit

Overall, the rate of new syphilis cases in the United States remained unchanged between 2010 and 2011; the rate decreased among women, but increased among men. CDC's new surveillance report shows that the rate of primary and secondary (P&S) syphilis cases (the early and more infectious stages of the disease) among blacks decreased by 6.6% from 2010 to 2011. However, blacks still account for almost half of all reported cases (43.8% or 6,119 cases).

In 2011, the P&S rate for black women was 17 times higher than the rate for white women, and the congenital syphilis rate for black infants (syphilis passed on in uterus or during childbirth to the infants of women with untreated syphilis) was approximately 15 times higher than the rate for white infants. Moreover, P&S syphilis cases among black men 20 to 24 years of age continued to increase significantly; over the last five years, syphilis cases increased 75 percent among this population.

The majority of P&S syphilis cases occur among men who have sex with men (72 percent of all reported cases). Other CDC data show an increase in syphilis of 167 percent among young black men who have sex with men from 2005 to 2008, indicating that new infections among men who have sex with men are driving the overall increase in syphilis among young black men. The finding is particularly concerning as there has also been a sharp increase in HIV among this population. CDC recommends that sexually active men who have sex with men be tested at least annually for syphilis, with more frequent testing recommended for men at high risk for infection. This is especially important because research shows that people with untreated syphilis are at an increased risk for acquiring HIV.

The data for 2011 are published in CDC's latest annual report, *Sexually Transmitted Disease Surveillance 2011* (available at http//www.cdc.gov/std/stats).

HIV and Black Men

CDC's new estimates show that African Americans, more than any other racial/ethnic group, continue to bear the greatest burden of HIV in the United States. While blacks represent approximately 14 percent of the total U.S. population, they accounted for almost half (44 percent) ofall new HIV infections in 2010 (20,900). HIV incidence among blacks was almost eight times higher than that of whites(68.9 v. 8.7 per 100,000 of the population). Comparing 2008to 2010, there was no statistically significant change inoverall HIV incidence among blacks.

Black Men: Black men represented almost one-third(31 percent) of all new HIV infections in the United States in 2010 (14,700) and accounted for 70 percent of new HIV infections among blacks. The rate of new infections among black men was the highest of any group by race and sex — more than six times that of white men (103.6 v. 15.8 per 100,000). The vast majority (72 percent) of infections among black men were among MSM. The largest percentage (38 percent) of new HIV infections among black males in 2010 occurred in those aged 13–24years — much higher than the proportion of new infections among Hispanic (25 percent) and white (16 percent) males that occurred in the same age group.

Black Women: Black women accounted for 13 percent of all new HIV infections in the United States in 2010 and nearly two-thirds(64 percent) of all new infections among women. Most black women(87 percent) were infected through heterosexual sex. While new infections among black women remain high, for the first time this analysis found indications of an encouraging trend. Comparing2008 to 2010, new HIV infections among black women decreased 21 percent, from 7,700 in 2008 to 6,100 in 2010. This decrease contributed to a 21 percent decline in new infections among women overall during the same time period. Additional years of data will be needed to determine if the decrease among black women is the beginning of a longer-term trend.

While the decline in HIV incidence is encouraging, the new data show that black women continue to be far more affected by HIV than women of other races/ethnicities. The rate of new HIV infections among black women in 2010 was 20 times that of white women and nearly 5 times that of Hispanic women (38.1 v. 1.9 and 8.0 per 100,000, respectively). This indicates an even greater disparity than shown in CDC's previous incidence analysis, in which the HIV infection rate among black women was 15 times that of white women and more than 3 times that of Hispanic women.

Centers for Disease Control and Prevention. Estimated HIV incidence among adults and adolescents in the United States, 2007–2010. *HIV SurveillanceSupplemental Report 2012*;17(No. 4). http://www.cdc.gov/hiv/topics/surveillance/resources/reports/#supplemental Published December 2012.

HIV/AIDS Information and Resources:

General information about HIV/AIDS: www.cdc.gov/HIV
HIV/AIDS news: www.cdc.gov/nchhstp/newsroom
Act Against AIDS campaign: **www.actagainstaids.org**

The African American Family
Marriage facts on Black Men:

From 1890 through 1950 the median age at first marriage for black men was lower than for white men.

The percent of those age 35 and older who were never married was higher from 1890 through 1930 for white men than black men, but by 1960, this had reversed, with black men age 35 and over having a higher percent never married.

By 1960, black men had a higher percentage age 45 and over who had never married. As of 2010, 20 percent of black men and 9 percent of white men have never been married by age 45 and over.

Marriage facts on Black Women:

After 1950, the median age at first marriage for black women was higher than for white women. Black women were more likely to have been married by age 35 than their white counterparts until 1970. The crossover happened in 1980, when 7 percent of black women had never married, compared with 5 percent of white women. By 2010, 20 percent of black women and 7 percent of white women had never been married by age 45 and over.

Overall US Census Bureau Conclusions:

The median age at first marriage in 2010 for all races is the highest on record, but didn't exceed the 1890 value until 1990.

There was a sharp increase in the proportion never married for Black men and women since 1980. Source: US Census Bureau

Historical Marriage Trends from 1890-2010: A Focus on Race Differences

In the 1950's and 1960's was an anomaly for men and women given the high proportions married at young ages. Race differences are particularly interesting, as black women were more often married than white women prior to World War II, yet since the 1980s, have been increasingly less likely to be married.

There are two historical trends in family studies and explicitly details sex and race differences using data from Decennial Censuses and the American Community Survey (ACS). First, we examine how the median age at first marriage has changed from 1890-2010 by sex and race. While the trend in age at first marriage has been examined previously by sex (U.S. Census Bureau 2010, National Center for Family & Marriage Research 2010, Norton & Moorman 1987), less research has examined these trends by both sex and race (Fitch & Ruggles 2000; Rodgers and Thornton 1985).

Black men and women were married in greater proportions than white men and women until 1960 for men and 1970 for women. Therefore, we make the argument that structural components are more influential than cultural components in determining race differences among never married individuals.

Historical evidence shows that until 1960, black men entered into first marriages at younger ages than white men. In 1890, the median age at first marriage for black men was 25.2 years, while it was 26.6 years for white men. In 1950, the median age at first marriage for black men was still lower at 22.8 years compared to 24.0 years for white men. By 1960, the trend changed and black men began entering into first marriages at later ages than white men. This trend has continued to the present, such that by 2010, the median age at first marriage for black men was 30.7 years, compared with 27.8 years for white men.

Decennial Census data show that the median age at first marriage was higher in decades before World War II than during 1950 to 1970. The proportions of never married men and women were also higher prior to 1950 than has been the case until only very recently. Our findings provide a justification for using a more extensive time frame to study marriage.

The second key finding centers on race differences in historical marriage trends. Looking from an extended historical frame of reference, we find that black men and women before World War II entered into first marriages at younger ages and were less likely to be never married than their white counterparts. Black men were less often never married compared with white men until 1960, whereas black women were less likely to be never married than white women up until 1970. The turning point comes in 1980, when both black men and women begin a sharp increase in the proportion never married by age 35 and age 45.

We discussed two theoretical explanations for the divergence in marriage rates over time by race: structural and cultural. Although our data cannot specifically address which of these is supported, or to what extent, our results present a baseline for future hypothesis testing between these two theories. We suggest that researchers examine the coincidence of structural factors of the 1980's and early 1990's such as drug and welfare policies and punitive prison sentences, and the steady increase in the proportion of never married black men and women from 1980 to 2000. Of particular importance for future studies is the examination of the association between the dramatic increase in black men's incarceration rates (Pettit & Western 2004) and the rise in the proportions of black individuals delaying and deferring marriage.

United States Census Bureau.(2010). America's Families and Living Arrangements, *Current Population Survey (CPS) Reports – Historical Time Series Marital Status Table MS-2*.Retrieved December 2, 2010, from http://www.census.gov/population/www/socdemo/hh-fam.html

Statistics Source: U.S. Decennial Census (1930-2000); National Center for Health Statistics, "Advance Report of Final Marriage Statistics, 1989 and 1990." Monthly Vital Statistics Report, Volume 43, No. 12. Supplement, 1995, Table 9.

Diana Elliott, Ph.D. is the Research Manager for Pew's Economic Mobility Project. The research included in this paper was conducted while she was a family demographer at the US Census Bureau.

African American Women and Poverty

Table 3 Shows Poverty Status by Family Relationship, Race, 1959 to 2011

Note: Numbers in Thousands. People of March of the Following Year

Year	Black Female Householder No Husband Present		
	Total	Below Poverty Level	
		Number	Percent
BLACK ALONE			
2011	14,145	5,980	42.3
2010	14,236	5,831	41.0
2009	13,680	5,427	39.7
2008	13,648	5,533	40.5
2007	13,741	5,459	39.7
2006	13,244	5,180	39.1
2005	13,481	5,303	39.3
2004	13,244	5,247	39.6
2003	13,118	5,115	39.0
2002	13,030	4,980	38.2
BLACK			
2001	12,550	4,694	37.4
2000	12,383	4,774	38.6
1999	12,823	5,232	40.8
1998	13,156	5,629	42.8
1997	13,218	5,654	42.8
1996	13,193	6,123	46.4
1995	13,604	6,553	48.2
1994	12,926	6,489	50.2
1993	13,132	6,955	53.0
1992	12,591	6,799	54.0
1991	11,960	6,557	54.8

Year	Black Female Householder No Husband Present		
		Below Poverty Level	
	Total	Number	Percent
1990	11,866	6,005	50.6
1989	11,190	5,530	49.4
1988	10,794	5,601	51.9
1987	10,701	5,789	54.1
1986	10,175	5,473	53.8
1985	10,041	5,342	53.2
1984	10,384	5,666	54.6
1983	10,059	5,736	57.0
1982	9,699	5,698	58.8
1981	9,214	5,222	56.7
1980	9,338	4,984	53.4
1979	9,065	4,816	53.1
1978	8,689	4,712	54.2
1977	8,315	4,595	55.3
1976	7,926	4,415	55.7
1975	7,679	4,168	54.3
1974	7,483	4,116	55.0
1973	7,188	4,064	56.5
1972	7,125	4,139	58.1
1971	6,398	3,587	56.1
1970	6,225	3,656	58.7
1969	5,537	3,225	58.2
1968	(NA)	3,312	58.9
1967	(NA)	3,362	61.6
1966	(NA)	3,160	65.3
1959	(NA)	2,416	70.6

SOURCE: U.S. Bureau of the Census, Current Population Survey, Annual Social and Economic Supplements.

For information on confidentiality protection, sampling error, nonsampling error, and definitions, see http://www.census.gov/apsd/techdoc/cps/cpsmar12.pdf

Footnotes are available at:
http://www.census.gov/hhes/www/poverty/histpov/footnotes.html

Pattern and Trends
Homicide Trends in the United States, 1980-2008
Annual Rates for 2009 and 2010

Blacks were disproportionately represented among homicide victims and offenders

In 2008, the homicide victimization rate for blacks (19.6homicides per 100,000) was 6 times higher than the rate for whites (3.3 homicides per 100,000).

The victimization rate for blacks peaked in the early 1990s, reaching a high of 39.4 homicides per 100,000 in 1991 (figure 17).

After 1991, the victimization rate for blacks fell until 1999, when it stabilized near 20 homicides per 100,000.

In 2008, the off ending rate for blacks (24.7 offenders per 100,000) was 7 times higher than the rate for whites (3.4offenders per 100,000)(Figure 18).

The offending rate for blacks showed a similar pattern to the victimization rate, peaking in the early 1990s at a high of 51.1offenders per 100,000 in 1991.

After 1991, the off ending rate for blacks declined until it reached 24 per 100,000 in 2004. The rate has since fluctuated, increasing to 28.4 offenders per 100,000 in 2006 before falling again to 24.7 offenders per 100,000 in 2008.

The race distribution of homicide victims and offenders differed by type of homicide
From 1980 to 2008—

Black victims were over-represented in homicides involving drugs, with 62.1% of all drug-related homicides involving black victims. By comparison, 36.9% of drug-related homicide victims were white and 1% were victims of other races.

Compared with the overall percentage of murder victims who were black (47.4%), blacks were less likely to be victims of sex-related homicides (30.4%), workplace killings (12.5%), or homicides of elders age 65 or older (28.6%) (Table 7).

While two-thirds of drug-related homicides were committed by black offenders (65.6%), black off enders were less likely to be involved in sex-related killings (43.4%), workplace homicides,(25.8%) or homicides of elders age 65 or older (41.9%) compared to their overall involvement as homicide off enders (52.5%).

Most murders were intraracial
From 1980 through 2008—
84% of white victims were killed by whites (Figure 19).
93% of black victims were killed by blacks.

The Bureau of Justice Statistics is the statistical agency of the US. Department of Justice. James P. Lynch is the director.

This report was written by Alexia Cooper and Erica L. Smith, Ron Malega and Kyle Harbacek provided statistical review and verification of the report.

Morgan Young and Jill Thomas edited the report, Barbara Quinn and Tina Dorsey produced the report, and Jayne E Robinson prepared the report for final printing and under the supervision of Doris J. James, November 20111, NCJ 236018. The Full text or each report is available in PDF and ASCII formats on the BJS website at **www.bjs.gov** Tables are also available in The PDF and CSV formats.

Made in the USA
Middletown, DE
09 November 2021